The Magical Practice
of
Talismans

The
MAGICAL PRACTICE
of
TALISMANS

Robin Skelton
illustrations by
Sylvia Skelton

BEACH HOLME PUBLISHERS

Victoria, B.C.

This edition is published by Beach Holme Publishers, 4252 Commerce Circle Circle, Victoria, B.C. V8Z 4M2, with the assistance of the Canada Council and the B.C. Ministry of Municipal Affairs, Recreation and Culture.

Cover Art: Robin Skelton
Illustrations by: Sylvia Skelton
Cover Design: Barbara Munzer
Production Editor: Antonia Banyard

Canadian Cataloguing in Publication Data

Skelton, Robin, 1925-
The magical practice of talismans

ISBN 0-88878-309-4

1. Talismans.   2. Witchcraft.   I. Title.
BF1561.S53 1991   133.4'4   C91-091556-3

to Jean Kozacari

Contents

Prefatory Note

In 1985 I published a book entitled *Talismanic Magic* which provided the first attempt at a comprehensive survey of the different kinds of talisman in Western Culture. In the period between 1985 and the present day I studied talismanic magic further and did, indeed, practice it. As a consequence I decided that once *Talismanic Magic* was out of print, I should revise it thoroughly and enlarge it considerably so that it would contain the results of my researches and also some account of my personal experience as a witch using talismans. This present book, therefore, contains all the information provided by the earlier book and a great deal more. Although I hope it is comprehensive enough, it cannot include details of all talismans in the world, of either the present or the past; that would require a library. I have therefore been obliged to select my examples. I have chosen, first of all, to deal mostly with talismans that are part of what we may loosely describe as Western Culture, including talismans from the civilizations of the Middle East where much of that culture began, though I have made some use of Chinese and Indian traditions. In tackling the talismans of popular rural belief I have restricted myself similarly, but have dealt more with the lore of the British Isles than elsewhere, for, while there are many differences in European practices they do not differ in principle. In writing this book I have, of course, leaned heavily upon the researches of others. I must, however, add that much of my material will not be found in books, and that in almost all cases the explanations of talismanic thinking are my own. An exception is the chapter on Talismanic Stones, for here I have gained a great deal from the researches of Margaret Blackwood and a good part of this chapter is taken directly from her notes. She should, indeed, be credited as co-author of this chapter. In working on the first version of this book I was helped by a great number of people, and must express my gratitude particularly to Jeffrey Gould, Sam Llewellyn, William David Thomas, John Robert Colombo, and Patrick Grant for directing my attention to matters that I might otherwise have missed. I am also, as always, deeply grateful to my wife Sylvia who has provided the illustrations and without whose constant and patient support this book would never have been written.

Robin Skelton

Introduction

Although there are many books about the history and practice of magic, there are very few about talismans alone, and there is no comprehensive survey of the subject. This book is an attempt to remedy this situation, to reveal the part talismanic magic has played and continues to play in human life, and to help people interested in exploring the subject to create talismans for themselves.

Magic itself has been defined by Aleister Crowley as "The science and art of causing change to occur in conformity with the will." In other words, magic is a way of making things happen without using physical or mechanical means, but by employing psychic energy. This energy may be directed by a person (as when a priest, shaman, or healer cures or alleviates a disease by means of a spell or the laying on of hands), or it may operate through an object which possesses and transmits the energy (as when the relics of a saint cause miracles to occur).

Belief in the "magical" has been supported by all religions. Holy objects and relics, including priestly vestments and ceremonial robes belonging to men of authority, have always been regarded as having magical power and as being talismans. It was not until the industrial revolution and the growth of so-called rationalism in Western Europe that magic began to be regarded as stupid superstition by large numbers of people, though the power of magic was never completely denied. In the twentieth century, however, man has come to realize that there are energies and forces at work that we know very little about, that the symbolic systems of the so-called "occult sciences" do give us a picture of forces that actually affect human existence, and that these forces may well be as closely connected to the movements of the stars and consequent changes in the natural rhythms of life as astrology supposes. It has also been shown that every thing possesses an energy field which can be photographed by Kirlian photography, and that the energy fields of living things are continually altering. These fields have been, in the case of plants, translated into electrical impulses which can either be seen on a screen or heard as sounds. If a plant is threatened by a person simply thinking of harming it, its energy field alters. It may even stop "transmitting". We now know therefore that all things transmit "vibrations" and that where living things are concerned, these vibrations can communicate emotional states at the very least. The nature of transmitted vibrations is not yet fully understood, but they are as real as radio waves, which were discovered and labelled not so long ago. Vibrations appear to communicate at unconscious or subconscious levels. They do not appeal to the conscious self. When we react against a house or even a person and speak of "bad vibes," we cannot explain the nature of the "vibes," however powerful the effect may be. We get the message, though, and those of us who are especially sensitive and intuitive get the message very clearly indeed.

Talismans send out vibrations. Sometimes these are made doubly effective and communicate with us at a deep level because we recognize consciously that the talisman is related to a religious belief, myth, or legend that has fascinated mankind for hundreds of years. We are moved, for example, by the image of the cross, not only because it may refer to Christianity, but because the cross has been an important symbol ever since records of man existed. Somewhere deep inside us we keep a personal record of our evolution as a race, and what moved us in the beginnings moves us now and is part of our psychological make up. Thus these ancient symbols form a language that speaks to what Paul Huson has called our "deep mind,"[1] and as it is the deep mind which is the very foundation of our beings, this language can affect us profoundly.

Modern psychology and parapsychology and the recent discover-

---

1. For more information regarding deep mind, refer to Paul Huson's *Mastering Witchcraft*, G.P.Putnam's Sons, New York, 1970

ies of the neuro-biologists and the practitioners of Kirlian photography explain in part why talismans can affect us, and perhaps why there is an increase in the popularity of talismans in our time. Nowadays the wearing of talismans, amulets and charms is not only socially acceptable, but fashionable. The ankh, the Egyptian symbol of everlasting life, is worn as a pendant as frequently as the cross. Many travellers and taxi drivers carry medallions of St. Christopher with them wherever they go. And the signs of the zodiac are present everywhere in the form of pendants, rings, brooches and stencilled T-shirts.

Most people would agreed that medals of St. Christopher and crosses and ankhs are generally regarded as having protective qualities. Few, however, would say that a coat of arms or a pin indicating membership of a particular club had any magical significance, and yet the reason for wearing or displaying these is to warn off some people and encourage others. They therefore do have a talisman-like effect. They make things happen "in conformity with the will." Moreover, although there is obviously a difference between using talismanic symbols as a form of social communication and using them for magical purposes, it is not always easy to make the distinction. A man may wear a military uniform because this establishes his social function, but the wearing of the uniform may give him an irrational sense of personal power. It has been said that "the uniform makes the man," and there are many instances where people have been punished for "insulting the uniform" as if the uniform were possessed of personality and had virtue in itself.

Talismans have long been a part of human life, and over the centuries many different kinds of talisman have been created, some of them extremely simple and some of them very sophisticated indeed. Not everyone will want to create the most sophisticated ones, but if we are to understand the nature of talismanic power and talismanic thought, we must explore these as well as the talismans in common use. In so doing we will find ourselves establishing a series of general principles that can be used in making talismans ourselves. Because I am not concerned to explore religious beliefs and practices as such, but only those talismanic beliefs and practices that, originating in a particular religion, become part of common practice, I have paid little attention to those talismans which are intended to play a part in ritual magic rather than simply to protect or otherwise affect the owner or wearer. I have done my best to explain the basic notions of astrology,

Kabbalism, and the doctrines of signature and correspondences which form the foundation of much ritual magic as well as of much talismanic theory.

It is, finally, my contention that while many people consider talismans as superstitious nonsense, we do, all of us, practice talismanic thinking in our daily lives, and while we may not make elaborate artifacts or empower found objects, we do have a sense of the fields of energy possessed by objects, and we do pay attention to them.

What is a Talisman?

*If God is the creator, and lord of created things, how is
it that the talismans of Apollonius have power over parts
of creation?*

Attributed to St. Justin Martyr
A.D. 150

Talismans, amulets, and charms are usually regarded as being
quite distinct from each other. Talismans are objects which confer
power of various kinds upon those who wear them or own them.
Amulets, properly speaking, are intended to protect their owners from
both physical and psychic illness and from misfortune. Charms combine the functions of both talismans and amulets but consist only of
written or inscribed words or symbols. Despite this, many objects
regarded as powerful talismans and amulets contain or include inscriptions. It is often difficult to say whether or not a given object is an
amulet or a talisman, for some objects have both active and protective
functions. For the purposes of this book I have used the general word
talisman for all these objects in order to avoid unnecessary complica-
tions and confusions.

A very long time ago, stone age man drew pictures of the bison hunt
on the walls of his cave in order to ensure a successful hunt. This is an
instance of sympathetic magic; by imagining a successful hunt the
stone age man felt that it was certain to occur, and by imitating it

15

graphically, he was bringing his image to life. The same kind of magic is at work in the ritual dance, in which the dancers act out the drama of the thunderclouds coming and the rain falling in order to cause rainfall, or the magic inherent in the country superstition that you can cause rain by spitting on a stone, imitating the arrival of the first raindrop. The drawing of the bison hunt, even though it is also an instance of sympathetic magic, is still talismanic, for it is an object with magical power.

It was not long after this first use of sympathetic magic that talismans began to appear. At first they were probably objects that represented the powers of nature which were regarded as gods or demons or other kinds of spiritual beings. The earliest objects were very simple, but as time went by they became increasingly elaborate. A crudely carved stone might at first be regarded as an image of a god and therefore as having the power of that god. Just as saying the name of the god was believed to bring that god into the speaker's presence, so every image of a god was thought to be imbued to some extent with the god's power. This is the kind of talisman we have in the St. Christopher medal, in ikons and in religious medals. Johannes Lalas of Antioch reported in A.D. 550 how Apollonius, in order to rid Antioch of scorpions, made a bronze image of a scorpion, buried it, and built a pillar over it. Soon after, all the scorpions left Antioch.

These talismans need not all bear actual representations of the god, saint, or sacred personality whose powers are intended to influence, or of the animals, insects or disasters they are made to affect. Some of them make use of graphic symbols which represent the god without portraying him; an obvious example is a Christian cross that does not have the figure of Christ upon it. Sometimes the symbol might refer to a particular incident in the life of a man of power or saint or a part of a god only. Thus there are Egyptian talismans depicting the Udjat, or Eye of the Moon God, and a Syriac talisman of King Solomon spearing a devil.

Such symbols were thought to have some power in themselves, but not very much. After all, they were not images in which the god or the power lived, but reminders of those images. The sacred images themselves could answer prayers and grant wishes only if treated well with food and drink and a good house, and some of them seemed to respond especially well to feasts that involved dancing and bonfires and the sacrifice of an animal or even a human being. Images which conferred power upon the possessor and which protected him from ill without his having to actually pray or worship probably developed from the belief in the ability of the gods to bless, or give power to an object, and that this power would then reside in the object itself. This kind of talisman is frequently found in societies that contain a powerful priesthood. The priest or shaman or witch doctor has the authority to give power to the object by blessing it in the name of the god, or by placing it in a holy place such as the god's shrine for a certain length of time. Talismans of this kind are usually created for protective purposes, either general or specific, depending on the nature and particular interest of the god concerned.

In the Middle Ages a great deal of trade was done in the bones of saints, pieces of the true cross, and fragments of saints' garments under the supposition that something once connected intimately with a person of psychic power and charisma would provide its new owner with some kind of protection against the powers of darkness. The relics themselves were also believed to have the power to bring prosperity and to heal sickness, and shrines containing relics were the object of many pilgrimages. Though we may nowadays scoff at this as superstitious nonsense, it might be as well to remember that a single cell of a human being does contain the whole map of that person's structure, and that this is what has led to many stories of cloning. We cannot yet clone a human creature but other living organisms have been cloned. Therefore it may not be entirely ridiculous to suggest that a fragment of a powerful dead person may contain the essence of that person's power.

Whether or not we accept this as possible, we must certainly take into account the way in which objects that have belonged to people retain something of their owner's character and feeling. A great many ghosts have been shown to have made nuisances of themselves because the house in which they died still contained some of their possessions, especially if these relics were ones which had a strong connection with their lives, either by being frequently worn clothing or jewellery, or by being objects for which they had a strong affection. A psychically sensitive person can often tell a great deal about the owner of a particular object, dead or alive, by using psychometry.

If we accept this view, then we can understand why, also, objects which symbolize one's guardian spirit or patron saint are talismanic. The image of a person calls that person to mind, and may do so with

17

a vividness that makes them to be felt as actually present, and a carving or painting or some object that symbolizes a god may be even more potent for making its message apparent to a true believer.

People do not only have a sense of deities spirits, angels or demons, populating the universe as discarnate entities. They also have a strong sense of their own past and of their inheritance, of their ancestors. After all, it is sometimes comically apparent that a child is the son of its father; the family resemblance is so strong. There are other inherited characteristics too. Consequently it is quite natural for people to think of their ancestors as either still a part of them or as spirits watching over them. In many societies the person who could claim people of power and charisma as ancestors was regarded as having inherited their power and being under their protection. Parents handed down personal objects of adornment to their children, not as wealth, but as symbols of the family's strength and importance. People also began to boast of their lineage, and to symbolize it in images and drawings. The Indian totem poles of the Pacific Northwest portray the lineage of the family or person to whom the pole belongs, usually in terms of the various guardian spirits that have been, as it were, "in the family." The banners and heraldic devices of nobility show by means of symbols something of the lineage of their owner. These symbols refer to historical events, to persons of consequence, and to people's trades or professions. They are talismanic in their assertions of the family power, the strength of the guardians. Those who carry them or wear them feel protected.

These kinds of talismans—the holy image, the blessed object, the relics and the heraldic device—seem to have been the first to be generally accepted. There were, however, others which had nothing to do with the worship of a god or with inherited power. These were simply "found objects" that were so strange or so interesting in shape that they made the finder think that they had magical power. They had personality; they had charisma; and mankind has always regarded personal charisma as being a kind of magical power. Roots shaped like the male genitals, silver or golden coins that have been pierced or twisted, stones which have holes through them—all these have been and still are regarded as having magical powers of one kind or another. Some found talimans may be quite without interest to anyone but the finder. Those of us who pick up pebbles and shells on the beach know well that every once in a while we find a "special" stone which we regard with great pleasure and treat as a treasure, and that the reason for this cannot usually be explained to other people.

All the kinds of talismans I have so far described are connected either with a straightforward belief in natural forces and spiritual powers or with a belief that oddity and charisma are themselves magical and we can all sympathize easily with these beliefs. It may be less easy to accept talismans which are based upon elaborate symbolic systems, such as the Kabbalah, or upon specific religions. Nevertheless, these talismans can be effective, for many of them make use of words, names and inscriptions which have universal significance. The use of words and names of power, perhaps the name or names of a god or spirit or a quotation from a holy book, was and still is extremely common. Many of these talismans are immediately intelligible. A talisman to protect one against blindness, for example, might contain the essential part of a story of Jesus healing the blind; a talisman to protect the wearer against ill fortune might include the name of a sun god, which, once recognized, could easily be accepted as significant.

When we move on from either the symbolism of a widely known religion or the simple use of easily identifiable names, to the use of talismans based upon the elaborate mystical systems of secret societies, we are brought face to face with a knotty problem. Is it essential to believe in or at least sympathize with the system of belief underlying the talisman for it to work? With talismans, are we dealing only with the magical, or psychic power of faith? Or, even if we do not believe in the system behind the talisman, does that talisman have power itself? Is it possible for an object to alter actuality by its spiritual energies?

There is no doubt at all that faith plays a great part in talismanic as in all kinds of magic. If you believe that a talisman has power, then you yourself adjust your own psyche so that it sends out the appropriate messages. If you feel you are protected, and feel it strongly, then you are granted self-confidence and courage. A great many of the ills of life are caused by our own psychic imbalance, and we can "refuse" to be healed and can "insist" on medicines being effective. The talisman against disease, either in general or particular terms, sends a message to the subconscious or "deep mind" of the individual and obliges it to respond by directing the body to heal itself or to counter the disorder. Thus faith in talismans is not simply superstition — it is a mode of directing psychic messages inward to the deep mind and commanding it to help and heal. Faith in the talisman is an important part of its power.

As with protective talismans, so with active ones. If you have a talisman which is credited with leading to success in love, and if you believe in the talisman, then your deep mind will transmit telepathic messages which are of the kind to make success in love possible or even probable. If you have a talisman for success in money affairs, then the wearing of it will cause your deep mind to so order your thinking and your attention that you will have the success you desire. In these instances the talisman derives its power from the wearer's belief in it.

What about talismans that are not believed in? This is a more difficult question to answer, for scepticism and downright disbelief will always fight against the success of any magical act. It is not much use wearing a talisman for prosperity if you don't believe in it. Your doubt of its efficacy is also a doubt as to the likelihood of prosperity arriving. Therefore, the deep mind may well get a negative rather than a positive message. If your doubt is particularly strong you may even find that the magic reverses itself and causes misfortune to befall you.

Not all talismans, however, require the faith of their possessor. It is possible to imbue a talisman with power, and for the talisman to function quite autonomously. Indeed, there are instances in which an object imbued with talismanic power has found its way into the hands of strangers and caused considerable distress. Jean Kozokari was once faced with the problem of a haunted house in which there were a great many artefacts and had to determine which one was causing the disturbance.[1] This she succeeded in doing, but the incident was another clear example of the way in which objects may have energy fields and carry messages long after the reason for the energy field or the message has vanished. Sometimes, of course, the message may not remain. It may only last a little while, though it may be very potent for that short period. Consider the love talisman. If you wish to give a love charm, you must first of all imbue it with the message you wish it to carry. You can do this simply by writing the words on the gift itself. A woman receives a bunch of red roses, which are emblematic of passion, together with a card that makes the message explicit. The explicit

---

1. See: Robin Skelton and Jean Kozacari, *A Gathering of Ghosts*, Western Producer Prarie Books, 1989.

message, because it is consciously understood, can be consciously rejected; the message that the roses transmit direct to the deep mind of the recipient is harder to deny because it is harder to identify. It is, as it were, in code.

That objects can be transmitting stations for psychic potential seems now to be generally accepted. As we have seen, the discovery of Kirlian photography has led to our realizing that every object on this earth has an energy field surrounding it, and that, in the case of living things, this energy field is constantly changing. The patterns of flares surrounding a living leaf alters if the leaf is damaged or even if it is threatened. The pattern of ever changing points and flares of light around a human body will intensify if the person is emotionally excited or disturbed and will become jagged and distorted if the person is unwell. These energy fields are called "auras" by mediums and other workers in the field of parapsychology, mysticism and magic. It is believed by some that this aura is radiated outward from a second body which is composed entirely of energy and which interpenetrates our physical bodies.

The aura perceived by clairvoyants changes as the mood or health of the individual changes, altering both its intensity and its colouring. It also seems capable of emitting messages, or "vibrations", as they are commonly called. When we say that we get "bad vibes" from a person we are saying that we are receiving messages we dislike, or even that we are being, in some way, attacked or threatened.

It is not yet proven that the energy field or aura is responsible for transmitting telepathic messages, but it seems likely since all other known energy fields emit "vibrations" and "radio waves." If this is the case, it is likely that the energy fields and transmissions of inanimate objects can be altered by charging the original energy field with energy messages of one's own. If this is the case, the talisman that has been "blessed", the "holy water" in the church font or the food one eats after blessing it in a Grace, do actually change as a result of the blessing.

Not all talismans are deliberately made. Some of them are found, and some objects not intended to be talismanic at all are used as talismans. This is particularly true of objects which send out messages because they have been, in the past, associated with some explosion of strong emotion, some psychic storm. The "unlucky" jewel or dagger is familiar to us from many stories; consider, for example, the story of the Hope Diamond. Its first owner was robbed by his son and died in

21

poverty; its second owner, Louis XIV of France, permitted his mistress, Madame de Montespan, to wear it and shortly afterwards she fell out of favour; Marie Antoinette wore it, and was executed and her friend, Madame Lamballe, who also wore it, suffered a similar fate. Later owners died in poverty, committed suicide, were murdered, or suffered other misfortunes. Just as familiar as the unlucky gemstone is the haunted house. In both instances one explanation of the phenomena is that "messages" of great power have been left behind in these objects or places by the psychic forces which at one time affected them.

This brings up an important point about talismans, and especially about those bought in stores: if a talisman has been in contact with strong emotional force fields of a kind foreign to the intention of the talisman's symbolism, then the talisman is likely to be weakened in power or even inoperative. Thus, if you buy a cross from a man who is a total sceptic you may find it useless. Ironically enough, it is the most widely believed in talismans that are most affected by this situation. For every shopkeeper who sells a St. Christopher medal or an ankh believing in their efficacy, there are hundreds who have no belief at all. Moreover, the manufacturer or craftsman who makes the talisman may well regard it simply as a gewgaw of no interest save as merchandise. It is for this reason that many people suggest that you should manufacture your own talismans or should use as talismans objects which, because their ostensible function is not talismanic, have not been drenched with negative impulses. On the other hand, a talisman (that has been negated in the way I describe) can be made positive again by the purchaser if he or she concentrates for a sufficient period upon the symbolism of it with great energy and intense belief in the power of the symbol.

We have seen the way in which the transmitting station of the talisman is powered by faith and/or powerful energy fields. Does the symbolism itself, however, have power? Here we are on delicate ground and there are two views to be put forward. The first one is that those symbols which have been important to man for a very long time have been made in response to needs of the "deep mind" and therefore themselves constitute a kind of language which speaks directly and potently to all of us at an unconscious and deep level. These symbols, which Jungians would call archetypes, include the mandala, the cross and the crown; the moon and the sun are also archetypes. We do not have to believe in a particular religion to feel the power of this language. We react intuitively and at a deep level. These images, which Jung at first called "primordial images" and later "archetypes", represent the fundamental forces at work in the "deep mind" and picture our most powerful instincts and intuitions about life. Jung says that they "occur with great regularity; everywhere we find the idea of a magical power or substance, of spirits and their doings, of heroes and gods and their legends."[2] He points out that these archetypes appear in many religions and differ only a little from one religion to another. He suggests that we have inherited the powers they represent and the experiences they symbolize along with everything else that makes us members of mankind, and says that "the deposit of mankind's whole ancestral experience—so rich in emotional imagery--of father, mother, child, husband and wife, of the magical personality, of dangers to body and soul, has exalted this group of archetypes into the supreme regulating principles of religious and even of political life, in unconscious recognition of their tremendous psychic power."[3]

These images are so rich in meaning that it is hard for us to see any of these as having only one significance. The symbols of Father, King, Queen, Sword, Cavern, and Mountain are so broadly significant that if we use them for talismanic purposes we must attempt to narrow down their symbolic possibilities to those that are relevant to the situation. Other symbols speak to us with only a little less power, and are almost as universally appreciated, because we associate them easily and immediately with aspects of our experience. We cannot but feel that anything golden has to do with the sun and with light; we cannot help feeling that bright green has a message of growth. We accept that black has to do with the loss of light, with darkness. And so forth. This kind of symbolism is almost universally understood, though it is obvious that green, for example, might be a more powerful colour to a desert dweller than to an inhabitant of a country where lush vegetation is taken for granted.

Irrespective of their method of operation, these symbols are powerful in that they present messages exactly as do verbal statements, but, unlike most verbal statements (with the exception of great poetry), they speak directly to the deep mind. I cannot emphasize too strongly that it is the deep mind which is the real source of magical messages

2. C.G.Jung, *The Structure and Dynamics of the Psyche*, 2nd edition, Princeton University Press, 1969, p.137
3. C.G.Jung, Op Cit. p.156

and powers. The deep mind is actually the transmitter and the receiver with which we deal when we speak of talimanic magic.

We now have three kinds of talismanic power to consider: that energized by belief; that created by deliberate or chance subjection to a strong energy field; and that caused by the presence of an ageless and universal symbolic language. We have surveyed, briefly, the origins of talismans and talismanic thinking and have seen how talismanic thought developed naturally from a belief in the power of the imagination and the reality of the spiritual world. We can now go on to look in more detail at the various kinds of talisman and discuss ways of making them, and of making them work.

Identity Talismans

... a Device exposeth the rare concepts and gallant resolutions of its Author, far more perspicuously, and with more certainty, than Physiognomy can, by the proportions and lineaments of the face.

Henri Estienne[1]

Perhaps the most common talismanic objects in use today are those which identify the wearer as a certain kind of person. Many of these devices are only minimally talismanic in that they are intended to display publicly and explicitly some personal characteristic or fantasy, or denote membership in some social group. They are talismans in that they protect the owner from misunderstandings and sometimes lead to useful or entertaining personal encounters. They might be called Identity Display or I.D. talismans.

We can pass quickly over such I.D. talismans as T-shirts labelled with facetious messages, but we should recognize that those which say "Gay Liberation", "Pennsylvania U", or "Up the I.R.A." do indicate significant social attitudes and can therefore lead to social contacts of

---

1. From *The Art of Making Devices*, translated by Thomas Blount, 1646.

the desired kind. They are displays similar to the mating displays of some birds and animals who endeavour to attract mates by "showing off."

Crests, badges and men's ties are I.D. talismans similar to T-shirts –albeit without the obvious written message. If we see a man wearing a regimental tie we know something of his background if he is entitled, of course, to wear it. The "old school tie" message has proven very effective in establishing relationships in the past, though nowadays many people may wear second-hand ties and are completely ignorant of their significance to someone who knows the symbolism.

Different societies have different I.D. talismans, some of which are intelligible only to members of the same group. Thus, only a Shriner is likely to understand all the various marks of rank and function that are worn in Shrine parades and only a boy scout will interpret correctly every one of the badges worn by another scout.

All I.D. talismans are related to the practice of heraldry which developed to its most sophisticated state in Western Europe. Heraldry began with the creation of seals that could be used to sign and authorize documents. Richard I of England was the first English king to use a Royal seal. This was in 1189. His second seal, of 1198, became the basis for the Royal Coat of Arms of England. These seals, which were sometimes large and weighty and sometimes in the form of rings, were I.D. talismans in that they displayed the personal identity of someone signing (and sealing) a document. Because these seals included symbols of power[2] they were truly talismanic; anyone disobeying the law or command thus sealed was opposing spiritual as well as earthly authority. Seals of this kind remain in use today and business corporations and societies have registered seals.

The first actual coat of arms that we know of is that of Geoffrey of Anjou, whose father-in-law, Henry I of England, gave him a shield on which were painted six golden lions. From this time onwards the nobility of Europe, the great landowners and feudal princes, began to make use of I.D. or heraldic shields and when members of two noble families married, their children combined the designs of their parents' families in another shield. The science of heraldry, or "armoury" as it

---

2. See the chapter, Inscriptive Talismans, for a more detailed description.

should more properly be called, developed rapidly after this. Soon the rules for creating and devising shields, badges and heraldic charges were regulated and it became an offence against the law to carry a shield or bear a device to which one was not entitled. In a number of countries there are still special courts to deal with these infringements. As recently as 1949 a French family successfully sued a champagne company for using the family arms on their labels!

We are not concerned here with legal aspects of heraldry, but with the way in which heraldic devices are I.D. talismans. In the fourteenth century, Joannes de Bado Aureo in his *Tractatus de Armis,* said that heraldry existed simply to distinguish one person from another. In the seventeenth century, Sir William Dugdale suggested that coats of arms were chiefly used to distinguish between families. One of the most important functions of these devices was to announce when a person was in residence in a particular house or castle, to whose family (or army, even) a person belonged and by whose authority things were being done. This was important at a time when few people could read or write.

Because people could not read or write it was important also to choose symbols that carried a message to both the conscious intelligence and the emotions of the beholder. Thus in early heraldry we find an abundance of lions, dragons, unicorns, eagles, crowns and castles. We also find arms that have been created by a kind of visual pun; these are called canting arms. The Applegarth arms contain three apples, for example and the arms of the Shelley family three whelk shells, while the Welwood arms display a tree growing up out of a well. Other symbols were derived from the often hereditary official positions held by the bearer of the arms; the Marquess of Ormonde, the hereditary Chief Butler of Ireland, has three cups in this shield. Many heraldic devices are based upon medieval lore. The lion was regarded as the king of the beasts and a symbol of kingship. Similarly, the oak was the king of the trees. This kind of symbolism depends very much upon one's accepting a certain hierarchy in the natural world and upon the belief that certain animals, plants, minerals, birds and fish have particular ranks and qualities. It was believed in the Middle Ages and well into the seventeenth century that everything on the face of the earth had a singular, identifying quality which it had in abundance over all others. It thus became possible to represent a certain quality with absolute accuracy. The animal kingdom was thought to excel over all other living things in instinct and sensuality; the plant kingdom exceeded the rest of creation in the ability to grow and the stones and minerals were the leaders in durability.

There was also the theory that every department of creation exactly paralleled all other departments, so that for every animal there was a corresponding bird, fish, or stone; for every creature a corresponding attribute in man; for every attribute or portion of man a corresponding planet, angel or other spiritual power. Moreover, mankind was re- garded as being structurally exactly parallel to the whole universe--a microcosm. In this system of correspondences, like affects like. Thus a storm in the heavens will cause or accompany social disorder, a falling star will lead to the fall of a great man. If a lion is found dead or found giving birth, then some great prince will face either disaster or prosperity. An eclipse of the sun, the king of the heavens, prophesies the eclipse of a king; that of the moon foretells the fall of a queen. The earth itself also parallels mankind; the rivers and streams are the blood, the air the breath, the grass the hair or beard and so forth.

This system of correspondences is far too elaborate and confused to explore in any detail here. It is, however, important to bring it into the picture for it not only lies behind many of the I.D. talismans of heraldry but also behind many other talismans. Obviously a lion will signify kingship or nobility, as will an eagle or an oak. It is less obvious however, until one thinks in terms of correspondences, that a new moon may symbolize a young princess, a star a nobleman and a bolt of lightning, war.

Many of these correspondences may seem arbitrary to us, but they are based upon the view that any two things which are in anyway similar can affect each other. This notion of the inner meaning of similarity was called the Doctrine of Signatures; each object, or person, bearing, as it were, the signature of the special power or virtue it possessed. Thus the lungwort, because its leaves are lung shaped and spotted like lungs, was regarded as a medicine for chest disease. Yellow flowers were helpful for urinary disorders. Roots shaped like genitalia were aphrodisiac. If a person has a chill he should be wrapped in a red blanket, for red is the colour of fire. If he is feverish his fever may be lessened by wrapping him in white, for white is the colour of snow. Young girls of marriageable age should wear light green or white, for green is the colour of spring and of the awakening of fertility and white is the colour of the earth before the spring has begun and therefore symbolizes purity. Men who have a store of wisdom, of secret knowledge, should wear black for it is the colour of night and of obscurity (academic gowns were all, until very recently, black). Red, being the colour of blood and also of Mars, the planet of war, is the appropriate colour for soldiers' uniforms.

As a result of all these medieval explorations we have a system of symbolism which can be used as a kind of pictorial language both in armoury and in the making of I.D. and other talismans. Unfortunately there is no one authoritative and comprehensive account of the system and there are many disagreements among researchers from the earliest times to the present day. However, to show simply how the system works, or fails to work, Table 2.1 and Table 2.2 provide lists of a few of the correspondences between the natural world and human attributes that were accepted in the past. Some of them derived from myths; some are based upon natural observation—the mole becomes an emblem of humility because of its refusal to emerge into the light of day. Talismanic correspondences are different in every culture. In the East, correspondences differ because of different flora and fauna as well as different religious and mythological systems.

Creature	Trait	Creature	Trait
ant	industry	lion	sovereignty
bee	order	magpie	aquisitiveness
dog	fidelity	mole	humility
eagle	sovereignty	owl	wisdom
eel	cunning	oyster	lechery
frog	fertility	pig	gluttony
grasshopper	frivolity	robin	loyalty
fox	cunning	scorpion	treachery
goat	lechery	snake	deceitfulness
hawk	pride and valour	sparrow	lechery
		spider	cunning
house marten	deceit	sturgeon	sovereignty
jackdaw	eloquence	tortoise	patience
lark	cunning		

Table 2.1. Creature Symbolism

By no means everyone would agree with these Tables of Corre-

29

spondences and, as we shall see when we look at other talismans, many of these creatures and plants have been given other and sometimes contrary significances by different people. Even in the most flourishing days of heraldry, symbols of this kind were fully understood only by those who had made a special study of them and, therefore, some heraldic devices had an esoteric significance as well as, or even instead of, a generally understood meaning. This aspect of I.D. talismans is, of course, still with us today as I have already pointed out in discussing regimental ties and the insignia of the Masonic orders. We do indeed have to realize that I.D. talismans can be either in plain language or in code.

The magical type of I.D. talisman is esoteric and intelligible only to a chosen few. Many are associated with membership in secret societies. We can separate this kind of I.D. talisman from the remainder by calling them Cypher talismans. They are, after all, in code.

For the most part anyone who wishes to wear an I.D. talisman will have little difficulty in finding symbols that are generally accepted and understood. The Cypher talisman is a little more difficult. You must ask yourself "By whom do I wish to be recognized?" and "What symbolic language shall I use?" More important still is the question which leads you from simply devising a mark of identification into creating a talisman proper. This is "How do I see myself?" or, to put it another way, "What will help me constantly to recognize who I am?"

You may feel completely satisfied by the public symbolism of an explicit I.D. talisman, having decided that you are, above all things, the member of a group and therefore you will wear the family tartan or crest, the school or university tie or badge and feel protected by the sense of group participation that these give you. It may, on the other hand, strike you that you will only feel comfortable if you are recognized by a select few and you will then choose to wear a Cypher talisman. You may, indeed, feel the need of an entirely personal talisman which may or may not have meaning for other people. Some people even conceal their personal talismans beneath their clothing. By doing this, the wearer provides himself with a talisman which reinforces his sense of his own identity and improves his confidence in himself, without running the risk of betraying himself to other people. He or she may carry it concealed in a pocket or purse rather than wear it.

How can you identify yourself to yourself in such a way that the talisman continually reinforces your sense of your own unique personality and gives you confidence? There are a number of existing symbolic languages which can be used. The most obvious of the systems is based upon astrology. You can identify yourself to yourself by wearing a talisman which carries the sun sign of the zodiac under which you were born. You can, of course, elaborate this by adding to the dominant sign the other signs and you can even, if you wish, create a written talisman which holds the astrological map of your horoscope. This is unusual. Most people create identity talismans that only bear one or perhaps two astrological symbols. This talisman is, of course, easily understood by many people these days, for astrology is popular. You may therefore prefer to create an astrological talisman by making use not of the signs themselves but of the precious metals and gemstones associated with them. I have given details of these correspondences in Chapter 5. But, as an example, I will pick the sign of Cancer, whose colour is green, whose metal is silver and whose precious stone is pearl. Therefore a person born under the sign of Cancer could contrive a talisman which was made of silver and pearl with a green background. Similarly a Taurean could contrive a talisman which included copper, sapphire and pale blue. The planets also have precious and semi-precious stones associated with them. Saturn, for example, is associated with jet, onyx, obsidian and diamonds and Venus is associated with emeralds and sapphires. There are also stones associated with the days of the week.

Table 2.2. Plants and Flowers

Plants and Flowers	Trait	Plants and Flowers	Trait
Acorn	Immortality	Asphodel	Regret
Adonis	Wealth, Longevity	Balm	Sympathy Love
Almond	Happy Marriage	Bay Tree	Glory
Aloe	Wisdom, Integrity	Birch	Fertility
Amaranth	Loyalty	Sloe	Austerity
Apple	Concord	Borage	Courage
Aspen	Lamentation	Box Tree	Stoicism
Aster	Elegance	Bramble	Envy
		Buttercup	Ingratitude

White		Mint	Consolation
Carnation	Pure Love	Mushroom	Wisdom
Cedar	Incorruptability	Nettle	Cruelty
Chrysanthe-		Orange	
mum	Optimism,	Blossom	Virginity
	Cheerfulness	Orange	
Clover	Fertility	Tree	Fecundity
Coltsfoot	Maternal	Pansy	Thoughtfulness
	Love	Pear	
Cyclamen	Resignation	Blossom	Hope
Cypress	Mourning	Pomegranate	Fruitfulness
Dahlia	Treachery	Red Rose	Desire
Daisy	Innocence	White Rose	Innocence
Elderberry	Humility	Yellow Rose	Infidelity
Primula	Inconstancy	Rue	Mercy
Fir	Boldness	St. John's	
Garlic	Strength	Wort	Suspicion
Goldenrod	Good Fortune	Snapdragon	Desperation
Liverwort	Confidence	Snowdrop	Hope
Hollyhock	Generosity	Speedwell	Fidelity
Iris	Faith	Sunflower	Devotion
Ivy	Friendship	Sycamore	Fertility
Jonquil	Desire	Thistle	Defiance
Lavender	Constancy	Thyme.	Courage
White Lily	Sincerity	Vine	Wealth and
Lily of the			Contentment
Valley	Humility	Violet	Modesty
Marigold	Jealousy	Walnut	Trickery
Marjoram	Comfort	Wormwood	Bitterness
Medlar	Timidity	Yew	Grief
Mimosa	Daintiness		

It is therefore possible to make up a talisman which includes symbols of the sign of the zodiac, the sign of the ascending planet and the day of the week on which you were born. The amount of labour and expense involved in making a talisman of this kind may well cause you to hesitate and, indeed, very few people choose to be so elaborate. Nevertheless, if you wish to create an identity talisman that precisely does state to yourself, if to no one else, who you are, it is hard to do so without taking some trouble over it. Astrology is not, of course, the only system that can be used to describe a personality though it is one of the most ancient.

Unless you inscribe a full horoscope on your talisman, however, it is unlikely to be unique to yourself, for many people are born under the same signs or even at the same moment. If you wish to ensure that your talisman is unique and totally personal, perhaps the best thing to do is to use the oldest magical trick of all and inscribe it with your name or monogram. If you feel that this is too public a message, you can easily "encode" your name by using one of the magical alphabets given in Chapter 6, "Inscriptive Talismans." You might also make use of the device of Gematria. If you do this you will have a personal talisman which includes symbols that spell out a message only to those very few who can read them. Thus you could, if a Libran with Venus ascending, inscribe on a disc of copper the sign of Venus together with a coded version of your name.

Of course this kind of identity talisman does not include, as do heraldic devices, any reference to your lineage, or your family tribe or race and you may wish to elaborate it by adding a symbol which refers to this or even to your job, trade or profession. In doing so, you would, of course, be creating a totally individual talisman which would carry conviction to your deep mind. You might, however, prefer to wear it concealed rather than openly. To announce one's membership in a group is one thing, but to announce publicly the whole of oneself is another. Indeed most people choose to wear their truly personal identity talismans either wholly or partly concealed. The best way to wear them is probably as pendants hung low enough to be situated over your heart.

There is, of course, one kind of talisman which could be said actually to become a part of the wearer. This is the talismanic tattoo. Many tattoos are identification talismans, some of them obvious in significance and some not. The man who has himself tattooed with the flag of his country, or an emblem of some naval ship or regiment in which he has served, identifies himself as belonging to a particular social group with certain definite attributes. The man who embellishes himself with the name of his girlfriend, or with some expression of his affection for his mother or his birth place, is not only expressing loyalties and affections but also asserting that these are a permanent part of his identity. Tattoos are unlike all other talismans in that they

33

are regarded as permanent. They are not; but the removal process is both painful and tedious, so when the tattoo is made the person getting it should think of it as remaining for life.

Because there is a certain amount of pain involved in being tattooed, the tattoo always implies to both the observer and the possessor that an act of courage has taken place. Consequently, a person wearing a tattoo feels protected by this emblem of hardihood. He may, indeed, actually be protected, for many feel a tattooed person might be dangerous to cross. We are not here concerned with the sociological effects of tattoos, however, but with their talismanic properties and these are firmly believed in by members of many societies who feel that by having the group emblem upon their skin they have acquired the collective strength of the whole group. The death's head tattoo common among motorcycle gangs, or other emblems such as dripping daggers labelled "death before dishonour" are more than mere insignia.

There is one further kind of identity talisman which is sometimes kept secret and sometimes not. It may take many forms. It may be, for a woman, a particular ring or bracelet without which she will say she feels undressed, naked. It is needed to complete her. It may be something so apparently trivial that it is never mentioned to anyone, a certain coin perhaps, or even a coloured bead which must be carried. It has no obvious symbolic significance. It has no name. It may be referred to as a "lucky piece", a "lucky coin". The word luck always comes into it. Luck, indeed, is the word most often associated with talismanic objects. This, we are told, will bring good luck and that is unlucky. We cannot go into all the many superstitions about good and bad luck, for they do not always involve talismans; they involve actions and places and words and such rituals as whistling in a theatre (don't!) or walking under ladders (be careful) or looking at the new moon through glass. Our concern is only with the talisman which is, essentially, a thing worn on the body or carried on the body or given by one person to another or hung on or in a building. If we do concentrate on these, then we can come to a definition of the "luck" which is mentioned. This "luck" is, surely, a sense of security and confidence, a self-assurance; it is a feeling that one's personality, one's identity, is complete, has no weaknesses and that all one's faculties are in such good shape that one may anticipate success in one's affairs, whether they are affairs of the heart or the head. Thus we find that many

34

members of insecure professions carry talismans or wear talismanic clothing. Peter Falk is reported as wearing the same crumpled mackintosh for all his television appearances as Colombo. Several actresses carry charms to their performances. Indeed it is quite usual for an actor to suffer a panic attack if his or her "luck" is missing.

These identity talismans differ from the identity displays of others in that they are not messages to outsiders but messages to the possessor. Nevertheless, the assertion of individual identity is at their core.

In many stories, some factual and some fictional, a person will hand something to another and say "Here is my lucky piece; keep it", or "You must have this for luck; it's always been lucky for me!" It would be extreme to suggest that this is a handing over of one's identity and yet, to some extent this is the case. If one hands over one's name in several cultures, one is putting oneself in the power of another. In some parts of East Asia a man never tells his true and secret name to anyone outside his family and if he says to a woman "Shall I tell you my name?" it amounts to a proposal of marriage. Thus, the giving of one's identity talisman to another person is, at the very least, an expression of trust, of friendship, if not something stronger. This giving may, of course be mutual. There are many instances of men exchanging ties; there are more of people exchanging rings to celebrate a marriage or other association. A contract, from one point of view, is an exchanging of names. And when a member of one aristocratic family marries a member of another, the children are shown as bearing coats of arms of both families.

While we are considering identity talismans that are particular to the individual rather than particular to a group, let us return to the subject of clothing. We have already noted that clothing is regarded as talismanic by many people. One always wears this buttonhole to meetings; one always wears this cloak when one goes out of an evening; one has a "lucky" petticoat or a "lucky" pair of suspenders or tie. Certainly one has a "lucky" pin, bracelet or ring. What one wears is always a part of one's sense of identity, even if one is in uniform when a certain group talismanic effect occurs, as we have already seen. The alarm and dismay of two elegant women meeting on a social occasion and discovering that they are wearing identical costumes stems from the talismanic significance of the clothes quite as much as from anything else, a point made with beautiful visual clarity in the Ascot

Races section of the movie *My Fair Lady*. Clothes are, indeed, very significant; they do carry the identity of the wearer and sometimes very powerfully, though it should be noted that clothes which are thoroughly cleaned and washed, lose their energy field; those that are not do not. Jewellery, of course and non-washable items retain their fields. Nevertheless, when a woman dies and bequeaths her furs, dresses, jewels to someone, the bequest is of more than finery. This view cannot easily be dismissed, for it is common to hear people wondering, somewhat nervously, who exactly had owned this second hand garment and some people simply will not buy anything second hand; the identity, the personality, of the previous owner is, they feel, still present in the garments.

We are habitually more aware of the energy fields around us than we usually care to admit. And we are, therefore, more inclined to countenance superstitious beliefs than we would like anyone to know. Moreover, most of us, in our ordinary day-to-day living, find ourselves sooner or later coming up against a certain kind of experience that is so irrational we call it childish. We are walking on a beach, let us say and we see a pretty pebble. We pick it up. It says something to us. We may look around guiltily to see if anyone is watching, but we slip it in a purse or a pocket. It is, we feel, a personal and private thing; it is part of us, of our "luck". And if that which we have found has attached to it some kind of folk-belief we feel even guiltier. Just suppose one found a cast-off horseshoe? Would one seek the horse out? I think not. Such traditional talismans of country lore are the subject of our next chapter.

Talismans In Country Lore

Chase evil spirit away by dint
Of sickle, horseshoe, hollow flint

Samuel Butler[1]

While many talismans are entirely personal to the finder, some are generally regarded as having talismanic power. Obvious examples are four-leaved clovers, cast horseshoes and stones with holes through them, these last being known variously as hag stones, holy stones, witch-stones, and mare-stones. These are all protective talismans that bring good fortune, and there are many such recorded in folklore. Some of these derive their power from having once been part of a creature with desirable attributes. The Inuit who sews the head or feet of a hawk into his son's clothing is intending to give the boy the strength, keen sightedness and hunting skill of the hawk, just as in adding a piece of fox dung or fox skin and a piece of skin from the roof of a bear's mouth he is commanding the fox's cunning and the bear's strength to assist the child. Some African tribes follow a similar practice by adorning the young male child with necklaces made of the teeth of predators. Sometimes these talismans are intended for protec-

---

1. From *Hudibras*, Book 2, Canto 3.

37

tion against the animals of whose bodies they are made. A man might wear a leopard's claw as a protection against leopards, a shark's tooth to ward off sharks. One explanation of this kind of talisman is that by wearing these talismans one is identifying oneself as kindred of the leopard or the shark and therefore as their friend and not their enemy. A further explanation is, of course, that by wearing a shark's tooth one is acquiring the energy field, the personal vitality, of the shark. Both elements are present in this kind of talisman, though sometimes one aspect is clearly more important than another. The Dogrib Indians, for example, wear a talisman of antler points which while intended magically to assist in luring deer within striking distance by suggesting to the deer that they are kindred, may also have the effect of partial disguise. For the most part, however, the talismans of this kind are usually sympathetic; the Indian girl who is given a necklace of beaver teeth is given it to make her as industrious as a beaver, and not to persuade beavers to regard her as one of the family. Keeping fragments of the animals one has killed on one's person or in one's house is certainly talismanic in origin. The fox hunter who has foxes' masks mounted on his walls may be displaying evidence of his prowess; he is also, however, bringing the fox's virtues into his home, and ensuring that he retains his hunter's cunning. Similarly, the big game hunter keeps the heads of lions, buffaloes, bears and elk, or makes footstools of elephants' feet and umbrella stands of ivory tusks. He is, whether he realizes it or not, indulging in sympathetic magic and in talismanic thinking. This is even more obviously true of the head-hunters whose culture involves them in keeping and displaying the heads of the enemies they have killed.

To take the whole matter one step further, it is surely a kind of talismanic thinking that lies behind ritual cannibalism, sacrificial feasts, and the Christian Mass or Holy Communion. Basically the belief is that to wear, consume or possess part of a creature is to take on the vital force and the virtues of that creature. Exactly what are the virtues of a particular creature, or object, is something which has occupied men's minds for centuries and we have noted some of these in the tables of correspondences already given. A complete listing of all traditional talismans and their correspondences would, however, be extremely large and involve many conflicting views. I only present an account of some of the most widely known talismans in country lore and popular belief, beginning with those that are either protective or increase the powers of the wearer. I have included some talismans that are to be "worn" by the house rather than the householder. Many of these while specifically intended to protect the place or the person from evil spirits, witches, the Evil Eye, do, of course have a positive effect in that they increase self-confidence and therefore lessen vulnerability. There are perhaps two modes of talismanic thinking involved here. The first and most obvious has already been noted; it is the belief that wearing part of a creature or even an image of that creature provides one with the creature's virtues. The second mode is less obvious, for many traditional talismans of country lore relate to religious beliefs; they stem from the pre-christian Old Religion which we now call Wicca, from ancient Mediterranean practices and rituals, and so forth. Clearly, if someone using these talismans were able to accept these religious beliefs the talisman would be all the more effective. Even if one does not accept these beliefs there is a human tendency to revere that which is old, to believe there may "be something in" a wisdom that has lasted from ancient times to the present. The very antiquity of a belief has, for many people, something persuasive about it.

To gain personal power: wear an eagle's feather. The eagle is generally regarded as the ruler of the sky and those that wear an eagle's feather will be able to fly high and far and be successful in their ambitions. The eagle was, of course, an image of the father god, Zeus or Jupiter or Jove, and a bronze eagle formed part of the standards of the Roman legions. This talisman therefore combines sympathetic magic with ancient reverence.

To gain courage and confidence: wear a sprig of stinging nettle or thyme, or provide yourself with a picture of snakes or dragons. The stinging nettle is an assertion, "*I too can sting!*" The snake and the dragon are both to be feared, are destructive; by wearing their image one takes on their fearsome qualities, makes them one's allies, maybe if the talisman is visible to the onlooker, makes the viewer nervous, as, presumably, did the lions and dragons upon the banners of warriors in the past. Incidentally, this particular type of talisman has its counterpart today in the rings worn by bikers and their associates, for some of these portray skulls, Death with a scythe, snarling wolves and snarling lions.

To protect yourself from theft: wear a sprig of mugwort or place it over the door of your house. Mugwort is used by practitioners of magic in many ways. It is a visionary herb and, if made up into a pillow, will cause mystical dreams. It is a herb of protection. It is also of use to ensure safe journeys. Talismans of mugwort are given to people setting out on a journey, to protect them from ill fortune and bring them back safely. The mugwort is sacred to Diana who was originally the goddess of the open sky, but who is also a woodland goddess. As originally journeys would be taken through wooded country and under the sky, a herb sacred to Diana seems appropriate to protect travellers. Another talisman to ensure safe journeys is the feather of a lark. The lark is associated with the Sun God whom he continually praises, rising high above the earth to sing when the sky is clear. The bird is thus associated with clear skies. The lark was later associated with St. Christopher the patron saint of travellers.

To get your wish: wear a cap woven from hazel leaves and twigs. These "wishing caps" are known in many European countries. The hazel is one of the seven Chieftain Trees of Celtic lore, and the tree of wisdom. Forked twigs of hazel have long been used for dowsing, not only for water but also for buried treasure. The hazel nuts, in Celtic mythology, when eaten, provided knowledge of all the arts and sciences.

To gain eloquence: wear a Jackdaw's feather. Jackdaw's feathers were often worn in the caps of itinerant beggars and entertainers in the Middle Ages. The jackdaw is, of course, a garrulous bird. Once again the principle of overcoming an opponent by wearing the opponent's symbol may be involved here, for the jackdaw has been widely considered a bird of ill omen, and this belief has been recorded as recently as 1969. Therefore, in talismanic thinking, wearing the jackdaw's feather will ensure no harm from the jackdaw, but will bring its eloquence.

To ensure success as a bullfighter: carry a clove of garlic into the bull ring; it will prevent the bull from harming you. This is a Bolivian belief. Garlic has been regarded as a herb of protection since ancient times. It is sacred to the goddess Cybele and the Greeks placed a clove of garlic on a pile of stones at a crossroads to call up Hecate. Its protection is against evil and it has enormous strength. Very possibly the conviction of its strength is caused by the experience of its odour.

To gain a lover: carry a mandrake root or a root of bryony in your pocket. This will bring you a new sexual partner. The mandrake root, to be most effective, should be carved into an appropriate, possibly phallic, shape and engraved with magical symbols under the full moon. The root should be cut from the plant with a consecrated knife and a little of the gatherer's blood should be left behind when the root is taken away. It should then first be dried over a slow fire of vervain leaves. It is said that the making of amulets from mandrake roots was not uncommon in the sixteenth century in Britain.

The mandrake, (or bryony as its substitute), has always been regarded as magical, partly because the roots look somewhat like images of human beings. In 1597 Gerard in his *Herball* complained of people who were carving bryony roots and deceiving people into thinking they were true mandrakes. In 1936, however, in Lincolnshire it was held that the black bryony was a mandrake and the white bryony was called a womandrake. The mandrake helps women to conceive according to *Genesis* 30:14-16. It has many other medical uses according to country lore. In 1966 Wilfred Pickles, in a BBC programme, discovered a London herbalist selling mandrake to help people stop smoking.[2]

To help overcome obstacles: carry a sprig of moonwort, springwort or chicory that has been gathered at midnight on St. James' Day (July 25th). Moonwort, according to Culpepper, "is an herb which (they say) will open locks and unshoe such horses as tread upon it. This some laugh to scorn and those no small fools neither; but country people that I know call it Unshoe-the-Horse. Besides, I have heard commanders say, that on White Down in Devonshire, near Tiverton, there were found thirty horseshoes ,pulled off from the feet of the Earl of Essex's horses, being there drawn up in a body, many of them being but newly shod, and no reason known, which caused much admiration; and the herb described usually grows upon heaths".

The springwort, in legend, opens up mountains and uncovers treasure. A shepherd driving his sheep over the Isenstein grew tired and leaned on his staff in which was a sprig or flower of springwort. The mountain opened and he saw a princess who told him to fill his pockets with the gold that lay around. This he did and was then about to leave when she said "Forget not the best" and he leaned his staff against the cavern wall and began to pick up more gold. As soon as he had let his staff go, however, the mountain came together again and cut

---

2. Much of this information is taken from *A Dictionary of Superstitions*, edited by Iona Opie and Moira Tatem, Oxford University Press, 1989.

him in two. In other versions of the story, because of the princess' words, the flower is not springwort but the forget-me-not.[3]

The chicory plant was regarded as luck-bringer and helper in exploration by early American settlers who used to carry roots of it in their pockets. It is still popularly credited with the ability to open locks and make people invisible, though it is not clear how.

St. James Day is the feast of St. James the Apostle, and a story of the seventh century has him sailing to Spain in a stone coffin and arriving at Compostella. The church at this time took over the shrine of the sea-goddess Brigit in that place, and it became a centre for pilgrims. The emblem of St. James of Compostella is a scallop shell; it was previously the emblem of the goddess. As midnight is the middle of the day according to the old pre-christian religion which operated on a moon calendar, it seems reasonable to suggest that the gathering of herbs at midnight on a day devoted originally to the goddess harks back to very old beliefs indeed.

To gain physical strength: provide yourself with a picture of dragons, or snakes, or eagles, and either hang it in your room or carry it on your person. A ring engraved with these symbols is particularly efficacious. Portraits of tigers, or tiger skins, have the same effect. Additional strength in the arms can be gained by tattooing hinges on the inside of the elbows. This is specially popular with sailors who also tattoo the injunction "Hold Fast" on the fingers of the hands, one letter on each finger, the thumbs being spared.

To ensure success in gambling: wear a tiger's tooth, or carry a four- leaved clover. Talismans carried by gamblers at Monte Carlo include holy relics, locks of hair (presumably of personal significance), hooves, coins, and bones. The tiger's tooth is easy enough to understand; the tiger is strong, cunning, and deals in surprise. The rest, apart from the four-leafed clover, clearly owe their existence to personal feelings.

The four-leafed clover has a long history as a talisman. In 1507 the *Gospelles of Dystaues* stated "He that fyndeth the trayfle with foure leues, and kept it in reuerence knowe for also true as the gospell yt he shall be ryche all his lyfe". The view that the four-leafed clover brings good fortune, not necessarily in gambling, has persisted to the present

---

3. A great deal of information about flower legends will be found in *Flowers and Flower Lore* by Rev. Hilderic Friend, F.L.S., 1884, reprinted by Para Research in 1981.

day, and plastic bubbles containing leaves can be found in many stores. The reason for the four-leafed clover's powers is not easy to determine. It has one other quality, however, which may help us. In the nineteenth century in Northern England and Scotland it was believed that the four-leafed clover enabled its wearer to perceive otherwise invisible fairies, and also to see through illusions. J. Napier reported in his *West of Scotland* (1879), "A certain man came to the village to exhibit the strength of a wonderful cock, which could draw, when attached to its leg by a rope, a large log of wood.... One of the spectators present on one occasion had in his possession a four-leafed clover and while others saw, as they supposed, a log of wood drawn through the yard, this person saw only a straw attached to the cock's leg by a small thread".

This suggests that the four-leafed clover brings good fortune because the wearer is no longer deluded by appearance. In Judeo-Christian tradition Eve is supposed to have taken a four-leafed clover with her when she left Eden. This story may partly account for the belief expressed by Lyly in 1580 that no serpent dare venture among clover. The clover was, however, significant in other traditions also. The Greeks considered it sacred, and in Germany both the two-leafed and the four-leafed clover were considered fortunate. Some authorities suggest that the normal trefoil or three-leafed clover symbolizes the Trinity and when the three leaves become four the wearer is given clairvoyant abilities. Others, delving for a further explanation, suggest that the three leaves present the symbol of the triple goddess in her three roles as maiden, woman and crone, and that the fourth leaf brings in Hecate the goddess of death, and therefore the death of all false appearances.

To keep ghosts away: scatter fernseed around the house or place hyacinths in the rooms. Hyacinths are flowers of grief and associated with death as the hyacinth is said to have sprung from the blood of a young man accidentally killed by Apollo with a discus. Other stories state that the flower arose from the blood of Ajax. The lamenting cry of "Ai Ai" is said to be readable on the petals, and so are the initials of the youth Hyacinth and the hero Ajax. Scholars have stated not only that the hyacinth formed part of the wreaths at funerals, but that is was sacred to the goddess Demeter. All these associations with death would seem to make it appropriate in keeping away ghosts as ghosts are discarnate spirits who have not come to terms with death.

43

Fernseed confers invisibility. This belief expressed by Shakespeare in 1596: "We have the receit of Fernseede, we walke invisible" (*Henry IV, ii, i*). In 1793, a countryman told how fernseed was gathered at midnight on St. John's Eve, which is the eve of Midsummers Day. It was a difficult task because the seed had to fall into the gatherer's plate of its own accord. The fern must not be shaken. In 1887, a man returned home to his wife and children and was not made welcome. He had walked through fern and the seed had got into his shoes and so he was invisible. It may be that ghosts do not haunt houses or people they cannot see.

The gathering of the seed on St. John's Eve is interesting as this is one of the great feast days, or sabbats, of the Old Religion and sacred to the Goddess. Thus in both these talismans we have a connection to the Old Religion.

Another way to keep ghosts away is to bring sprigs of hawthorn into the house. Hawthorn is a most ambiguous symbol. On the one hand it is associated with the worship of the goddess, being carried around the villages and pinned above the house doorways on Mayday which is the Celtic feast of Beltaine and a Sabbat. It is also associated with the faerie, especially in Ireland, where the chopping down of a thorn tree brings extremely ill fortune, and there are many recorded instances of this. However, on the other hand, one of the Christian legends states that Christ's crown was made of hawthorn, and therefore it would seem logical for thorns to keep anything evil away from the house. In the Middle Ages it was thought good to use hawthorn blossom, or "may", to keep away witches, even though the "may" was very much part of the witchcraft religion. This is another instance of the way in which the Christian church turned pre-christian beliefs and symbols to its own use.

Yet another talismanic practice to keep ghosts away is to plant lilies in the garden. The lily is also connected to the pre-christian goddess, and many kinds of lily were later dedicated to the Virgin Mary. In Buckinghamshire, for example, the White Lily is called Lady-lily. The White Lily is often shown with the Virgin Mary in paintings, and is generally considered an emblem of purity. It is therefore reasonable to suggest that the lily is an excellent protection against dark forces.

To keep away evil spirits: decorate your house with peach branches and blossoms, or hang branches of elder or mistletoe over the doors and windows. Branches of arbutus, a tree once considered sacred to the Roman goddess Cardea, if hung in a child's room, will give protection from evil.

Cardea was a minor Roman goddess and associated with the threshold of the house, indeed with the hinges of the door; she was invoked when matters of entrance or departure needed attention. She therefore would be an admirable deity to prevent evil entering a room or a house.

The peach is a symbol of longevity and immortality in Chinese tradition, and peach blossoms over the door are said to ensure this.

With the elder we face two traditions as we did when considering the hawthorn. In one Christian tradition elder was the wood of which Christ's cross was made, and the tree from which Judas hung himself was an elder. In 1656 we are told that elder leaves were gathered on May Eve and fixed to doors and windows to keep witches away. This belief is reported right up to the twentieth century. Elder is also, however, a magical tree in pagan tradition. If you spend Midsummer Night (St. John's Eve) in an elder grove you will see fairies. It is considered sacred to the moon and its berries should be picked by moonlight. In Ireland there was a belief that witches used staffs of elder as their steeds; it is also associated with death in many legends. It is, according to Robert Graves, the doom aspect of the White Goddess.[4]

Mistletoe has long been considered magical. The Druids cut mistletoe from the oak with a sickle, the shape of the new moon, although the sickle, according to others, may have been of gold, the colour of the sun, in which case perhaps the sickle should be considered the emblem of the waning moon. Mistletoe is associated with death; in one myth Heracles is impaled upon a mistletoe bough. In Scandinavian myth Balder was killed by a spear of mistletoe. Nevertheless, it is not death but rebirth and renewal which is the central significance of the mistletoe; the god-hero rises again from the dead. The mistletoe also has phallic and sexual connotations, its white berries being considered representations of male semen, just as the red berries of the holly are considered to symbolize menstrual blood. As regards this particular house talisman, however, it would seem that its association with death and rebirth would give it the power to keep away evil spirits.

To banish witches from the house: hide a root of the male shield

---

4. For this and other references to Graves' views, see Robert Graves: *The White Goddess*, Faber and Faber, 3rd edition, 1952.

fern in the room; this will make any witch feel ill and obliged to leave. In Wales a bunch of fern would be stuck in horse-collars or over horses' ears in order to frustrate witches. The fern is associated with witches in many ways, and with the devil. One name for the fern is Devil's Brush. It is also however associated with the Goddess in her persona as the Virgin Mary for one fern *(Polypodium Vulgare)* is thought in Germany to have sprung up from her milk. The Royal Fern is dedicated to Saint James whose feast day, as we have seen, is July 25th; it is also the feast day of St. Christopher who bore the infant Christ across the river, and another name for the fern is Herb Christopher. Witches are popularly supposed not to be able to cross running water; there maybe a connection here, for many symbols and practices of the Old Religion were inverted by the Christian church, so that (for example) the caul, which was greatly prized by followers of the Old Religion, became regarded as a protection against witches. Witches not only could cross running water, they made their sacred places wherever possible by wells, over underground streams and especially where streams cross underground. Herb Christopher therefore would, in the Churches inverted thinking, present a phantasmal stream that witches could not cross.

To detect the presence of evil: Keep a toadstone at your side. The toadstone is a dark grey or light brown stone that sweats in the presence of evil. You can identify it by placing it in front of a toad, for if it is a true toadstone the toad will immediately leap towards it. That is, at least, one belief. The toadstone has, however many virtues; it can cure rat bites and the stings of wasps or ants; it can protect pregnant women from demons; it can cure the scrofula and fits. In the presence of poison it becomes hot. Its origin is variously given, but the general view is that it is a stone found in a toad's head. It has had various names. In 1488 it was called a paddockstane, paddock being another name for toad. In 1558 it was called a Crapon or Toad Stone. In 1579 it was termed a Crapandina or Craupaundina. The stone was extracted from the toad by burying the creature in an ant hill. Toadstones were used to heal as recently as 1879.

The toad has long been associated with the Old Religion and with magic. Toads were kept as pets by countryfolk and they were regarded as witches' familiars. Witches could change themselves into toads, it is reported. Not only the toadstone, but many other bones of the toad are reputed to have magical properties. One bone from the toad's side, will calm angry dogs, and if put into a drink soothe bad tempers and end quarrels. If worn, this bone is an aphrodisiac. If grey toads are eaten clean in an ant hill and their bones ground to a powder, the powder will help you to control horses. A toad's breastbone will give power over cattle and horses as well as people. If you get the bones of a black toad, throw the bones in a running stream at midnight and pick out the one bone that does not go downstream, which will be the breast bone, then wear it or put it in your pocket; you can then bewitch people and work magic but you yourself cannot be bewitched.

All this makes it clear that the toadstone is connected fundamentally with the Old Religion and the belief in magic powers. It is only fair to point out that those toadstones which have been examined have usually turned out to be fossilized teeth of one kind or another, usually those of fish.

To protect a newly born child: Give the child salt, matchboxes, eggs, and coins of silver. Salt is symbolic of the element of earth and is the great cleanser; it is used to dispel the energy fields of objects. Silver is sacred to the Goddess and silver coins therefore bring her blessing. The matchbox (it would have been a piece of coal or peat earlier) symbolizes the elements of fire and air and the egg, which is a symbol of the Goddess as creator is a water symbol for it is filled with liquid. It is also, and obviously, an allusion to a successful birth. There are many gifts that tradition prescribes to be given to newborn children and almost all of them relate to pre-christian beliefs in one way of another.

To protect horses: Tie a hagstone, which is to say a stone which is pierced through by a hole, to the key of the stable door or a sickle in the stable. A horse whose rider carries a whip with a stock made of rowan will also be protected from danger. If you fasten hazel wands to a horse's harness it will protect it from witchcraft.

As we've already seen, the hazel was very much a part of the equipment of witches, so that this suggestion is another instance of inversion. The Roman, or mountain ash, is sacred in the Old Religion and there is much lore about it.

Robert Graves tells us that the rowan is also known as the quickbeam or quicken or witch-wand. The rowan was used for metal divining and its berries were believed to heal the wounded and add years to a man's life-span. It was important to the Druids and the red rowan berry was regarded in Celtic tradition as the food of the gods. With all this behind it, it is not surprising that in 1597 cattle were protected from evil by having rowan twigs plaited in their tails, and in 1685 Aubrey reported that rowan trees are a protection against witchcraft. In the eighteenth century in Scotland lambs and sheep were sent through a hoop made of rowan on the mornings and evenings of the two feasts of Beltaine (May Day) and "Hallowday" (Samhain or All Hallows) two of the great sabbats of the witches' year. As one can see, there is nothing specifically appropriate to horses in the rowan. In Lancashire in the ninteenth century people would have a branch of the "Wiggen Tree" at the head of their beds, and bowls and cups were made out of the tree. The rowan commanded reverence in country districts of Britain in the 1930s, and is, indeed, still respected today. It must be realized that some talismanic trees and shrubs considered to be most effective turn up as recommended for a number of virtues. They are all purpose, and in 1884 Hilderic Friend reported that highlanders still inserted crosses of rowan bound together with red thread in their clothing, and that in Cornwall rowan was carried in pockets and tied to the horns of cattle to ward of the Evil Eye.

Hagstones have been considered lucky for over five hundred years; they are mentioned in a Bodleian manuscript of the second quarter of the fifteenth century. Traditionally the hagstone should be a flint, but this does not seem to have been insisted upon after the sixteenth century. It is called a hagstone because its function is to prevent a witch or hag riding a horse away; it is also a specific against being hag-ridden in a nightmare. Stones of this kind are found not infrequently on beaches and in fields, and are more often chalk or limestone than flint. The hagstone—or holystone or mare stone—is usually suspended by a red thread or red ribbon at the head of a bed, over a stable door or over a cattle byre. The belief is as strong now as it was in the sixteenth century.

It is hard to determine why perforated stones should be thought so powerful. They not only are protections against witches, but also protect ships from storms, and ease labour pains. It may be that here we have a symbol that reaches very far back indeed, that may be part of our psychic inheritance, for the belief in the perforated stone as good luck seems to be world-wide and universal. It may well be a Jungian archetype. If we consider the image the perforated stone presents we soon realize that, because it is stone, the image is of a cave or cavern , the cavern, however, passing right through the stone. We might then recall many of the rites of different cultures. Initiation rites frequently involve the crawling, or even wriggling, through a narrow passage. This has, of course, been related to the birth-passage. In climbing through the huge holed stone of the Men-an-tol in Cornwall we are being reborn without the affliction that we climbed through the stone to cure. The hagstone, though small enough to wear as a pendant or hang on a byre or bedhead, still gives us that image of passage, of transition, and therefore presents us with a sense of controlling birth and death; it is a kind of initiation. Thus it may be that the hagstone's significance derives from very ancient practices and beliefs and should be considered alongside other allusions to megalithic tombs and passages.

To prevent harm to a child: hang a peachstone around its neck or place leaves of hawthorn in its cradle. We have already noted the virtues of these talismans.

To protect yourself against danger while sleeping: have the picture of an open eye tattooed on each nipple. The open eye is considered talismanic in many cultures. Its significance is obvious, but the placing of it may need a comment. The nightmare often takes the form of the feeling of a great weight upon the chest and, indeed, some ghosts have afflicted people this way. The heart also is affected and made to palpitate by night-terrors. Therefore the placing of the tattooed eyes makes sense.

To protect yourself from lightning: carry acorns in your pocket or place some in your window. The oak is supposedly the tree most frequently struck by lightning, and therefore has an affinity with it and can protect against it. Moreover, the oak is sacred to Zeus, to Jove, who uses the lightning as a weapon. Sprigs of stinging nettle will also protect you, for the sting of the nettle is as sharp and sudden as a stroke of lightning. A number of other generally protective talismans are also in the lists of protectors against lightning.

Having surveyed by no means all but the most common talismans of country lore in terms of specific requirements, we must turn to the general talismans, those which are credited with either ensuring good fortune or protecting against witchcraft and the Evil Eye.

To ensure good fortune: There are numerous talismans for this general purpose. You should carry a sprig of holly that has been used in Christmas decorations, a lotus blossom, a sprig of mayweed, a leaf

49

of shamrock or a four-leaved clover. Holly was sacred to the Druids, and they would have holly in their houses during the cold months so that the people of the woodland, the fairies and little people, could have refuge until the spring. In folklore the holly is a sacred tree that must not be cut down and this belief has persisted to the present day in Britain. Walking sticks of holly keep witches away, nevertheless, and holly is a great protection against lightning. Here again we see that a sacred tree of the pre-christian religions is turned into a means to keep practitioners of that Old Religion away. The lotus is also associated with pre-christian beliefs; it is used to call up Isis, Osiris, and Hermes and its pods are used for incense. The lotus was the symbol for almost all the goddesses of ancient Egypt. In Hinduism the lotus was seen as the goddess Padmi whose body is the Universe. It has erotic implications because it is seen as resembling the vulva, the feminine life-principle. The Mayweed was sacred to Pallas Athene in Greek culture; it was later renamed St. Mary's Herb and given to Mary Magdalene. So far, it seems that all the good fortune talismans stem from pre-christian beliefs.

A further bringer of good fortune is the image of a black cat tattooed on your body. The black cat, of course, has long been associated with witches, and with female deity. Freya, the Teutonic mother goddess had cats drawing her chariot. Bast was the Egyptian cat-goddess and Artemis and Diana often appeared in the form of cats. In Scotland the Goddess of the Witches was called the Mother of the Cats (or Hares). The witch burners used also to burn cats and cats in the Middle Ages were not only regarded as witches' familiars, but as the devil in animal form.

Another charm to bring good fortune is a pace egg, an egg coloured for Easter. If kept from one Easter to the next it will bring good luck. The word *Easter* is taken from the name of the Saxon Goddess Eostre who is identified as being another name for Astarte and the Great Mother Goddess Kali. Eggs are symbols of rebirth and pace eggs are traditionally coloured red, the colour of vitality and of blood. The egg is a symbol of creation; in Orphism the World Egg was brought forth by Mother Night, the great Goddess of Darkness. Once again it seems the Goddess lies behind the talisman.

The house and household may be assured of good fortune by decorating the walls with bay or laurel, though for the most part it is supposed to ensure good fortune by being protective; it is defensive rather than constructive and keeps away witches—a belief recorded in Britain as recently as 1983. The bay/laurel was used by the Delphic Priestesses to send them into a visionary trance and it was used to invoke Apollo. Laurel/bay has long been used to celebrate achievements from Greek times to the present day. The laurel is sacred to Apollo because he was the cause of its creation; the nymph Daphne, pursued by the god, wished to be changed into a tree to escape him and thus became the laurel. According to Robert Graves this myth records the way in which the followers of Apollo captured the shrine of the Goddess at Tempe, near Olympus. The laurel/bay was, in fact, sacred to the Goddess before it was taken over by Apollo, and it was used as a drug by the Goddess' followers to incite vision. It was indeed used in exactly the same way as witches used their hallucinogenic ointments, according to report. Once again there has been an inversion of significance.

A really well known house talisman is the horseshoe. This should be a cast horseshoe found in the road, and it should be nailed up over the threshold with the ends pointing upwards, otherwise the luck will run out. It has been regarded as a defence against witchcraft, the devil and all kinds of bewitchment since the Middle Ages; it is mentioned by Scot in his *Discoveries of Witchcraft* in 1584 and it is still very much in evidence. Barbara G. Walker's explanation[5] of the horseshoe symbol is succinct and could not be bettered:

> **Horseshoe:** Hindus, Arabs, and Celts regarded the ionic shape of the horseshoe as a symbol of the Goddess's "Great Gate," thus it was always esteemed as a prophylactic door charm. Druidic temples were constructed in the shape of a horseshoe. So were some Hindu temples with the frank intention of representing the yoni. The horseshoe arch of Arabic sacred architecture developed from the same tradition.
>
> Greeks assigned the ionic shape to the last letter of their sacred alphabet, Omega, literally, "Great Om," the Word of Creation beginning the next cycle of becoming. The implication of the horseshoe symbol was that, having entered the yonic Door at the end of life (Omega), man would

5. Barbara G. Walker: *The Woman's Encyclopedia of Myths and Secrets*, Harper & Row, 1983.

be reborn as a new child (Alpha) through the same Door. It was everywhere represented as "a horseshoe, the very figure that is nailed to so many doors in various parts of the world, as an emblem of luck. Mighty few of those who live in such houses know that the horseshoe is only a symbol of the yoni and that by nailing it to their doors, they follow out a custom older than the history of their race."

The Christian God who claimed to be the "Alpha and Omega" (Revelation 1:8) was only copying one version of this very ancient symbolism, whose meaning seems not to have been understood by the biblical writer.

There are, of course, other ways of viewing the horseshoe, and the image of a cup comes to mind. One nineteenth century view was that the horseshoe kept the devil away because he always travels in circles and is frustrated when he cannot complete the circle around the horseshoe. Another attempt to Christianise the symbol was to suggest the horseshoe was a capital C for Christ, but this explanation had little or no currency. Yet other explanations of the symbol's power allude to the blacksmith's forge; the smith is a significant figure in pre-christian religion—a god in all religions—for he works with the four elements of earth, air, fire and water and makes weapons, chains, household implements and cauldrons. The horse that wears the horseshoes, and who discarded the shoe for us to find, must also be considered; the horse is sacred to the Celtic goddess Epona and to the Teutonic moon goddess Horsel (later transformed to St. Ursula). Once again, it seems that the most widely accepted protective talisman for the house and household reaches back into pre-christian times and derives from ancient religious beliefs and practices.

To protect yourself against witchcraft and the Evil Eye: Many of these talisman's have already been noted for specific powers. A twig of rowan with berries on it, a sprig of holly picked at Christmas, sprigs of mugwort and cloves of garlic are listed. Other talismans recommended in country lore are rue, kingfisher feathers, and garlands of birch, bracken stems or juniper.

Rue used to be grown around Roman temples and in the Middle Ages was strewn around the house to keep disease away. Sometimes a bunch of it is hung in the kitchen and sometimes it is combined with a piece of bread, ash from the hearth and personal items from the members of the family and hidden in the house. It is used in consecrating iron for magical purposes and mediums or channellers wear it to protect them from the unpleasant and untoward. Rue was also believed to cause clairvoyance and, according to Hilderic Friend, missionaries used to sprinkle holy water from brushes made of rue, which is how it came by the name "Herb of Grace" which is alluded to in *Hamlet*. Once again it seems that a talisman which enables one to see the invisible or become clairvoyant is valuable as a protection against evil. One might deduce that evil is therefore regarded as the manipulation of the illusory, as fundamentally untruth—a view which is expressed in the description of Satan as "The Father of Lies".

Birch has been called the "Lady of the Woods" and is therefore a symbol or even an embodiment of the Earth Goddess. It is also sacred to Thor, the Germanic god of fertility, thunder and lightning. Birch twigs were used to beat delinquents and lunatics to drive evil out of them and the birch became a common implement of punishment in British schools. According to Graves the witches' besom was made of birch twigs. In Celtic tradition, the birch was allotted Sunday as its particular day.

Bracken, or fern has already been noted, but it is worth recalling that it too, like rue, is associated with clear seeing.

The significance of juniper appears to derive from a Christian legend, though berries and branches of juniper were burned by the Greeks to protect them against the gods of the underworld and juniper berries were burned at funerals to fend off evil spirits. Hilderic Friend in her *Flower Lore* published in 1884 wrote: "On the Continent the Juniper is also regarded with great veneration, because, as the tradition affirms, it saved the life of the Madonna and the infant Jesus when they fled into Egypt. In order to screen her son from the assassins employed by Herod to put the children of Bethlehem to death, the Virgin Mother is said to have hid him under certain plants and trees, which naturally received her blessing in return for the shelter they afforded. Among the plants thus blest (says A. de Gubernatis), the Juniper has been peculiarly invested with the power and privilege of putting to flight the spirits of evil, and destroying the charms of the magician."

The talisman of kingfisher's feathers is clearly intended rather to bring calm and peace than to oppose anything at all, for the Kingfisher is also known as the Halcyon. The Greek story tells how Halcyone, having been warned in a dream of the imminent death of her lover,

Ceyx, kept watch on the seashore and his body was washed up at her feet. Her grief and longing were so great that she was suddenly transformed into a bird, the first kingfisher, and Ceyx returned to life and, also transformed, joined her as her mate. The Greek gods and goddesses blessed the couple and now, when the halcyone or kingfisher is ready to lay, calm descends upon the waters. Thus kingfishers are regarded as bringing calm and peace. If a dead kingfisher is hung up by its beak the way it twists and turns will tell the weather.

St. John's Wort has been regarded as a powerful protective talisman since the Middle Ages, and probably earlier. A fifteenth century manuscript states that the Devil cannot approach anyone carrying a sprig of it. Some say it should be gathered on a Friday—the day of Venus incidentally—but others say it should be picked on St. John's Day, Midsummer Day, the midsummer fire festival of Europe. In Sir Walter Scott's *Guy Mannering* we get the rhyme:

Trefoil, vervain, John's wort, dill,
Hinders witches of their will.

We have looked at the trefoil or clover already. Vervain (or Verbena) is credited with so many virtues that it is difficult to list them; it is a visionary herb; it is used in consecrations; it was used by Druids as a cleanser and in consecrating the altar; it is included in philtres for attracting lovers; it was used in Persian celebrations honouring the Sun, and is thrown into the midsummer fires. It is also sacred to Diana. Other virtues abound; it cures scrofula or the Kings Evil; it not only brings visions, but may prevent bad dreams; it protects soldiers in battle, and protects against snakebite.

Dill is a herb of protection and used in blessing the house and especially the kitchen. It clears the mind and protects the wearer from the consequences of false beliefs and superstitions. Dill is sometimes considered to have the same virtues as Fennel, which should be collected on Midsummer Eve and supposedly improves the eyesight and even returns sight to the blind. Again the theme of clarity of vision returns.

One of the most fortunate of talismans is the caul, the thin membrane that covers the faces of some children at birth. Children born with a caul were believed to become clairvoyant in later years. That someone carrying a caul can never be drowned is a belief recorded as early as the fifteenth century and as late as the twentieth. In the seventeenth century the caul had the alternative name of Silly How, according to Sir Thomas Browne and in 1816 the term was hallihoo, which is to say holy hood. Those born with a caul have great good fortune; those who buy a caul also have good luck and cauls have been known to fetch very high prices. In 1779 a child's caul was advertised as on sale to gentlemen of the Navy at a price of twenty guineas. In 1919 in London the price was only three guineas, however. A person's caul must be kept safe; if it is destroyed its original wearer will die.

The talismans surveyed so far are all protective in one way or another, and while they deal with specific kinds of insecurity and different desires, they do not tackle the common problems of bodily health. There are many talisman's recommended for bodily health. Many of these seem at first to be inexplicable and arbitrary. There is usually, however, some reason for the belief in talismanic power. There is some logic behind the advice to wear a wreath of rosemary **to improve your memory,** for rosemary is recommended by herbalists for a number of disorders. Rosemary tea helps to bring comfortable sleep and it is also a cure for headaches, migraines and stomach upsets caused by nervous tension. Rosemary has a long history of talismanic use also. "Rosemarie is for remembrance" a writer stated in 1584. It is given to mourners at funerals; in some places these sprigs of rosemary were thrown into the grave. It was believed as late as 1879 that this would bring peace to the departed spirit. It is not clear whether this has anything to do with rosemary as an aid to memory, or because it also has the reputation of keeping illness away. It also brings success in love, and if hung on the house threshold it drives away both diseases and devils. It seems that rosemary as a talisman to improve the memory is not wholly unconnected with its actual medicinal properties. This leads to realizing that talismans for improving or preserving health often make use of plants that do have medical uses as teas, poultices, unguents. Spruce, for example, which, as a talisman is recommended **to ease muscular pain,** has been used to make a spruce tea which cures scurvy, and the water in which plantain leaves have been boiled has been used to bathe inflamed eyes. If a plant has a medical virtue of any kind, it was believed that this virtue would also operate talismanically. Many doctors in rural areas in both Europe and Africa have told how their patients have chosen to make necklaces of pills and capsules rather than to take them internally; some have even used bottles of medicine as pendants. These talismans have sometimes proved to be effective; presumably they work in the same way as placebos. It would be pleasing to discover that all medical talismans were utilizing herbs and plants of real medical value, but this is not always the case and in some instances the medical value of the plant appears to have absolutely nothing to do with its talismanic function. Thus mugwort, which is recommended **to cure back pains** and which we are told to wear in the part of the back that is aching, is used for feverish colds, helps **to ease childbirth pains and menstrual pains** and is a tonic for pregnant women. Since labour pains do give women aching backs, it seems that this aspect of the mugwort has led to its use as a talisman, but the mugwort's other uses seem irrelevant.

To cure insomnia and ensure good dreams one is advised to hang a wreath of violets at the head of the bed. Violets belong to the viola family and members of this family, especially Hearts Ease, are useful to cure skin irritations including eczema. It has also been used to treat epilepsy and asthma, and was considered a cure for venereal disease, as well as a necessary ingredient of a love potion. Here the only possible connection between medical and talismanic powers appears to be the way the violet—actually Hearts Ease—can cure itching of the skin which certainly could well keep one awake.

Swellings and boils may be cured by hanging a plantain root around the neck. Culpepper said that plantain juice "clarified and drank for days together by itself, or with other drink, helps excoriations or pains in the bowels, the distillations of rheum from the head, and it stays all manner of fluxes, even women's courses, when too abundant". It has also been used to treat both internal and external ulcers. Nowadays its main use is to reduce fever. Its talismanic use obviously derives from its posed power to cure ulcers.

To increase the flow of milk of a nursing mother saxifrage should be placed between her breasts. Saxifrage root is diuretic; the seeds are carminative and disperse wind in the stomach. One variety *(Pimpinella Saxifraga)* is, however, said to increase the milk flow of cows which feed upon it, and this is clearly the relevant attribute. It is strange to note, however, that to increase the milk yield of cows saxifrage is not recommended as a talisman; boughs of flowering blackthorn are hung above the entrance to the cowshed on the first of May. The whiteness of the blossom must be presumed to do the job.

To prevent the ague one is advised to carry teazles in one's pocket or sprigs of polar or aspen. Water collected in a teazle is supposed to cure warts. Teazles hung outside one's door are supposed to be able to foretell a change in the weather. The aspen—yet another tree that has been credited with providing the wood for the cross and the branch from which Judas hung—is notable for its continual trembling. As the ague causes trembling it is logical, in talismanic thinking, to use the trembling aspen to control it. The teazle's connection with changes in the weather may be relevant, as the ague often occurs when the climate becomes cold and damp.

If a baby has **teething trouble**, he or she should be given a necklace made of elder or of alligator's teeth. The reason for alligator's teeth is clear. The pain of growing teeth can be countered by fully grown teeth. We have already looked at the elder from the mythological point of view. From the viewpoint of the herbalist the elder is one of the great herbs. Paul Beyerl[6] tells us "the leaves of the elder may be made into an ointment mixed with one part elder to two parts fixative, either animal fat or vegetable shortening. This is an excellent ointment for treating bruises, wounds and damages to the body which require soothing and healing." Elder is also sacred to the Goddess and has been used in the blessing of the new born children in both pagan and Christian tradition. Elder will also enable one to see fairies, and can be used to protect cattle by hanging twigs bound together with red thread outside the byre. Clearly it is an appropriate talisman for teething.

To ensure an easy childbirth the mother-to-be should wear hyacinth, and, when in labour, bind an Eagle stone (*Lapis Acquilaris*, light brown aetites) round her thigh in a cloth bag. The hyacinth does not appear to have much medical value, but it is associated with many rituals. On the Greek Islands young brides and their female attendants used to wear wreaths of hyacinth in the nineteenth century, just as they did in the days of Theocritus around 282 BC. It is also, as we have seen, associated with grief and used as a talisman to keep ghosts away. It is thus associated with marriage as well as grief; in talismanic thinking death and birth are often closely related, both being gateways into another dimension of life.

The Eagle stone is also recommended to women to ensure a safe pregnancy and should be placed in a cloth bag and worn round the

6. See Paul Beryl, *The Master Book of Herbalism*, Phoenix Publishing Co., 1984.

neck. In 77 AD Pliny said that eagles used aetites in constructing their aeries and that the eagle stone has no medical properties except immediately after it has been removed from the nest. In the thirteenth century it was believed that the eagle could not be fertile without these stones and that it brought on labour quickly and easily if tied to the woman's thigh. The Eagle stone was believed also to contain another stone within it, thus presenting an image of birth. This talisman is therefore an instance of sympathetic magic.

Colour is the key to a talisman **to cure lunacy**, which, as the word indicates, derives from the influence of the moon (lunar). The recipe is to place buttercup flowers in a linen bag and hang the bag around the patient's neck. The buttercup, being the colour of a newly risen full moon, will counter the moon's influence and ease the patient's mind. It should be noted that in the villages of the British Midlands in the nineteenth century another name for the buttercup was "crazy" because the smell of the flower was believed to send people mad. The talisman may therefore be based upon the principle of fighting fire with fire as in the use of stinging nettles as a protection against lightning.

There are many talismans to promote fertility and to ensure pregnancy.

To ensure pregnancy: Place a root of mandrake or bryony beneath the bed before you make love. Pots of basil in the house will bring children to those who wish for them. Japanese women carry fragments of stone to ensure fertility. If the lady is a virgin, she should wear, on her wedding day, a bracelet of shells or a garter of straw—wheat for a boy, oats for a girl. If she is not a virgin this will not work. Mandrake and bryony have already been noted earlier. Basil has long been regarded as a fertility herb and also as an incense to invoke dragons, the word "basil" being reminiscent of the basilisk. It is however associated with love and romance in the folk lore of Italy, Crete and Moldavia. It is considered useful at funerals in helping the spirit move on to its next existence and it causes compassion in those who eat it in their dishes. It soothes nervous disorders, especially dyspepsia caused by tension and, in the form of snuff, it has been used to cure headaches.

Setting aside the association with dragons, basil seems appropriate. A woman to conceive should, perhaps, not be in a state of nervous tension, and, after all, a birth is as much a journey of the spirit from one dimension to another as is a death. Birth and death are both gateways and it should not surprise us to find the same herb or talisman considered suitable for both births and deaths. Basil is a widely venerated herb in Hindu tradition and also in Malaysia as a herb to be strewn on graves.

Stone talismans are numerous, but the note about the Japanese custom does not specify any particular stone, therefore it must be stone as such that is significant. Here the explanation may once again be that sympathetic magic is in play, for in a great many cultures stones are thought to be born by the earth mother. Thus a stone is a proper talisman for bringing a birth.

Shells have often been associated with fertility possibly because they come from the sea and are therefore part of the moon-tugged tidal rhythms that affect women. Aphrodite, after all, is shown riding shorewards on a shell; the conch is a symbol of richness and wealth in the form of the cornucopia; cowrie shells are regarded as wealth in many cultures and also as sexual symbols. Indeed, if the shells referred to in oral tradition are cowrie shells the appropriateness of this talisman becomes very clear indeed. Cowrie shells, in their appearance, remind one of the vulva and have been used as a symbol of rebirth for thousands of years. Bodies were ornamented with cowrie shells as early as 20,000 BC. and Egyptians used them as charms on sarcophagi. In Islam the cowrie is worn by pregnant women. Gypsies regard the cowrie as a potent charm for good fortune.

The cowrie, however, does not only resemble a vulva but also an eye. Many ancestor figures or figures of gods in a number of cultures have been given cowrie shells for eyes, as were the skulls of ancestors by the people of Jericho in the seventh century BC. The cowrie was associated with the great Goddess in Roman times.

Straw is, clearly, a product of harvest and therefore a good talisman to bring harvest, to bring growth and completion. Wheat for a boy and oats for a girl seems arbitrary unless one retreats to traditional views of the sexes and sees the woman as delicate, trembling, dancing, as are the heads of oats, and the man as compact and sturdy as are the ears of wheat. The ears of wheat might also be regarded as phallic and the ears of oats, because of their formation, as somewhat vaginal.

It is interesting to see how the number of talismans for a particular problem or disorder reflects something about the way of life of the countryfolk in the past. There are many talismans to cause fertility, for example, and many to ease cramps and prevent rheumatism. Rheumatism must have been a serious disorder for the country folk for the list of talismans is long.

To prevent rheumatism: Carry a nutmeg, potato, horse chestnut, walnut or carrot in your pocket, or wear around your neck a bag containing elder pith or a twig of elder tied into three or four knots. Alder twigs in the vest pocket are also effective and on going to bed you should place a pillow stuffed with hops under the bed. Rheumatism may also be warded off by carrying the right foot of a hare in your left hand pocket, or carrying a mole's foot.

Oil made from powdered nutmeg is used as a laxative and nutmeg ointment is used to treat haemorrhoids. It is thus associated with easing bodily functions. The wild potato is diuretic, but actually does have some use in the curing of rheumatism. In *A Modern Herbal*, Mrs. M. Grieve[7] tells us:

> Successful experiments in the treatment of rheumatism and gout have in the last few years been made with preparations of raw potato juice. In cases of gout, rheumatism and lumbago the acute pain is much relieved by fomentations of the prepared juice followed by an application of liniment and ointment. Sprains and bruises have also been successfully treated by the Potato-juice preparations.

Horse chestnuts have also been used in the treatment of rheumatism, neuralgia, and haemorrhoids. There is no connection with horses here; the word horse probably derives from the Welsh word "gwrres" which means "hot" and distinguishes this tree from the sweet chestnut which is of quite a different species.

Walnuts have been credited with many virtues over the centuries. Oil extracted from the kernels has been used in the treatment of skin diseases, wounds and gangrene.

Tea made from the wild carrot eases gout and the seeds help to deal with flatulence, colic, hiccups, dysentery and chronic coughs--the latter explaining why to cure asthma and croup one should carry a carrot in the pocket. A strong decoction of carrot tea is a cure for gravel and stone—which explains why another virtue of the pocket carrot is

---

7. Mrs. M. Grieve: *A Modern Herbal*, Penguin Books, 1978.

the curing of gallstones.

We have looked at the elder already from the mythological and religious point of view. From the medical viewpoint elder is extraordinarily rich in virtue. Elderberry juice eases the pain of sciatica and neuralgia generally and may even cause an actual cure. Almost every part of the elder has some medical use. The bark is a purgative or emetic and was known to Hippocrates. The berries have many uses and wine made from the flowers can be splendid.

A decoction of alder bark has been used to bathe inflammations and swellings and ease sore throats and reputedly has cured the ague. Alpine peasants, we are told, have been cured of rheumatism by being wrapped around by bags of heated alder leaves. Hops maybe used similarly; a pillow made of warm hops will take away the pains of toothache or earache and cure nervous tension, thus bring comfortable sleep. Hop juice cleanses the blood. If it were used to ease rheumatism it would clearly be because of its qualities as a pain killer and soporific.

All these talismans to cure rheumatism are clearly derived from the belief that a herb with medical powers does not have to be turned into a drink or unguent or poultice to be effective. The virtue is strong enough to work simply because of the presence of the healing object. This is, at least, one explanation. Another one may be that as all this knowledge was passed down orally though the generations and was also kept relatively secret as the medical profession looked askance upon herbal remedies that derived from the wise women--or witches --of rural communities, the information became garbled. Told that the potato is good for rheumatism, the listener assumed that it was good for rheumatism in the same way that a religious symbol was good for keeping evil away. The two kinds of information became confused. The potato is a particularly interesting case as it did not reach Britain until the Elizabethan period and therefore its medical value must have been discovered well after that, for it was initially a luxury. I myself suspect its origin in Ireland where Sir Walter Raleigh first planted it in the 1580s and where it became a staple of diet and therefore, most probably, was tried out for as many uses as possible.

If this is the case, then we must deduce that at least some of our herbal talismans did not originate in medieval or pre-christian times, but much later, and therefore that talismanic thinking was habitual in the rural communities up to modern times.

When we turn to the mole's foot and the hare's foot we move from one kind of talismanic thinking to another, however. The mole has always been regarded as a magical creature. Pliny stated in 77 AD. "Of all animals it is the mole that the magicians admire most.... There is no animal in the entrails of which they put such implicit faith, no animal....better suited for the rites of religion". Indeed molehills are supposed to presage death; a tooth from a live mole will cure toothache, and mole blood in wine drunk at the time of the new moon and then the full moon will cure epilepsy, according to seventeenth century belief. The feet, according to one source, should be cut off a live mole and the mole should then be freed. A pair of mole's feet round the neck cures the toothache or the King's Evil. As the maimed mole dies, the disease will disappear. This is a form of dwindling magic rather than strictly talismanic. Why are moles so magical? I would suggest that they are first of all creatures from beneath the earth and are not only creatures of the dark but also blind. Called originally not mole but moldiwarp and, in some places, unt, the mole is doubly strange because of his small humanlike black hands. Hands are among the most ancient of talismans. The mole spends his time burrowing, building hills, and it may be that his energy makes him an appropriate talisman for easing stiff and painful joints.

The hare is a representative of the moon goddess in many cultures and witches are supposed to turn themselves into hares from time to time. There are many stories of a hare being lamed by shot and of a woman of the village then appearing with a lame leg. Thus the hare as a talisman derives from the Old Religion.

In a talisman to prevent convulsions there is an interesting mixture of pre-christian and Christian elements.

To prevent convulsions: wear a ring made of a silver coin collected at the Communion Service or Mass, or one made of three nails or screws taken from a coffin buried in a cemetery. If the person to be protected is a girl, the talisman should be made from five silver sixpences, or other silver coins, given by five unmarried men, who are not to be told the reason for the gifts. Silver is sacred to the Moon Goddess and to the Goddess as Diana and has been considered lucky since ancient times. In Britain the lucky threepenny piece, the lucky sixpence and the lucky silver shilling were all highly esteemed. It is interesting to note that, because silver is sacred to the Goddess, a silver bullet is the only way of destroying a witch who has transformed herself into a hare and that a silver bullet is believed to be able to pierce a lead-proof jacket. Silver hung around the neck will ward off many ailments in Scottish belief. A silver sixpence should be placed in the left shoe of a girl on her wedding day; it has also been used to help children pass school examinations.

It would appear that it is the roundness that makes the silver particularly effective against convulsions, perhaps because it is an image of the moon which controls the tides of the body as of the sea.

The ring of coffin nails or screws may have the same effect for the same reason. A ring made of a coffin hinge was thought to cure cramps in the eighteenth century as was a piece of coffin carried in the pocket. In Wales a circular amulet made from a coffin taken from a reopened grave was a specific against epilepsy. Toothache could be cured by placing a coffin nail against the afflicted molar. The coffin quite clearly relates to death, to losing one's bodily functions; consequently the coffin operates to prevent bodily functions failing by countering like with like. Coffin nails originally would be iron, and iron, because of its association with the magical forge, always has power.

Both these talismans may derive part of their power from their association with Christian rituals, the Eucharist of the Funeral Mass. Another Christian cure, which is not strictly talismanic makes use of the image of the cross on the back of a donkey, and which, of course, was the consequence of Christ riding a donkey into Jerusalem. Riding a donkey is supposed to cure or prevent haemorrhoids and also cure toothache. Another talisman to cure toothache is to carry a double hazelnut in the pocket or a nutmeg round the neck. We have looked at the virtues of the hazel and nutmeg already so it is only necessary to point out that any tooth that can crack a nut must be fairly sound. A tooth from a deadman's skull accompanied with a mole's foot and hung in a bag in the fireplace is also effective. The mole we have already surveyed and the thinking behind curing toothache with a tooth is obvious. The nutmeg round the neck will also cure a head-cold. This seems not to relate at all to the medicinal uses of the nutmeg. One must come to the conclusion that this is a talisman made of a curative herb or fruit or tree that has a specific virtue and is then regarded as having general powers. Over time, a talisman that does relate to a specific disease, such as the potato and rheumatism, becomes one for general use as an all-healer or bringer of good fortune. Some talismans, being religious in origin, are properly regarded as having wide powers to protect and bless. Samuel Pepys carried a hare's foot to prevent colic, for example.

The talismans to prevent or cure sickness in general include a number we have already seen as having specific purposes and virtues.

To prevent or cure sickness in general: Keep a pot of basil in the house or carry a pebble that has been boiled in a pot with potatoes. A string of onions hung in a house will also keep away disease; this is at least based upon fact as the powerful odour of the onion does destroy some bacteria. If you wish to protect a child from sickness you should hang a bag of hair from the cross on a donkey's back around his or her neck. If you wish to protect the child for a whole year you should hang a sprig of St. John's Wort round his or her neck on St. John's Day. On St. John's Day you should also, to protect all members of the household for a year, hang wreaths of yarrow in the house. You can get the same results by keeping, for a year, some hot cross buns or a loaf baked on Good Friday or a sacramental wafer that was blessed on Easter Sunday. Another general and long lasting talisman against all sickness is made by first collecting thirteen coins from as many friends and then exchanging them for a more valuable and larger coin (preferably silver) which has been given to the church; this large coin should then be hammered into a suitable shape by the blacksmith and worn around the neck.

Some of these talismans demand a footnote. The Easter reference is understandable as it is a reference to death and rebirth. The coin made of thirteen silver coins is, however, more interesting. The number thirteen is often regarded as unlucky because it is taken as referring to the thirteen present at the last supper. Thirteen, however, was significant long before that legendary event, for there are thirteen moons in the lunar year, the old calendar, and (of course) silver is the metal of the moon goddess. Thus this talisman mingles pre-christian with Christian belief even before we arrive at the magical figure of the blacksmith. One wonders into what "suitable shape" he would hammer the coin. It would be perfectly reasonable in some traditions for the shape to be phallic.

St. John's Wort is indeed a medical marvel and is also rich in traditional beliefs. Let us take the medical uses first; these are given by Mrs. Grieve in her *A Modern Herbal* as follows:

> *Medicinal Action and Uses.* Aromatic, astringent, resolvent, expectorant and nervine. Used in all pulmonary complaints,

bladder troubles, in suppression of urine, dysentery, worms, diarrhoea, hysteria and nervous depression, haemoptysis and other haemorrhages and jaundice. For children troubled with incontinence of urine at night an infusion or tea given before retiring will be found effectual; it is also useful in pulmonary consumption, chronic catarrh of the lungs, bowels or urinary passages. Externally for fomentations to dispel hard tumours, caked breasts, ecchymosis, etc.

St. John's Wort has been regarded as a herb of protection ever since the days of the Greeks. It is clearly connected to the Old Religion, for St. John's Eve is, as has already been pointed out, one of the great Sabbats.

Yarrow is sacred to the horned god of the Old Religion and in Chinese culture is used in divination. The horned god relationship is revealed in three of its popular names: Devil's Nettle, Devil's Plaything, Bad Man's Plaything. On the other hand its virtues as a vulnerary and astringent are obvious from its also being called Soldier's Woundwort, Knight's Milfoil, Herbe Militaris, Bloodwort, Staunchweed and Sanguinary. Its pungency and its use as snuff are revealed in its being called Old Man's Pepper. Yarrow, usually in the form of tea, has been recommended for use in dealing with ague, cramps, severe colds, measles, bleeding piles, kidney disorders and baldness. Certainly, it is sufficiently versatile to have gained a place in a catalogue of all-heal talismans.

With one or two exceptions, such as the rings made of silver coins and horseshoes, the talismans generally accepted in country lore are not man-made. They are an expression of a relationship with the natural world and, while this involves in some instances a series of beliefs in one or another religion, these beliefs are not particularly specific. A great many talismans, however, are not only manufactured but are made in terms of definite religious beliefs and dogmas. Some of these have, admittedly, changed in significance over the years because of religious upheavals, and many talismans are common to widely different cultures. These are the subject of the next chapter.

Traditional Talismans

Then I asked: "Does a firm persuasion that a thing is so, make it so?" He replied: "All Poets believe that it does, and in ages of imagination this form of persuasion removed mountains..."
William Blake[1]

Manufactured talismans are distinct from organic and found talismans and they were common in all civilizations. They were intended to give protection against ill fortune of all kinds, some being more specific in intent than others. It was widely believed that all misfortune, or at least a substantial portion of all misfortune, was caused by psychic influences–those of demons, devils, dark angels, ill-wishing shamans, witch-doctors or witches. Indeed right up to the fifteenth century the Christian church regarded all disease as a form of demonic possession. Consequently those people who treated disease with anything other than Christian exorcism were suspect. While this view of illness may now strike many as somewhat melodramatic, we do know that just as we can inflict diseases upon ourselves psychosomatically, so others can affect us by the telepathic messages they send and by directing psychic energies towards us. That psychic energy can be used to affect actuality has been shown over and over again by experiments in

1. From "The Marriage of Heaven and Hell" in *The Poetry and Prose of William Blake*, edited by David V. Erdman, Doubleday, New York, 1965.

psychokinesis in which a person, simply by concentration of the will, can move an object from one place to another. The evidence for psychokinetic power is considerable. The form of psychic attack that most talismans were generally regarded as countering can be summed up simply in the phrase "the Evil Eye." The Evil Eye is a term for ill-wishing by some particular person or persons. Many people in rural communities in Europe were believed to have the Evil Eye simply because they had a peculiarly intent gaze or a squint. They were often ostracized, sometimes beaten, and, in time of general misfortune, frequently killed. The Evil Eye was, it was believed, used equally against people, domestic beasts, and vegetables. If a man fell sick, or a cow ceased giving milk, or the butter would not come or the apple tree failed to fruit, these disasters were likely to be blamed on the "Evil Eye" of some ill-wisher. There are more spells against the Evil Eye in the various collections of verbal magic than there are of any other kind. Unfortunately, however, the possessor of the Evil Eye is not always in control of this energy force. The bewitcher of young children, of babies, called in Italy, *jettore di bambini,* may well not intend evil at all. A Neapolitan gentleman, with all good intentions, sponsored three babies and all three died; he was then regarded as possessing the *malocchio* and children were kept away from him thereafter. In Rome there was once a man who appeared to carry ill luck with him wherever he went. The point I am trying to make here is that psychic attack is not always intentional, and while we may scout the notion of the person, the *jettore,* who continually causes disaster by his or her very presence, the supposed existence of such people makes it sensible to wear talismans against the Evil Eye and other kinds of psychic attack in general.[2]

While the Evil Eye is not the only kind of psychic attack, it seems to be the most universally recognized. Many societies have names for it: the Sumerian word was *Igi-Hul* (eye-evil); the Arabs call it *Ain al-hasad* (if they wish to avoid drawing its attention to themselves they refer to is as *Ain al-Jamal,* the eye of beauty); the Copts called it *Bon,* the Ethiopians *Ayenat;* the Greeks *Baskanos;* the Syrians *Aina bisha;* the Armenians *Paterak.* In Europe today it is called *Bose blick* in Germany, *Booze blik* in the Netherlands, *Mal de ojo* in Spain, *Innocchiatura* in

2. For a fascinating survey of the Evil Eye, see Lawrence Distasi, *Mal Occhio, The Underside of Vision,* North Point Press, 1981

Corsica, *Mauvais oeil* in France, *Droch-shuil* in Ireland, *Szemverses* in Hungary, *Skjoertunge* in Norway–the list is vast.

Belief in the Evil Eye was, of course, no more than a recognition of the power of psychic energy, combined with a belief that any disruption of normally harmonious existence must have been caused by some malign person or spirit. The ability of shamans and witch doctors

Figure 4.1 Hand of Fatima

to detect the presence of a malign influence, to deduce its source and to counter it with magical rituals and blessings made them important and powerful members of their communities. It was, however, necessary not only to counter an evil activity already in progress, but also to provide people with means to prevent such attacks. Thus the shamans and the witchdoctors provided protective talismans as well as talismans that conferred blessings. As time went by some talismans became generally accepted as effective in themselves and the shaman or witch doctor was not required to provide them. The cross became such a talisman for Christians, as did the *cornu* for Italians.

Several otherwise quite different social groups and magico-religious traditions have talismans in common. One instance of this is the talisman generally known as the Hand of Fatima (see Figure 4.1). This image of an open hand can be found among Egyptian talismans where it is regarded as a symbol of openheartedness and generosity, and as a protection against envy and all evil arising from emotions akin to envy. The Etruscans considered it symbolic of justice and victory. Sometimes combined with other images, such as an eye or other powerful symbols in the palm, the Hand of Fatima is a protection against envy or the Evil Eye.

The Mohammedans gave this talisman its name. Fatima was the

Prophet's daughter by his first wife, Khadijah. She married Mohammed's cousin Ali and bore him three sons, Hasan, Husain, and Muhain. Even after having these children she was called Virgin or Clean Maid (Al-Batul) and was also called by one of the names for Venus, Al-Zahra. This talisman is regarded as symbolizing Mohammed's family, the thumb being Mohammed himself, the first finger Fatima, the second finger Ali, and the last two Hasan and Husain. It therefore carries an enormous power for good. It also symbolizes the five main duties of Mohammedans: to observe the fast of Ramadan, to make a pilgrimage to Mecca, to give alms, to practice all the rites of ablution and to be an enemy to infidels. The Hand of Fatima should, according to some authorities, be made of pottery or bronze, though the association with Venus might suggest that copper would be more appropriate. In modern times, however, it is usually made out of silver or a base metal or alloy of a silver colour.

Figure 4.2. The Egyptian talismans of the udjat (eye).

The Mohammedans use another hand talisman which is made out of blue glass, one finger extended. It is hung around the necks of children to protect them from evil. An Etruscan hand amulet shows the hand closed with the thumb placed between the second and third fingers; worn as a pendant with the thumb pointing down, it protects the wearer from the Evil Eye, as does the talisman of the cornu, or horns, in which the hand is closed save for the first and last fingers which are extended. This talisman is used as a highly insulting gesture today in Italy. Another variety is an Egyptian amulet made simply of two straight fingers; this brings the wearer strength and power.

The Christian blessing gesture of the hand with the thumb and two fingers extended has been found in the form of carvings in many Roman archeological sites. Called the *Mano Pantea*, the hand usually also contains a serpent and was associated with the worship of both

Serapis who is a combination of the Egyptian gods Osiris and Apis, and the moon goddess.

The hand talisman was often given additional power by making it the carrier of other symbols. The serpent is usually connected either to the third finger, which is associated with medicine and Aesculapius, or with the middle finger the *digitus infamis* or *obscenus*, which in Roman times was considered phallic as well as the finger of Jupiter, and was the finger used by prostitutes to beckon customers. A frog was also sometimes placed near this finger, the frog being regarded as aphrodisiac, as we will see later. It would be tedious to go through all the symbols that have been attached to the hand talisman over the ages. It is perhaps sufficient here to point out that to the hand of blessing, which is general in intent and protective, particular blessing talismans may be added.

The hand amulet is typical in being not only attached, at one stage in its history, to a particular set of religious beliefs, but also in being accepted and trusted outside that system of beliefs. The talisman of the eye is similar in this. The Egyptian talisman of the *udjat* (Figure 4.2), which means simply eye, provided defence against the evil and provided its wearer with good health and physical protection. The *udjat* is

Figure 4.3 The Scarab. An Egyptian talisman used for general protective purposes.

the Eye of Ra the sun god, which according to legend was once blinded by the evil powers during an eclipse, its sight being restored by Thoth. The Eye of Ra is sometimes combined with a second udjat, the eye of Aah the moon god, to form the Udjatti, a talisman in whose presence no evil person or thing can have power. The Eye of Ra is only one of many eyes to be found throughout the world. An eye is frequently painted on the prows of boats, in order to ensure successful navigation, as the eye symbolizes being able to see the way. In the Middle East, an eye talisman is sometimes placed over the left eye of a horse to protect it from harm.

Another Egyptian talisman used for general protective purposes is the *scarab* (see Figure 4.3). This beetle collects dung, then lays an egg in it and molds it into a ball which it then pushes into a sunny place where the heat will hatch the egg. It symbolizes the god of creation rolling the ball of the sun across the sky. The model of the beetle, the scarab, is therefore a talisman not only to protect the wearer against evil but also to give him vitality and strength, the energy and drive of the god of creation. The Egyptians made scarabs of all sizes and of almost all materials, creating statues as well as talismanic rings, brooches and pendants, but the favourite materials were green stone and black basalt.

Egyptian talismans face us with a problem, for all of them were placed with the mummified bodies of the dead to protect and help them on their after-death journey, and it is by no means certain that every one of them was used by the living. There are so many of them, moreover, that even Wallis Budge in his *Survey* [3] had to admit that he had not enough space to mention them all. In a like predicament, I must therefore choose those that do appear to have been used by the living and not solely for religious rituals.

Although green and black stones were most popular for talismans, some talismans were red.

The *Tjet* presents a conventionalized image of the vulva of the goddess Isis, and it was made most usually of red stones such as red jasper, bloodstone, red porphyry, carnelian or red agate. It might also be made of red sand, and some gold ones are known, though these would seem a little off target as the amulet talisman was credited with giving the wearer all the powers and virtues of the blood of Isis.

The talisman of the serpent's head was also made of a red stone or red glass and was naturally regarded as a protection from snakebites. This was certainly worn by the living as well as placed on the mummies to protect them from worms.

---

3. E.A.Wallis Budge: *Amulets and Talismans*, University Books, 1968 edition.

Other creatures are used for amulets, as are all the gods, but the majority of Egyptian talismans refer directly to religion and there is no space for a prolonged discussion of them here. The most popular creature talismans also became important to other cultures, and some talismans of Greece and Western Europe may derive from Egypt.

An insect talisman that may be derived from the scarab is that of a ladybird, which protects against poverty and indeed is supposed to bring wealth. It is traditionally made of gold but there are many made of other metals. In Germany, the ladybird is associated with the Virgin Mary and called *Mariankafer*. In other places it is also called "God Almighty's Cow." It is thus associated with ideas of creation and bringing to life.

Talismans in the shapes of both insects and animals are very widespread. The Etruscans believed that a spider talisman brought wisdom, foresight and riches. The Burmese believe that frog talismans can protect children from evil; the Egyptians considered them talismans for fruitfulness. In Chinese tradition, images of the stork and the crane bring health and long life, those of two bats ensure good fortune and that of a goose domestic happiness. The image of the phoenix in China is believed to bring longevity and marital happiness, while in Japan it is supposed to endow the wearer with the virtues of rectitude, fidelity and obedience to divine law. The Egyptians used a talisman of a vulture to prevent scorpion bites. The Chinese regarded the tortoise talisman as a protection against black magic and a bringer of health and long life.

Whether or not one understands or shares the religious beliefs of these various countries and peoples, a great many of their talismanic images still impress us. They appear to carry with them a kind of power accumulated from centuries of belief. It is as if our deep minds have been in some way conditioned to accept them. Once we know that a pretty little beetle badge has been, in the past, an object of religious importance, and that many millions of people have regarded it with awe, we tend to regard it with awe also. Once we view anything with awe, we admit the possibility that it has magical power, that it transmits messages, and the objects will have an effect on us and for us.

It is perhaps because the traditional symbol can be easily understood in terms of a powerful message and wondered at as something that has played an important part in many human lives, that it is more effective as a talisman than many more recent creations. Moreover, many of these traditional symbols are still part of our lives and have meaning for us in contemporary terms as well as in terms of ancient beliefs. Such talismans are those of the heart, the key and the knot.

The heart talisman is of great antiquity. The Egyptians called it the *Ab* and it symbolized the vital power of the person, perhaps the power of the unconscious and immortality. Shown as Figure 4.4, it was usually made of some red stone such as jasper, or of red glass, porcelain, wax or paste. Later societies accepted it as symbolic of the vital force of life, but gradually it developed a more limited popular significance as symbolic of love, affection and passion. Because it gives

Figure 4.4 The Ab. This heart-shaped talisman symbolized the vital power of the person.

the wearer a constant sense of the power and importance of love, it protects him against hatred. It is also, of course, used as a love talisman in an active sense. Modern heart talismans are usually made of gold.

The key has been used as a talisman ever since keys came into being. The Greeks regarded the key image as a powerful talisman symbolizing knowledge and possessing the ability to open a door to the unknown. The key was sacred to Apollo and Diana. The Romans, who thought it sacred to Janus and Jana, believed it effective in promoting prudence, memory of the past and perception of the future as well as ease in childbirth. The Japanese have a talisman of three keys, the keys of the granary, which brings the wearer happiness, riches and love. In other countries the three keys are said to ensure love, wealth and health. The emblem of Saint Peter is two crossed keys and Saint Zita, the patron saint of domestic servants, has a bunch of keys as her device.

The key has appeared in different guises in many societies. Figure 4.5 shows the Egyptian *Ankh*, which is formed of a letter T, or Tau, with a loop above the cross piece; it has been called "the key of life," and is a powerful protective amulet. Although in the first century AD. it was placed alongside the Christian cross on tombs, it is not truly a cross, although some people have said it is a cross with a handle, a *crux ansata*. Others have believed it to represent a gibbet and yet others the hammer of Thor. Some believe it to be a representation of a phallus, which seems not unlikely, for it is clear that it symbolized the life force itself; all the Egyptian gods are seen carrying it in their right hands and presenting it to those who serve them. Indeed, some pictures show a god putting it to the nostrils of a corpse in order to awaken the dead to life. Another view is that the loop represents the open mouth of a fish giving birth to the waters of the Nile and therefore to life itself. Used as the symbol of Venus, the Ankh has also been said to symbolize the triumph of spirit (the loop or circle) over matter (the Tau cross). The Ankh is not only generally protective, therefore, but also brings the wearer long life. It

Figure 4.5 The Egyptian Ankh.

is interesting to note that it has come back into favour in the twentieth century and is now one of the most popular pendants in existence.

Because of its loop, the Ankh may be related to the talismanic knot. The knot was also an Egyptian talisman and it has been used in many forms by many people from antiquity to the present. It is, of course, a symbol of that which joins and unifies and is common in the form of lovers' knots which symbolize the joining of two people. It is also a protection, therefore, against the disruption of relationships, and a talisman to preserve the status quo; something that the talisman owner or maker has "tied" into the knot will also be preserved. In India and Tibet the knot talisman is protective against evil, for it is believed to secure the good forces and bind them together, and to provide a hindrance to the evil ones. Knot talismans are used in weddings, both in China and elsewhere, for the above reason. A person at death's door, however, must have no knots upon him, as they will prevent the departure of the spirit. Similarly, knots in the clothing of a woman in labour may prevent the coming of the child.

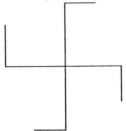

Figure 4.6   The swastika, gammodion or fylfot

Not all talismans retain their original symbolic meanings, or remain generally acceptable. Some become trivialized by popular misunderstandings; some fall victim to commerce and are recognized only as trademarks; some become so closely associated with particular social groups or sects as to lose their general universal meanings. One of the most ancient and powerful talismans, the *swastika*, has been affected in this way.

The swastika originated in ancient India. It is a cross, all of whose arms are of equal length, and made of "L" signs reversed, so that the ends of the arms all point to the right and suggest a clockwise spinning motion. This symbol, shown as Figure 4.6, is also known as the *gammadion* because the "L" reversed can also be read as the Greek letter gamma. It has also been known as the *fylfot*, which is a term taken from ancient designs for windows in which the symbol was used. A French term for it is *croix-pattee*. The fylfot sometimes exists in reversed form, which is to say that the arms point in a counter-clockwise direction. This counter-clockwise form is properly a *sauvastika* (see Figure 4.7).

The swastika has been interpreted in many different ways by commentators. Some have believed it to be a fire symbol portraying the crossing of two fire-sticks. Some have taken the swastika to represent the springtime sun, and the sauvastika the sun in autumn. Some think that it symbolizes the four quarters of the heaven or the four quarters of the earth. Others have seen it as the symbol of Indra, or Zeus, or Thor, or summed them all up in one and called it the symbol of the Supreme God. In general, it is accepted because of the wheel-like appearance, as a symbol both of the sun and of the Supreme Being, and as a good luck symbol.

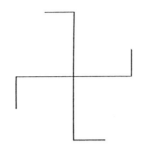

Figure 4.7 The sauvastika.

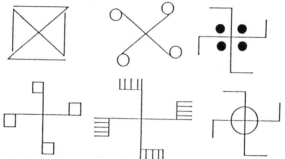

Figure 4.8 Some variations of the sauvastika

The symbol itself appears with some variation in many civilizations. (See Figure 4.8.) A Scythian swastika has little squares, like flags,
tucked onto the ends of the arms. Another version turns the short parts
of the arms into circles. On pottery, the sauvastika appears with four
dots added, one in each of the angles made by the crossing of the arms
at the centre. It appears as a symbol of the Buddha on many statues and
is also shown adorning the breast of Bodhisattvas. The Chinese name
for the swastika is "thunderscroll" *(Lei-wen)*, and when used as a
written character means not only good luck, but prosperity and long
life. In Sanskrit it means "purveyor of good fortune or well being." It
is also known as the Wheel of the Law, and taken to represent both the
cycle of the seasons and the human cycle of death and rebirth.

The swastika was used as an emblem by the Nazis in Germany;
since it is an ancient Aryan symbol, it was therefore appropriate to the
Nazi insistence upon what they chose to call Aryanism. It was also
recognized by them as a power symbol. The Nazis caused the swastika

to change in symbolism—it is now associated in our minds with so much tyranny, cruelty and evil that many of us cannot get beyond these associations to the real and timeless significance of the symbol itself. What happened to the swastika has happened, to different effect, with the cross. The sign of the cross predates Christianity by many thousands of years and it may even be the oldest talismanic symbol in the world. In the earliest known examples, the arms are all of equal length and at right angles to each other; this is known as the Greek or equilateral cross shown in Figure 4.9. It is clear, however, that the cross itself, and usually a form of equilateral cross, was a meaningful and potent symbol to mankind long before the days of Greek civilization. The cross has been interpreted as symbolizing the four quarters of heaven, and therefore, as a symbol of the power of the heavens and especially of the sun. Columbus was astonished to find it in America. It appears on many ancient Mexican and Peruvian artifacts and experts say that there it symbolized the four directions of the wind.

The cross on which Christ was crucified was probably one in which the horizontal arm was shorter than the vertical one and placed above the centre of the vertical. Figure 4.10 shows this cross, the Latin Cross (*crux immissa* or *crux capitata*) which has become the commonest form of the cross talisman. There are however other versions, such as those in Figure 4.11: the Cross of Lorraine, which has two cross pieces, the higher one being shorter than the lower, and an oriental version which adds a third short cross piece to the Cross of Lorraine near the foot of the vertical. There is also Saint Andrew's Cross which is in the form of an X (the *crux decussada*), and the Tau cross (or *crux commissa*), which is really not a cross at all, but the letter T or Greek Tau.

The cross did not become inextricably attached to Christianity until the fourth century when the Empress Helena is popularly supposed to have discovered the true cross. Thereafter, it became a sign of great protective power for Christians and was re-adopted, or revived, as a talismanic sign also by many non-Christians.

Figure 4.9 Greek or Equilateral Cross

77

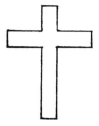

Figure 4.10 The Latin Cross (crux immissa or crux capitata)

The Latin cross is now regarded as essentially Christian, but other forms of the cross are used without specific religious significance as powerful talismans against evil and talismans of supreme power. It is interesting to note how Saint Andrew's cross is used to "cross out" errors, which is to say to cancel and to defend against wrongs.

Crossroads are, in all civilizations, regarded as places of magical power. The Romans even had a goddess of the crossroads called Trivia. Suicides are often buried at crossroads where their spirits are prevented by the sign of the cross from wandering from that place. Gallows were often erected at crossroads. The widespread notion that crossroads are haunted by evil spirits owes more to these practices than to any feeling that the sign of the cross is itself malign. Money is sometimes cached at crossroads, for there the cross will protect the treasure. In the Western world the sign for the kiss of love is a St. Andrew's cross. In folklore, before the advent of mechanical street cleaners, there existed a profession of crossing sweepers—they, like

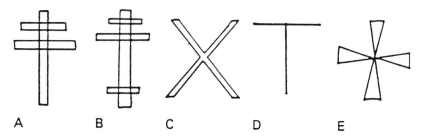

A   B   C   D   E

Figure 4.11 Other variations of the Latin Cross: a) Cross of Lorraine; b) Oriental version of the Cross of Lorraine; c) St. Andrew's Cross (the crux decussada); d) Tau Cross (the crux commissa); e) Maltese, Coptic or Rayed Cross

chimney sweeps, were regarded as lucky people to meet. Crossing one's fingers is a talismanic gesture against misfortune, as of course is making the sign of the cross. People who are unable to write make a cross as their signature on documents. The cross, indeed, remains a powerful talisman even though one form of it has, like the swastika, become attached to a particular group of people.

The cross is regarded as a sun symbol, and, like all sun symbols, as a powerful protection against evil. Moon symbols are equally protective. The symbol of the crescent moon in its first quarter, which is to say with the horns of the moon pointing to the left, is a talisman against misfortune and the Evil Eye. (It is important to have the horns pointing left for this shows the moon on the increase and therefore is also a symbol of growing prosperity. Crescents pointing the other way portray a waning moon and are negative in effect.) The crescent was known as the *Saharon* by the Hebrews and was worn by women, presumably because of its fertility inducing powers, and by kings, because the king stands for the country and the country must be fertile. It was also tied around camels' necks as a protection against the Evil Eye.

Another ancient talismanic symbol is the *mandala*, shown in Figure 4.12. In its most simple form it is a circle divided into four quarters by a cross, and it symbolizes unity and wholeness. The four segments may be read as thought, intuition, feeling and sensation; they may also be read as the four quarters of the heavens, the directions of the winds and so forth. This basic form has been used to create extremely elaborate symbolic figures, some for aids to mediation and some as protective talismans. Frequently these talismans have a representation of the sun, which is the centre of the universe, the all powerful god, and the human heart, at the middle of the design. Sometimes the circle includes a square which symbolizes the conscious controlling and ordering of the unity presented. All mandalas are protective.

In Figure 4.13 we see another mandalan talisman, the Chinese talisman of the Yang and Yin. It presents the unity of the universe and of the self in terms of the complementary interlocking of the feminine and the masculine, the dark and the light, night and day, above and below, in a form which also suggests, like the swastika, the turning wheel.

This, again, is used as much for meditative as talismanic purposes, and is a wholly protective symbol.

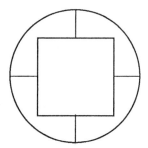

Figure 4.12   The Mandala (very simple form)

The two most widely used talismanic signs are of course the five pointed star which is also known as the *pentacle* or *pentagram,* and the *hexagon* or *hexagram.* The pentacle (Figure 4.14) is also called the Seal of Solomon because, together with other signs, it is supposed to have been engraved on his signet ring. It is, however, of great antiquity and was found on Babylonian vessels long before the time of Solomon, presumably as a preservative or protective device. The Greek followers of Pythagoras called it the Pentalpha, because it can be seen as five alphas intertwined. It should be made with one stroke of the pen, brush or engraving tool. If it is made of metal—preferably silver, the metal of the moon goddess—it should be made of one unbroken strip with only the one join to complete it. Because there is no opening in it, it was believed in the Middle Ages that the Devil could not enter it. This unbroken aspect of the pentacle is often reinforced by placing it within a circle. Occultists make use of this pentacle's protective powers by working from within one painted on the floor or on a sheet or rug, in which case many other symbols are arranged in the design. Medieval folk called the pentacle by many names indicating this aspect of the symbol such as Goblin's Cross, Devil's Sign and Wizard's Star. The pentacle was regarded as a sign of the earth goddess by the Celts, and this view is still held by witches. The pentacle with one point upwards is the sign of the goddess, of spirit ruling matter; the pentacle with two points upwards signifies the horned god and the rule of matter over spirit. The pentacle has also been seen as a symbol of man as microcosm, for it can be regarded as a schematic figure of man with legs apart and arms outstretched, and occultists use this symbol. Other interpretations of the pentacle include the view that with one point upwards it is a talisman for good fortune and with two points upwards it is unlucky, or even the identity talisman of a satanist, though it is hard to see why unless the pre-christian horned god is equated with Satan as he was in medieval witch-hunting days. The pentacle has also been seen as representing the interlocking of the male and female principles, the five senses, the five books of Moses and of God. It is sometimes worn by travellers to ensure a successful return home or as a talisman against the Evil Eye and demons.

Figure 4.13 The Yin and Yang

Figure 4.14 The Pentagram

This is in its simplest form, unadorned by letters and other signs. It can be used in combination with other inscriptions such as the name of angels, the signs of the zodiac and of the planets, and the name of God for more specific purposes.

Figure 4.15 shows an almost equally common talismanic sign, the *hexagram*, or six-pointed star, which should be made of one piece of material, or with one stroke of the pen. This figure has been called the Shield of Solomon, and like the pentagram, has many uses when inscribed in various ways. A talisman against fire, for example, is a hexagram inscribed in the middle with AGLA, the initial letters of the four Hebrew words that spell out "Thou art mighty forever, Adonai," and the short and long versions of the name of God (YH and YHWH) written round the sides. Finally, a text from Numbers 11:2 is inscribed on the reverse in such a way as to form a triangle–the top of the page is the base of the triangle, so that when it is read from right to left and downwards the message dwindles as, presumably, the power of the fire will dwindle.

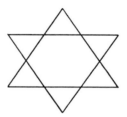

Figure 4.15 The Hexagram

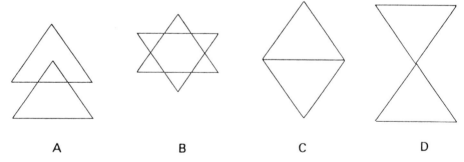

| A | B | C | D |

Figure 4.16 Hexagrams of the Elements: a) fire; b) earth; c) air; d) water

Though nowadays the hexagram is considered an identifying badge (or talisman) for a Jew and known as the Shield or Star of David, it was not considered an emblem of Jewry until the seventeenth century. The hexagram appears in many cultures with different meanings. In Tantric Hinduism the downward pointing triangle symbolizes essential womanhood and the upwards pointing triangle manhood. This Union of the Mother Goddess with her consort is called the Great Yantra. The down pointing triangle is the goddess Shakti, the upwards pointing triangle the god Shiva. The goddess in Tantrism is considered the source of all active energy and is therefore on top of the male god and giving him the energy to complete the union. Shiva is associated with fire and the upward pointing triangle in the Middle Ages was regarded as a symbol for fire, and the down pointing triangle the symbol for water. Thus the hexagram images a union of opposites from this point of view also. In Jewish tradition the mystical discipline of the Kabbala also saw the hexagram as unity, as the union of the Female Force or Power with the God, the union of Shekina (the Jewish Shakti) who was also viewed as the Torah, the Law or Truth with her consort. The hexagram therefore stands for wisdom--hence, most probably, its name of Solomon's Seal. It also, however, stands for sexual union, and the Kabbalists took the view that the Ark of the covenant contained a picture of a man and woman in sexual union in the form of a hexagram.

Pentagrams and hexagrams have been used as protective talismans for centuries and also as the ground plan for other talismans. Some practitioners of ceremonial magic make use of variations on the hexagram form to symbolize the four elements of Fire, Air, Water and Earth. (See Figure 4.16.)

The symbol of the fish has been used as a talisman for many centuries and was used as a badge by the early Christians. The derivation for this use comes from the Greek word for fish, *ichthus*, which is also an acronym for the Greek phrase *Iesuous Christos, Theou Uios Soter* (Jesus Christ, the Son of God, the Saviour). Both before and after the birth of Christianity, however, it was regarded as a talisman of good fortune that protects from poverty and promotes fertility and riches.

The Egyptians also considered the fish to be a talisman to bring abundance, wealth and domestic happiness because the fish was the symbol of the god Hathor who controlled the waters of the Nile. The fish as a god—Dagon, the sun fish—was worshipped by the Syrians. The Egyptians revered the Abtu fish and the Ant fish—they were believed to protect the boat in which Ra the Sun God sails by swimming beside it to drive away evil. Some talismans show the Christian cross with two fish swimming beside it, thus combining both Christian and Egyptian

83

symbolism.

The fish is one of the eight emblems of Buddhism; the god Vishnu's first incarnation took this form and the fish talisman is considered to bring wealth. The Romans regarded the fish talisman as a protection against colic, dropsy and other "watery" diseases. The simple yoni shape of the fish also directs us straight away towards the Great Mother Goddess, and to the vulva and the womb. Indeed, the word Delphos in Greek meant both womb and fish. The Christian Church took over a most powerful symbol when it created the Icthus symbol. When the Catholic Church instituted the eating of fish on Fridays it was doing no more than following the pagan custom of revering Friday, the day of the goddess Freya, or, in Roman times, the *Dies Veneris* or Day of Venus, and the day of the fish goddess and goddess of sexual activity Aphrodite Salacia. Indeed, the goddess as fish mother can be seen in many cultures.

The fish is not the only creature to be engraved, drawn, carved or cast into talismanic brooches, pendants or bracelets or rings. Another which, nowadays, is found not infrequently in the form of rings of silver is the frog. The frog was regarded as sacred in Egypt and a symbol of fertility because of the huge quantity of its eggs and of the consequent tadpoles. They saw the frog as a symbol of strength growing from frailty and/or rebirth, for the frog can suspend animation for years if trapped beneath the earth and can then come to life again without any difficulty. Because, like Venus/Aphrodite the frog appears to be born of foam, the Romans considered the creature sacred to Venus. Pliny believed that the frog talisman strengthened love and made for good friendships. The Babylonians carved nine frogs on cylinder seals to promote fertility, the number nine obviously referring to the nine months of gestation.

The casual observer of talismans cannot always distinguish a frog from a toad, the only visual difference being that the toad is warted and the frog is not. Toad talisman's are regarded as having much the same attributes as the frog ones, especially the death-rebirth significance, and for the same reason. Toads were very much respected in many cultures; in Latin America and in China they were deities. In Europe, however, they became associated with witches, as witches were supposed to use toads in their spells and kept them as pets. Indeed the talismanic power of toads was used, as we have seen, not by creating models of them but by using their toadstones and their bones.

Many of these talismans are obviously created because of specific attributes of the creatures. The bull was an important talisman to the Etruscans who engraved bull heads on metal discs to produce success in all things, strength and long life. There have been several bull-gods or gods with whom bulls are associated. There were bull deities in Phoenicia, Crete, Rome, Persia and India; Zeus, according to Ovid, used a bull disguise. For all that, the bull talisman is not particularly prevalent today and, in any case, it seems to have derived from simple observation rather than ancient religion.

Though this may be the case, it must be pointed out that many creatures in common knowledge sooner or later developed into a deity of one kind or another and therefore became represented in statuary or in talisman form. The elephant appears in the head of the great Hindu god Ganesa, and Ganesa talismans are worn to produce wisdom as well as to remove obstacles and help in authorship, for he is the god of writers. Sometimes the talisman is simply in the form of an elephant and not a full portrait of round bellied Ganesa seated upon a rat with emblems in all his four hands.

The cat, already mentioned in another context, is often presented as a talisman and the cat, as we have seen, was a deity of Egypt. The Lion, usually credited with bringing strength and power and the ability to heal fevers if carved on jasper, gave its head to the Egyptian goddess Hathor in her shape as the Sphynx. Cybele is reported as travelling in a chariot drawn by two lions. The lion is associated with the sun because of its mane. In the fifth century BC. the Lion Goddess of what is now Israel was ritually married to the Jewish Jehovah and their worship was combined.

Horses appear on talismans not infrequently, but these pins and brooches are worn more often by race goers than by the generality. The British worshipped their goddess Epona in the form of a white mare and her image is still to be seen cut into the hillside. Giraldus Cambrensis tells of a twelfth century coronation in Ulster which involved the king-to-be coupling with a white mare. Epona, the horse brooch, brings therefore good fortune and power.

As we have seen, the religious background of some of these creatures is not always very important. The attributes of the creature are what counts. Thus the talisman of a fox brings success, probably because of the foxes, reputation for ruthlessness, deviousness and cunning.

The talisman of the scorpion is a powerful protection against an enemy and can also be used as an active talisman to destroy an ill-wisher. Arrowheads and axes are also protective against ill-wishers.
Most of the above talismans are visual representations. Not all talismans are of this kind. Fringed clothing has been worn in many societies to avert the influence of evil spirits. Bells sewn to garments have the same function; the Romans used to attach rattles to the garments of their children. Some societies have used jangling bracelets and anklets for the same reason. These are often worn during ritual dances, as are the anklets made of deer hooves of the Haida and Kwakiutl Indians. The bells attached to the clothes of the Morris dancers in Britain, and the bell attached to the hobby horse of the professional jester, probably had originally the same functions as do the coins sewn on gypsies clothing, and the pearl buttons on the outfits of London costermongers or "pearlies." Bells and noisemakers every-where are regarded as having talismanic and protective properties. The Chinese use firecrackers to keep off evil spirits. Other societies have used gongs, drums and wind instruments. These are talismanic rather than true talismans in that it is the sound which does the work and the power does not reside in the objects themselves. Nevertheless, by association, bells have come to be regarded in themselves as talismans; many of them are inscribed with the swastika to make their protective influence even more certain, even in Christian churches.
Other manufactured talismans have more specific protective quali-ties. In the Punjab one wears copper rings, bracelets or earrings as a protection against rheumatism and sciatica, and in the western world copper is regarded as a defence against rheumatism. Rings of iron are worn or carried in both India and the western world as a protection against witchcraft. According to western folklore, witches of evil disposition are repelled by cold iron. The Chinese protect their chil-dren from misfortune by making them wear bracelets and anklets of jade. Jade rings have become popular once again in the twentieth century in the West, though only a few wearers know the talismanic reason for wearing them.
Many manufactured talismans are simply metal models of natural objects which have been long regarded as having talismanic power, or of objects which are too clumsy or awkward to wear in themselves. Thus there are more models of horseshoes worn for good fortune than there are real horseshoes and metal models of rabbit's feet are more

commonly carried than rabbit's feet themselves. The vast majority of traditional talismanic symbols, however, appear to relate to some central mystery of existence and to attitudes and beliefs which form a part of almost all religious systems. Many of them, such as the cross and the heart, go back thousands of years and appear to derive their power from the symbolic language in which they speak to the deep mind and from the awe with which we regard objects that have been venerated in one way or another for many centuries. It also seems true that any talisman which has passed through the hands of many people, all of whom have used its talismanic powers, has gathered a powerful energy field and will therefore be more effective than one of modern manufacture. The age of talismans is always a matter of interest to those who seek them out; the older they are the more credible they are felt to be and, therefore, the more powerful.

Not all talismans make their appeal only to the deep mind. Those Egyptians who wore the scarab and the ankh and those Babylonians who inscribed the cross and the swastika on their pottery were consciously aware of the place these symbols had in their religious beliefs. Conscious understanding of the symbolism helps to direct the deep mind, of course, for conscious and intuitive response are then combined. This is especially the case with talismans made in the figures of the gods. These are extremely numerous, for they occur in all cultures and societies and it would require a book to list even half of them. Perhaps here it is only necessary to say that all the images of Indian, Chinese, Japanese and other gods that can be seen in stores devoted to antiques and curios are talismanic, and that if you purchase one you should look up its significance in a book on the religion and mythology of the country concerned. The appearance of the god is often of little help. Many that look ferocious are benevolent; some that appear to be harmless have harmful uses. Who would suppose that the Ganesa, the elephant-headed god of India, was a god of wisdom and literature, and, as a talisman, powerful in the removal of obstacles and difficulties and of great help when beginning important business? Who would think that Hanuman, the monkey god, was a powerful good fortune talisman? These talismans are indeed difficult to understand at first glance, as are all esoteric visual symbols.

Talismanic Stones

When the soul of the world, by its virtue, does make all things (that are generated or artificially made) fruitful, by sealing and impressing on them Celestial Virtues for the work of some wonderful effect, then things themselves...when they are conveniently bound to, or wrapped up, or suspended about the neck, or any other way applied although by ever so easy a contact, they do impress their virtue upon us.

Albertus Magnus: Egyptian Secrets

From time immemorial, talismans have been made from precious and semi-precious stones and there is a considerable amount of lore connected with them. Some of this is purely medical lore, involving the stone being crushed into powder or burned in the fire and eaten.[1] There are other medical uses for stones which are talismanic, such as the laying of particular stones upon different parts of the body to cure illness, or the holding of stones in the hand when sick, or the dipping of stones in water or wine which is afterwards drunk. Most talismans are worn on the body and often next to the skin and many people believe that no talisman can be effective unless it is in contact with their

---

1. Practices which involve the alteration of the stone from its original state do not concern us here, since this chapter will address talismanic uses of stones that may have been cut or engraved but otherwise not been altered.

bodies. Therefore, the dipping of a stone or any other talisman in water may be thought of as the transference of some power or virtue from the talisman proper into a medicine. Some stones are regarded as having medical properties which may or may not be truly talismanic and these are often carved into goblets from which wine or water may be drunk. There is a grey area here as no real distinction was made by the early users of talismans, or indeed by early medical practitioners between psychic and physical operations. Some cures which we now know to be based upon the physical properties of plants and herbs were regarded as being just as magical as the cures we now regard as entirely psychic or psychological. These days, the world of medicine is slowly coming around to the views of its forebears in that doctors are no longer regarding psychological and psychic methods of healing as outside the province of medicine proper.

Precious and semi-precious stones are also effective curative talismans because of the shapes into which they have been cut or carved–certain shapes can contain, resonate and transmit energy in the same way as the pyramid. The interesting phenomenon of "pyramid power" has shown us that blunt razor blades, when placed under cardboard replicas of the Cheops pyramid and oriented in the same way, north to south, can regain their edge. It has also been shown that the pyramid will keep meat fresh, aid in the healthy growth of plants, and if suspended over a bed will help sick people to sleep and assist the healing process. Pyramids are now in use at several hospitals.[2] It is apparently not the material of the pyramid that matters, but the pyramid's shape. This would go some way towards explaining why cut diamonds and crystals of all kinds are considered powerful talismans. Of course, the properties of crystals are well known to science and crystals are used in many ways by technology. We may, therefore, in listing talismanic stones and especially precious stones be touching upon something which may, like so many "magical" beliefs of the past, come to be explored and understood in terms of physical properties.

In addition to their medical properties, talismans made of precious and semi-precious stones in various combinations have been popular for centuries. Perhaps the most famous one of these is Aaron's

---

2. For a more in-depth discussion of the medical uses of pyramids, readers should see Lyle Watson's fascinating book, *Supernature*, Bantam Books, New York, 1974.

Breastplate, which was to be worn as a talismanic aid to making correct judgements in disputes. It is described in Exodus 28:15-21:

> *And thou shalt make the breastplate of judgement with cunning work...of gold, of blue, and of purple, and of scarlet, and of fine twisted linen, shalt thou make it .*
>
> *Foursquare it shall be, being doubled; a span shall be the length thereof, and a span shall be the breadth thereof.*
>
> *And thou shalt set in it settings of stones, even four rows of stones: the first row shall be a sardius, a topaz, and a carbuncle: this shall be the first row.*
>
> *And the second row shall be an emerald, a sapphire, and a diamond.*
>
> *And the third row a ligure, an agate, and an amethyst.*
>
> *And the fourth row a beryl, and an onyx, and a jasper; they shall be set in gold in their inclosings.*
>
> *And the stones shall be with the names of the children of Israel, twelve according to their names, like the engravings of a signet; every one with his name shall they be according to the twelve tribes.*

This text is that of the Authorized Version of 1611. There are other versions. In G.F. Herbert Smith's authoritative *Gemstones* [3] we read:

Besides this description, which in the Hebrew original perhaps goes back to about 1500 BC, four others have come down to us: in the Septuagint Version, the Greek translation which was made at Alexandria in the early half of the third century BC; in the Vulgate Version, the Latin translation made by St. Jerome about 400 AD[4]; and

---

3. G.F.Herbert Smith: *Gemstones*, Methuen 1912 (Revised Edition by C.F.Philips, 1958)
4. Eusebius Hieronymus 340-430 AD.

in Josephus's two works, *The Jewish Wars*, written originally in Hebrew about 75 AD, shortly after the destruction of Jerusalem, and subsequently translated into
Greek, and The *Jewish Antiquities*, written in Greek
about 93 AD[5].

The gemstones and their position on the Breastplate as described in
the five versions are given in the following table, the English equivalent
always being used.

GEMSTONES ON THE HIGH-PRIEST'S BREASTPLATE

	FIRST ROW		
Authorized	sard	topaz	carbuncle
Septuagint	sard	topaz	emerald
Vulgate	sard	topaz	emerald
Jewish Wars	sard	topaz	emerald
Jewish Antiquities	sardonyx	topaz	emerald

	SECOND ROW		
Authorized	emerald	sapphire	diamond
Septuagint	carbuncle	sapphire	jasper
Vulgate	carbuncle	sapphire	jasper
Jewish Wars	carbuncle	jasper	sapphire
Jewish Antiquities	carbuncle	jasper	sapphire

	THIRD ROW		
Authorized	ligure	agate	amethyst
Septuagint	ligure	agate	amethyst
Vulgate	ligure	agate	amethyst
Jewish Wars	agate	amethyst	ligure
Jewish Antiquities	ligure	amethyst	agate

	FOURTH ROW		
Authorized	beryl	onyx	jasper
Septuagint	chrysolite	beryl	onyx

---

5. Flavius Josephus 37-100 (?) AD.

Vulgate	chrysolite	onyx	beryl
Jewish Wars	onyx	beryl	chrysolite
Jewish Antiquities	chrysolite	onyx	beryl

The description in *The Jewish Wars,* which in an English translation is as follows, is not so precise as in the other sources and it has been assumed above that the order of the gemstones in the text corresponded to the arrangement on the Breastplate:

> On the other part there hung twelve stones, three in a row one way and four in the other: sard, topaz, emerald, carbuncle, jasper, sapphire, agate, amethyst, ligure, onyx, beryl, chrysolite. (Book V, ch. 5, par. 7.)

We notice that, ignoring the order, the species of gemstones mentioned in the several versions are identical with two exceptions: diamond in the Authorized Version replaces chrysolite in the others, and sardonynx appears in *The Jewish Antiquities* instead of sard. The diamond in the Authorized Version clearly could not have been the gemstone known by that name to-day, because the latter would have been too hard to be engraved with the name of one of the tribes, apart from the fact that diamonds of the size required for the Breastplate are uncommon. It is, indeed, doubtful if our diamond was generally known much before about 1000 AD. Sardonynx, however, might well have been the more correct name if the piece had a streak in it, and may therefore be considered as an alternative to sard.

The New English Bible gives the stones as First Row: sardin, chrysolite and green feldspar. Second Row: purple garnet, lapis lazuli, jade. Third Row: turquoise, agate, jasper. Fourth Row: topaz, carnelian, green jasper. This version states also that the stones should be set in rosettes made of gold.

The significance of Aaron's breastplate lies in its later development. The stones were conceived as standing for the twelve tribes of Israel in Rabbinical tradition and therefore as being rather heraldic than talismanic. It was, of course, inevitable that they should be given talismanic powers eventually. In Revelations 21: 9-21, the stones of the breastplate, and the breastplate itself, by implication were made to form the foundation of the New Jerusalem. The description runs:

And there came unto me one of the seven angels which had the seven vials full of the seven last plagues, and talked with me, saying, Come hither, I will show thee the bride, the Lamb's wife:

And he carried me away in the spirit to a great and high mountain, and showed me that great city, the holy Jerusalem, descending out of heaven from God.

Having the glory of God: and her light was like unto a stone most precious, even like a jasper-stone, clear as crystal;

And had a wall great and high, and had twelve gates, and at the gates twelve angels, and names written thereon, which are the names of the twelve tribes of the children of Israel:

On the east, three gates; on the north, three gates; on the south, three gates; and on the west, three gates.

And the wall of the city had twelve foundations, and in them the names of the twelve apostles of the Lamb.

And he that talked with me had a golden reed to measure the city, and the gates thereof, and the wall thereof.

And the city lieth foursquare, and the length is as large as the breadth; and he measured the city with the reed, twelve thousand furlongs. The length and the breath and the height of it are equal.

And he measured the wall thereof, an hundred and forty and four cubits, according to the measure of a man, that is, of the angel.

And the building of the wall of it was of jasper: and the city was pure gold, like unto clear glass.

And the foundations of the wall of the city were garnished with all manner of precious stones. The first foundation was jasper; the second, sapphire; the third, a chalcedony; the fourth, an emerald;

The fifth, sardonynx; the sixth, sardius; the seventh, chrysolite; the eighth, beryl; the ninth, a topaz; the tenth, a chrysoprasus; the eleventh, a jacinth; the twelfth, an amethyst.

And the twelve gates were twelve pearls; every

several gate was of one pearl: and the street of the city was pure gold, as it were transparent glass.

The twelve tribes have now become the twelve apostles. And Rabanus Maurus, Archbishop of Mainz, (786-856 AD) is reported by G.F. Kunz[6] as saying:

> In the jasper is figured the truth of faith; in the sapphire, the height of celestial hope; in the chalcedony, the flame of inner charity. In the emerald is expressed the strength of faith in adversity; in the sardonynx, the humility of the saints in spite of their virtues; in the sard, the venerable blood of the martyrs. In the chrysolite, indeed, is shown true spiritual preaching accompanied by miracles; in the beryl, the perfect operation of prophecy; in the topaz, the ardent contemplation of the prophecies. Lastly, in the chrysoprase is demonstrated the work of the blessed martyrs and their reward; in the jacinth, the celestial rapture of the learned in their high thoughts and their humble descent to human things out of regard for the weak; in the amethyst, the constant thought of the heavenly kingdom in humble souls.

The stones are still, here, more heraldic than talismanic, telling of powers and virtues rather than possessing them. But by now the stones had also been allotted by Josephus in the first century AD and by St. Jerome in the fifth, to particular months as birth-stones and also to signs of the zodiac. Kunz tells us that the custom of actually wearing natal stones may not have begun until the eighteenth century. The difficulty was that the stones had now been given particular healing powers and the powers of one's birthstone might not apply to one's own particular health. It seems that some people changed the stones month by month, that some wore all of them together because of their astrological power. Moreover different traditions allotted the stones differently. Kunz gives us the count using the order selections given by the Jews, Romans, Arabians, Poles, Russians, Italian, Isidore, Bishop of Seville and the generally agreed list of modern times, though his list of

6. G.F.Kunz: *The Curious Lore of Precious Stones*. J.B.Lippincott, 1913.

1913 differs slightly from that agreed upon by the National Association of Goldsmiths of Great Britain in 1912. If we alter his list accordingly we get:

January:	garnet 8, hyacinth 2
February:	amethyst 9, hyacinth 1, pearl 1
March	jasper 5, bloodstone 5, aquamarine 1
April:	sapphire 7, diamond 3
May:	agate 5, emerald 5, chalcedony 1, carnelian 1, chrysoprase 1
June:	emerald 4, agate 4, chalcedony 3, turquoise 1, pearl 1, cats-eye 1
July:	onyx 5, carnelian 2, ruby 2, sardonynx 1, turquoise 1
August:	carnelian 5, sardonynx 4, moonstone 1, topaz 1, alexandrite 1, peridot 1
September:	chrysolite 6, sardonynx 2, sapphire 1, lapis lazuli 1
October:	beryl 8, aquamarine 5, opal 2
November:	topaz 9, pearl 1
December:	ruby 6, turquoise 3, chrysoprase 1, bloodstone 1

Apart from details of naming and so forth this may be all that need concern us here, except to point out that the situation is further complicated by each month having a guardian angel and that angel having a stone apportioned to him, and each month also having an apostle who has a gem. This information is to be found further on in this chapter.

The importance of the gems as power is shown in another tradition. The Hindus, who also allocate gems to the months and to the zodiac, combine them in a nine-gem jewel. Kunz writes:

> "One of the oldest and perhaps the most interesting talismanic jewels is that known as the *naoratna* or *nararatna*, the "nine-gem" jewel. It is mentioned in the old Hindu *ratnacastras*, or treatises on gems, for example, in the *Nararatnapariksha*, where it is described as follows:

Manner of composing the setting of a ring:

In the centre	The Sun	The Ruby
To the East	Venus	The Diamond
To the Southeast	The Moon	The Pearl
To the South	Mars	The Coral
To the Southwest	Rahu	The Jacinth
To the West	Saturn	The Sapphire
To the Northwest	Jupiter	The Topaz
To the North	The descending node	The Cat's-eye
To the Northwest	Mercury	The Emerald

Such is the planetary setting.

From this description we learn that the jewel was designed to combine all the powerful astrological influences. The gems chosen to correspond with the various heavenly bodies, and with the aspects known as the ascending and descending nodes, differ in some cases from those selected in the West. For instance, the emerald is here assigned to Mercury, whereas in Western tradition this stone was usually the representative of Venus, although it is sometimes associated with Mercury also. On the other hand, the diamond is dedicated to Venus instead of to the Sun as in the Western world.

It is easy to understand that such a talisman as the *naoratna*, combining the favourable influences of all the celestial bodies supposed to govern the destinies of man, must have been highly prized and we may well assume that only the rich and powerful could own this talisman in a form ensuring its greatest efficacy. For the Hindus believed that the virtue of every gem depended upon its perfection and they regarded a poor or defective stone as a source of unhappiness and misfortune.

In modern times this talisman is sometimes differently composed. A specimen shown in the Indian Court of the Paris Exposition of 1878 consisted of the following stones: coral, topaz, sapphire, ruby, flat diamond, cut diamond, emerald, amethyst and carbuncle.

Talismanic stones are regarded as having power in themselves, but when they are mounted in brooches, formed into pendants or set in rings their power is frequently increased by means of inscriptions. These inscriptions may simply spell out the particular one of their attributes that the wearer wishes to emphasize and call into play. It may consist of the appropriate sign of the zodiac. Many gems are inscribed, however, with symbols that have been significant to humanity for thousands of years and a great many precious and semi-precious stones are used to create carved images which combine the power of the material used with the power of the symbol--we will look at the subject of inscribed talismans later. Many stones are also associated with the seven energy wheels of the human body, the chakras, and I have given this information also. The chakras are seven in number. The first group of four begins at the base of the spine with the Root Chakra which corresponds to the element of earth. The second chakra at the sexual organs is the Sacral Chakra and corresponds with the element of water. The third situated at the solar plexus is the Solar Chakra and its element is fire, and the fourth chakra, the Heart Chakra, corresponds with the element of air. The next three chakras form a trinity. The first is that of the throat which is the Chakra of the Earth; the second is the Chakra of the Brow, of the third eye, and is that of thought, and the third chakra is that of the Crown of the Head and spirit.

This system is, of course, a study in itself.[7] For our purposes it is only perhaps necessary to state that each chakra sends energy to the next one in the ladder and that when the energy of a particular chakra is weakened, or blocked, when its wheel no longer turns smoothly, then the person is sick and needs help. Essentially in contemplating the chakras we are surveying energy fields and different densities of vibration and so it is perfectly reasonable for talismans that deal in energies to be related to these energy centres in the body.

Agate
The agate comes in so many different forms and is coloured so variously that a survey of its talismanic properties amounts to a survey of many different stones. Moreover, the various authorities disagree quite sharply about it, as they disagree about many of the attributes of precious and semi-precious stones which are listed here. I have done my best to include the beliefs of all the major traditions but some viewpoints will certainly not be represented.

The astrology agate has been regarded as one of the stones of

---

7. For a sensible and lucid short survey of this subject see Peter Rendel: *Introduction to the Chakras*, The Aquarian Press, 1979

Gemini, the House of the Twins. The sun enters this house on/or about May 22nd and leaves it on the 21st of June approximately. It is also one of the stones associated with the planet Mercury. A traditional rhyme runs:

> Who comes with summer to this earth
> And owes to June her hour of birth,
> With ring of Agate on her hand
> Can health, wealth, and long life command.

Nostradamus (1502-1566), taking his views from a supposed poem by the alchemist Pierre de Boniface (ob.1323) says that "the Agate of India or Crete" renders a man "eloquent and prudent, amiable and agreeable".

In Aleister Crowley's Table of Correspondences[8] the Agate is associated with Yellow, the Juggler Card in the Tarot pack, the Egyptian gods Thoth and Cynocephalus, Indigo, Grey and Purple, Hermes (or Mercury), the Hindu gods Hanuman and Vishnu (in his role as Parasa-Rama), Vervain, Herb Mercury, Marjoland, Palm, the Swallow, the Ibis, the Ape, the perfumes Mastic, White Mandal, Mace, Strorax, the vegetable drugs Juniper and Penny Royal, with falsehood and dishonesty, and with the Sun as well was with the miracles of healing, the gift of speaking with tongues, and scientific knowledge. This is a sufficiently confusing list and it seems from it that the agate has many attributes, not all of them consistent with each other. The agate is also listed as a birthstone for June, whose Guardian angel is Muriel, who rules Cancer. Muriel is, surprisingly, masculine and has the ability to supply his supplicants with magic carpets. He should be invoked from the south. Agate is also the personal stone of the angel Bariel, the ruler of the eleventh hour or the day. In Jewish tradition the agate is the stone of the Tribe of Naphtali and of the month of May; its zodiacal sign is Scorpio, and its angel Barbiel, otherwise known as Barbuel or Baruel, the angel of the month of October. One authority equates him with Barakiel which would make him also the angel for February who rules the lightning (see also Amethyst) and can help in games of chance.

The similarity of the various angelic names leads one to think that

---

8. See Aleister Crowley: *777 And Other Quabalistic Writings* Edited by Israel Regardie, Samuel Weiser, 1977.

there may be some confusion here. In Kabbalistic Numerology the Agate's number is fourteens.

The calming effect of agates has been believed by many people over the centuries. Pliny tells us that the Magi of Persia used to burn agates in order to keep storms away. One wonders whether this belief has anything to do with the frequent use of both real and imitation agate as umbrella handles in our own time. It's also interesting to note that agate is still used for mortars and pestles as it was by the physicians of old, and is also used for burnishers, paper knives, seals, brooches and necklaces.

The belief in agate averting storm and lightning appears to have been widespread. Marbodeus, otherwise known as Marboeuf, the Bishop of Rennes (1067-1081 AD) gave Aeneas's agate talisman the credit for enabling him to escape unscathed from his many adventures, and Camillo Leonardo, in his *Speculum Lapidum* of 1502, not only agreed about the agate's capacity to fend off storms but also believed that it brought vigour and success to those who wore it. Throughout the Middle East agate was in great demand. The Persians considered that it conferred eloquence, clarified the mental processes, improved the sight, increased amiability and brought good fortune in matters concerning legacies and wills. If pressed to the forehead of a sick person it would cure fever. It was also, they believed, helpful in the finding of hidden treasure. Its ability to clarify the mental processes led to the Mohammedans believing that if powdered and drunk in apple juice or, some say, water, it would cure insanity. There is a belief that if an agate is pressed on the wound caused by the bite of a poisonous insect, a scorpion or snake, the bite will do no harm. Camel drivers would put agate in their mouths to prevent thirst during their long journeys. It also was supported to provide security. Queen Elizabeth I was given an agate engraved with a picture of Vulcan at his forge with Venus watching him. Considering the marital difficulties of Vulcan and Venus it is not easy to understand why Archbishop Parker, who gave the stone to the Queen together with a long list of its qualities in Latin, told her that as long as she had it she would always have a reliable friend. Agates were often carved and engraved to form talismans. In the year 1701 a rectangular slice of agate with bevelled corners was made for a follower of the prophet Mohammed's son-in-law, Ali. In each corner, according to Sir Wallis Budge's book *Amulets and Talismans* was "a circle containing a divine name and the first border i.e. that with diamond shaped ornaments contains forty-eight of the ninety-nine "Beautiful Names" of God. The second and fourth borders, which are separated by an ornamental border, contain extracts from the Koran, viz the Fatihah, and the Throne Verses, the Declaration of the Unity of God etc."

Agates were frequently used for such religious amulets in Arabia, Syria, Mesopotamia and North Africa. The agates usually chosen were ones crossed by white bands or dark grey and semi-transparent ones. They would be carved into the required shape then engraved with a lapidarists wheel or engraving tool. In the nineteenth century they were sometimes coated with wax and the text was then inscribed through the wax and the agate placed in a bath of hydrochloric acid. Agates and carnelians were used most frequently because they were believed to have magic properties.

One of the magical properties is found in the Breton belief that if a young woman were given a mixture of powdered agate and beer and was unable to keep it on her stomach she was a virgin; if she digested it she was not. Oddly, in this context, the agate was considered in the nineteenth century to be of use in achieving a successful seduction; this may, however, connect merely with its reputation for increasing eloquence. In general, apart from Aleister Crowley's curious association of it with deceit and dishonesty—though Crowley's correspondences often reveal more of his mischievous contrariness than his scholarship—there seems to be some general agreement among writers on this subject. The agate is a healing and calming stone; it lowers fevers and reduces anxieties. In its various special forms it increases vitality both in human beings and the world of nature.

Each kind of agate is credited with individual powers. The names of these agates commonly refer to their colours or the patterns in the stone. The Bearded Agate, which portrays something that could conceivably be a beard, brings strength to its wearer, presumably because men are associated with physical strength. The Eye Agate, (so called because it resembles a human eye) is believed to cure eye trouble of all kinds and to protect its wearer against the Evil Eye: this is clearly an instance of sympathetic magic. A Mexican Agate portraying a single human eye with remarkable clarity was called a Cyclops. An iridescent form has been called the Iris or Rainbow Agate. An agate with zig-zag bands that suggest the outer walls of an ancient fortress has been called the Fortification or Ruin Agate. Its fortification rather than its ruin aspect are reflected in its power, which is to protect in general. The Moss Agate is so called because its markings look like fronds of vegetation, often rather moss or fern-like, and sometimes like a wooded landscape, in which case the stones are referred to as Tree Agates or Wood Agates—which should not be confused with agatized wood. When these markings are black or brown it may be called Mocha-Stone, the name being derived from a port on the Red Sea called Mokha. The Moss Agate, and its variants, is used by Gypsies and, in the Far East, to help speakers to improve their powers of persuasion. The Moss Agate has fascinated many people over the ages because it so often looks as if it contains a quite specific image. In the British Museum there is a remarkable moss agate which looks like a portrait of Chaucer. William Pavitt[9] states that "the Strawberry Hill Collection has another with a portrait of Voltaire and a third showing the profile of a woman".

The Tree Agate was regarded with awe by the Romans as it was felt that, because of its markings, it had been singled out as a special stone by the Creator. Pavitt states "According to Orpheus, if thou wear a piece of Tree Agate upon thine hand, the Immortal Gods shall be well pleased with thee; if the same be tied to the harness of thy oxen when ploughing, or about the ploughman's sturdy arm, wheat-crowned Ceres shall descend from heaven with full lap upon thy furrows." Another tradition states that the agate should be worn on the upper part of a man's right arm and upon the right horn of each of his oxen. Presumably tractor drivers will be able to work something out. This is one of those rare instances of a talisman being bound on the right rather than the left arm. An explanation may be that while the left arm, being on the heart side of the body, is associated with the animating life spirit, the right arm is associated more with physical strength and labour.

Presumably because the Moss Agate interests the eye more particularly than many other stones it was considered a valuable eye medicine and was used for mortars and pestles on which physicians ground the herbs for eye lotions. The Red Moss Agate helps to create a balance in the wearer's physical energy and the Green Moss Agate gives balance to the emotions. Other agates have been given descriptive names: the cloud-agate has cloudy patches that contrast with its background of transparency; the star-agate has star-shaped figures; the coral-agate

---

9. William Pavitt: *The Book of Talismans, Amulets and Zodiacal Gems,* The Aquarian Press, 1914 (New Edition 1970).

appears to contain coral or shells. And there are a number of others scarcely less fanciful.

The Red Agate is a very positive stone. As we have noted, it was one of the several red stones that the Egyptians used to make their most sacred amulet, the *Tjet*, the stylized image of the vulva of the goddess Isis, that was supposed to bring the virtues of Isis' menstrual blood to the wearer. Together with the *Tet*, which was a stylized image of the lower part of the human spine, it was placed in the hands of statues and also on coffins to help the dead person to be prepared to face the judgement Hall of Osiris. The one hundred and fifty-sixth chapter of the *Egyptian Book of the Dead* was often carved upon the Tjet.

The red agate also symbolizes the spiritual love of good, peace, longevity, health and wealth. In addition, it protects the wearer from lightning, thunderbolts and the bites of snakes and insects. The White Agate is called the Milk Stone in Italy, and it was believed to increase the flow of mother's milk, again and obviously following the rules of sympathetic magic. Its smoothness and whiteness make it also of value as a sleepstone; when properly empowered by a spell-caster with thoughts and images of calm and rest it should be placed under the pillow of a sufferer from insomnia, who should hold it in his hand when he wakes up in the middle of the night or before he goes to sleep. The Black Agate is traditionally associated with courage, vigour and prosperity. It provides success in games.

Tawny Agate has all the properties of Black and Red Agate and also increases the wearer's intelligence, brings good fortune in love, protects against insanity and fever and gives victory in battle. If held in the hand when one is ill, it will speed up recovery and make it certain. It also gives the wearer longevity. Grey Agate cut into a triangular shape and worn as a pendant protects the wearer from indigestion, intestinal disorder and stiffness of the neck. If a woman wishes to prevent herself ever becoming sterile she should drink water in which a Green Agate ring has been washed. Black Agate with white veins strengthens the wearer's heart.

The agate is, perhaps, the most widely used talismanic stone because of its many different appearances. Not all the talismanic minerals used as talismans are precious or even semi-precious stones, however. For example, **Alum,** if sewn into a person's clothing or tied into their head coverings, protects against the Evil Eye. If placed at the threshold of a house it will give the house the same protection. These are Middle Eastern beliefs. **Amber** is a fossilized resin, not a stone, but it has been used in talismans for centuries. It is associated with the sun and with the planet Leo and those born under that sign should wear amber bracelets, rings or necklaces. Amber, of course, retains electrical charges, and can emit sparks. This is probably one reason why the Greeks had a high regard for it. They called it Elektron, from which our word electricity derives. It was associated with the sun because it was believed that it was created by the heat of the sun's rays. It has been used talismanically for thousands of years. Amber beads were found in Egyptian tombs. Amber phalluses were considered powerful protections against the Evil Eye. In the Far East amber, being relatively soft, was carved into the forms of animals--those animal forms we have already noted--lions, hares, frogs, fish and so forth. The electrical power of amber was considered, and is still considered by some, a most efficient healing force. Amber necklaces are held to prevent or cure goiter and throat ailments and also to prevent a baby having convulsions while teething. If held in the mouth amber will stave off infection, which may explain why so many cigarette holders and tobacco pipes have amber mouthpieces. If one gazes through a piece of amber, one's vision will be strengthened and eye disorders will be cured. Amber is also useful to cure rheumatism and alleviate pain in general. It soothes the nerves and calms the disposition, which may be why Greek worry-beads are often made of amber at the present time. In general, amber revitalizes the body, absorbs negative energies, and is beneficial to the internal organs of the body if placed over them. It stabilizes and decreases suicidal impulses and relates to the third Chakra, the navel. When carved in the form of frogs, fish or hares amber will make men virile and women fertile. Amber also protects the wearer from digestive disorders, toothache and migraine.

Amethyst

The amethyst ranges in colour from pale violet to purple. According to some authorities, the amethyst is a stone of the twelfth House of the zodiac, Pisces, the fishes. The sun enters Pisces on February 19th and leaves it on March 20th. Consequently, the amethyst is the birthstone for February and a traditional rhyme runs:

The February born shall find
Sincerity and peace of mind,
Freedom from passion and from care
If they the Amethyst will wear.

Other authorities say that the amethyst is the stone of Aquarius (January 21-February 19). This is less of a disagreement than might appear at first, for both signs are associated with water and both have blue as their associated colour. The colour associated with the planet Jupiter is also blue, and its stones are amethyst and lapis lazuli. In Jewish tradition, the Amethyst is the stone of the tribe of Gad and of February; its zodiacal sign is Sagittarius and its Angel Adnachiel, otherwise known as Advanchiel or Adernahael, the angel of the month of November. In another tradition it is the stone of February and Pisces and of the angel Barchiel whose personal gemstone is Jasper, and who has also been called Barachiel, Barakiel, Barbiel, Baraqiel. He rules over lightning, the planet Jupiter and Scorpio and is useful in helping gamblers to be successful. The Amethyst is also the stone for Wednesday and the personal stone of the Apostle Matthias.

In the comprehensive Table of Correspondences provided by Aleister Crowley in 777, a collection of his "qabbalistic writings" the amethyst is regarded as corresponding with: Jupiter, Mercy, Deep Violet, four fours of the Tarot deck, the Egyptian Gods Amoun and Isis, the Greek God Poseidon, the Scandinavian God Wotan, the shamrock, the unicorn, Jehovah in his capacity as rainmaker, opium, cedar and the virtue of obedience among other less immediately intelligible matters.

Whether or not the connection with water has anything to do with it, the name Amethyst is derived from the Greek *a* (not), *methuein* (to be drunken). The amethyst was, indeed, regarded by both Greeks and Romans as an amulet to prevent drunkenness. It was also very highly prized and it seems probable that this was because of its rarity. Persia was at that time the only major source for the stone though others are reported as being Britain, Spain and India and supplies were limited.

The amethyst's effectiveness as a controller of inebriety is reflected in a legend. In its Roman form the legend tells that Bacchus, the god of wine, came across a beautiful maiden, named Amethyst, who was on her way to worship at the shrine of Diana. Bacchus, who was angry with Diana at the time, had vowed that the next mortal he should see on the way to her shrine would be devoured by tigers. On hearing the bad news Amethyst appealed for help to Diana who transformed her into a white statue, whereupon Bacchus, seeing the girls beauty and regretting what had happened, poured a libation of wine over her and thus gave the statue its colour. Like many legends this one is a little hard to swallow; tigers were not plentiful in either Greece or Rome. One suspects that the story was constructed to explain and justify a belief for which any other explanation would be hard to find. A variant of this story has Bacchus intending to rape Amethyst and Diana changing the maiden into a gem, and makes it clear that Bacchus, himself, presumably in a spasm of guilt, gave it the quality of protecting its wearers from the ill effects of wine among which one must number lust.

The amethyst was worn by both Greek and Romans and frequently engraved with the figure of a god. One such ring is described by the Greek poet, Antipater of Thessalonica probably around 25 BC.

> I am Drunkenness engraved
> upon a sober amethyst
> quite inappropriately I'd say,
> but I'm on Cleopatra's fist,
> the ring of that immortal queen,
> and since I am thus owned,
> although a goddess, I've not been
> entitled to get stoned.   (Translation, R.S.)

It seems that the amethyst was often engraved with the figure of either the god of wine or the god of love. Plato the Younger, writing sometime in the first or second century AD used the same subject.

> I, the drunkard Dionysus,
> am carved upon this amethyst.
> Either this engraved device is
> going to teach me to desist
> or in time it will have learned
> itself to get completely stoned.
>   (Translation, R.S.)

Plato, of course, missed the point. The amethyst was engraved with the God of Wine because it was he who had given the amethyst its protective power; his image, therefore, would rather reinforce than lessen its influence. Logically enough, amethyst was also carved into drinking vessels.

The connection between drunkenness and sex was clear to both Greeks and Romans, and some amethyst rings were engraved with the figure of cupid, the God of Love, presumably as a protection against mere lust. Saint Valentine who was martyred on February 14th, the day on which it was believed in folklore that birds mated, is supposed to have worn just such a ring. That amethysts are associated with true love and fidelity rather than wantonness is shown by the belief of Roman wives that amethysts could ensure that their husbands remained affectionate. The amethysts are, indeed, associated with the quelling of any kind of intemperance or any strong passion. It has been said to repress all evil thoughts and all excesses. The Arabians believed that it could prevent not only gout which is associated, rightly or wrongly, with excessive wine drinking, but also nightmares. Pliny says that the Magi thought that if an amethyst were engraved with symbols of the sun and moon, it would prove a powerful charm against malign witches—though not all witches were regarded as malign in that time--and bring good fortune and the favour of the authorities. If the sun and moon amethyst were worn on a necklace of swallow feathers or baboon hair, it would protect the wearer from hailstorms as well as the Evil Eye. The Egyptian soldiers used to wear talismans of amethyst to bring them success in battle and keep them calm at times of danger.

Two other gods are associated with the amethyst, the Greek Hermes and the Egyptian Thoth. Both these gods are responsible for conducting souls into the underworld. The amethyst colour, purple, was in many cultures regarded as the colour of mourning. It has also long been considered a royal colour, a colour signifying dignity and power. Purple amethysts were included in the gems laid in the tombs of the Pharaohs, and there was a Byzantine custom that when the Empress was due to give birth, she should be put to bed in a room with walls of purple hangings or of porphyry, which is a purple marble. Purple is the colour not only of mourning in the Christian church but also the colour of penitence; purple vestments are therefore worn during Lent, and one wonders if this has anything to do with Bacchus's penitence over the maiden Amethyst. Probably not. The word purple derives from the Greek Porphyria, which means both the shellfish that provided the dye, Tyrian purple, a species of Murex and the marble. The child of a king or emperor is said to have been "born into the purple".

It may be that the symbolic significance of purple as much as the power of the amethyst as a gem is partly responsible for the use of amethysts in the rings of Christian bishops since the sixth century. The amethyst has, indeed, been called "Bishops stone" by the Roman Catholic church. The ring is worn on the second finger of the right hand and the ring is kissed ritually by supplicants. In the sixteenth century, a custom of breaking the Pope's amethyst ring after his death and fashioning a new one for his successor began. The amethyst is considered to be a gem of healing. Its long believed attribute of inducing temperance and balance has led to its being regarded as able to bring into harmony, the mental, emotional, physical and spiritual in man. It helps those who are set in their ways to become less rigid and it helps those of the opposite temperament to become disciplined. It calms the impatient and soothes any who suffer from feelings of martyrdom.

When used in physical healing it is first moved all around the body of the sufferer and then placed upon the part affected. It is useful for dealing with blood clots and if used as a talisman it should be worn as a pendant near the heart or in a choker around the throat. Long associated with spiritual power it aids in meditation, increases second sight and prevents insomnia. It is also said that, like many other gems of the quartz family, it has the power to change molecular structure. It is equally effective whether set in silver or gold. It is a talisman to bring peace of mind and tranquillity and to prevent temper tantrums, and during the Middle Ages when war and plague were disturbing people, rosaries were made of amethyst, for the rosary would thus bring the user peace of mind and dispel anxiety. In point of fact the purple rays of light passing through an amethyst have been found to exert a calming effect on hysterical patients and also to ease the pain of nervous disorders such as neuralgia and migraines if drawn lightly over the forehead of the sufferer. Worn as a talisman it is said to cure gout and will give pleasant and comforting dreams if placed under the pillow; it will also improve memory. Lawyers and sailors should wear amethyst rings for protection; the ring should be worn on the third finger of the left hand. The amethyst increases the wearer's powers of intuition and is helpful in practising meditation. It eases the grief of those mourning the death of a loved one, and it helps in ameliorating the bad effects of overwork and stress. It not only is a stone of the Sixth Chakra, the third eye which is the eye of psychic vision, but also all chakras. Some think the amethyst helps people to keep vows of chastity or celibacy. In Kabbalistic Numerology the Amethyst has the number nine.

Asphalt or **Bitumen** may seem an odd choice for a talisman, but Wallis Budge tells us that the Egyptians believed it has strong powers, and that a quantity taken from the skulls of mummies could prevent "sprains, fractures of the bones, blows, fallings down, headache, epilepsy, dizziness, palpitation of the heart, etc." A cross made with asphalt on a man or beast protects it from witchcraft and the Evil Eye. He adds that the Aztecs would tie small bags of asphalt round the necks of their children to keep sickness away.

Alexandrite

This stone is so named because it was discovered in the Ural mountains in 1839 on the birthday of the Crown Prince Alexander of Russia. It changes colour from olive green in daylight to a reddish violet in artificial light. It is said to stimulate love and pleasure at night and bring good fortune during the day. It increases refinement and sensibility in the wearer, and, if worn in a ring on the left hand, it will limit the energy of those people with whom the wearer does not wish to become involved. It is also said to bring a sense of discipline and restraint to the wearer of it in ring form, but if it is worn as a pendant on or near the chest it will inhibit or restrict the wearer's wishes and actions.

Aquamarine

The aquamarine is associated with Neptune and Pisces, which may be so simply because of its name. It is the birth stone for those born under the sign of Scorpio and for the month of March, though some say October. The aquamarine helps those who are to procrastinate to become decisive and brings the wearer courage and bravery as well as quick decisiveness. It promotes constancy of feeling and therefore makes a good wedding gift. Necklaces of aquamarine were considered helpful in curing toothache and preventing disorders of the stomach or liver in the Middle Ages. The aquamarine is also a great protective talisman for sailors and earrings of aquamarine are supposed to bring the wearer friendship and love. It calms nerves, reduces the retention of fluids and is good for the eyesight. It helps in meditation and is associated with the Fifth Chakra, the throat.

Aventurine

The name of this stone comes from the Italian, *avventura* meaning chance. Green aventurine is associated with the sign of Cancer, and, in some parts of Europe, with the month of August. It is regarded as a healing stone; when placed on the body above the site of some internal trouble, its green ray emits a healing influence. It deals effectively with psychosomatic disorders, increases perception and lives up to its name by being lucky for games of chance. It brings its wearers a sense of balance. Green aventurine is associated with the Third Chakra, the solar plexus and the Fourth Chakra, the heart. Red and brown adventurines are most effective for the Second Chakra which is placed just above the sex organs, and also the Fifth Chakra, the throat. Some authorities state that green aventurine tunes up the Sixth Chakra, the Third Eye, and the Seventh, the crown of the head. Aventurine, in general, is useful for keeping the chakras unblocked and aligned properly with one another.

Azurite

Azurite is sometimes called Chessylite and is a blue copper carbonate. Being blue it is associated with Venus. It is a clarifier of the mind and helps the wearer to understand and control his or her emotions. It enables the wearer to face his or her private and secret fears successfully and it enables the wearer to deal with the subconscious. It stimulates inspiration and psychic perception, is useful as an aid in hypnotizing and it is, in general, an enormous help in increasing both intellectual and psychic perception. It is a stone of the Sixth Chakra, which is the Third Eye.

Beryl

Beryl is the gem of Saint Thomas, who is one of the guardians of the month of June. It is also the stone of Humiel, the guardian Angel of December, who governs Capricorn and the birthstone of October whose Guardian Angel is Bariel who rules the eleventh hour of the day and is one of the angels of Jupiter.

Beryl is a stone of Scorpio and of October. It has many colours and therefore many names, one of which for pale blue beryl we have noted under aquamarine. When golden it may be called Heliodor, when clear Goshenite, when rose-coloured Morganite and when blue-green it is beryl simply. Beryl, when very green, is good for curing diseases of the eye, and the greenish-yellow variety is helpful in cases of jaundice and liver disorder.

Beryl symbolizes hope and protects against the Evil Eye. It sharpens intelligence, cures laziness and brings peace of mind. If it is carved in the shape of a frog or has a frog engraved on it, it makes peace between enemies and promotes friendship and marital love. It heals illnesses of the stomach and eases soreness of the throat and pain in the jaws. It preserves sailors and travellers from danger and is useful in discovering anything hidden. If worn as a ring or a pendant it should be set in gold.

Bloodstone or Heliotrope

The name bloodstone has, in the past, been used to refer to a variety of stones, so, in this instance, it might be as well to sort this problem out. Though in talismanic studies the term bloodstone is used most frequently, probably because of the connotation of blood as the life fluid, it should really be regarded as simply one variety of heliotrope. Heliotrope is a green chalcedony spotted with red caused by the presence of iron oxide. Green chalcedony without blotches or spots is called plasma and ranges in colour from almost white through apple green to dark leek green, which is the most common colour. The heliotrope has the same colour range, but only those of a deep green with blood red spots are valued. The most valued are the stones in which the spots are round rather than streaks or blotches and regularly disposed, so that they look as if they have been caused by drops of blood. Because of this the heliotrope has also been called bloodstone, and stones with yellow spots or patches have been looked upon with some scorn.

The name bloodstone has, unfortunately, also been used over the ages to label almost every red stone, including red jasper, red agate, red coral, red marble, and carnelian. The German bloodstone (blutstein) is, in fact, hematite. Consequently when reading the older writers it is not easy to be certain whether or not the reference is to heliotrope. This is made a more tiresome problem because of the conviction held by many that heliotrope is a simple green jasper flecked or spotted with red. Jasper, however, is not a chalcedony but a compact quartz; heliotrope relates to plasma not jasper.

Be that as it may, the name heliotrope supposedly derives from the Greek words for the sun, *Helios* and for direction, *tropos*, because it is said that if one particularly thickly spotted with red is dipped in water it produces an image of the sun.

In astrology heliotrope is associated with the house of Aries, the planet Mars and the month of March whose guardian Angel is Malchediel, Machidiel, Malahadiel, Malchedael, Melkeial or Melkejal. In grimoires, the books of ritual used by occultists, this angel is invoked to bring the person commanding him the woman he desires and if the precise time and place is stated she will certainly appear. Heliotrope is also associated with the sign of Pisces; this is not much of a contradiction as the sun enters Pisces on February 20th and leaves it for the house of Aries on March 21st. It is also said that the stone is more suitable for wear by men than women and is of most benefit to those born under the sign of Pisces. Occultists have also said that the heliotrope can make one invisible and Plato tells the story of Gyges whose heliotrope ring made him invisible when the ring was turned inward; this ability has also been credited to the eye-agate, the diamond and the opal.

The bloodstone is said to have originated at the crucifixion of Christ when drops of blood from the Roman soldier's spear that pierced Christ's side fell upon some green jasper. As we have seen it could not have been jasper, but must have been plasma. This is said to account for its magical properties which are numerous. The connection with the crucifixion was, however, embodied in a statue of the scourging of Christ made in Heliotrope, the red spots being used to display the drops of blood on Christ's clothing. The statue was on display in the National Library of France in Paris in the early years of this century.

The bloodstone has been worn in pins, brooches and rings for centuries and is credited with very considerable powers. It was popular among the Egyptians for thumb rings, the thumb being under the rule of Mars. The Egyptian king Nechepsos wore bloodstone engraved with the figure of a dragon emitting rays of light; this was in order to strengthen his digestion. The gnostics wore bloodstones for the same purpose and to make them wealthy. The Romans considered the bloodstone a help in gaining the favour of powerful people, as well as being a charm against insect and scorpion bites. Roman athletes, following a general belief that bloodstones increase constancy and endurance, wore bloodstones to achieve success in the games. Roman soldiers wore bloodstones in order to reduce the flow of blood from wounds acquired in battle. It is believed still in parts of India that if a bloodstone is dipped in water and then pressed upon a wound or cut it will stop bleeding; this is not entirely without reason, for the iron oxide in the stone is an astringent and was used for this purpose by surgeons. Powdered bloodstone was used by the ancients to cure both internal and external bleeding, especially in the lungs and uterus. Bloodstone is said to cure disorders of the urinary tract, and a bloodstone, if engraved with the figure of a scorpion at the time the sun is entering the house of Scorpio, will prevent the formation of bladder stones. The bloodstone wards off disease, prevents melancholy, prolongs life and strengthens the digestion. It clears up bloodshot eyes and dries eyes afflicted with the rheum. It helps to cure the dropsy and the ague and was popular in the Middle Ages with farmers breeding cattle. It prevents the wearer from being deceived or cheated and also makes the wearer's own words and arguments convincing. In parts of the Sudan it was, and is still, believed to provide protection from headaches or sunstroke. Almost everywhere it appears to have been regarded as a help in making its wearers both rich and brave, and in Mediterranean countries it is thought to be a protection from the Evil Eye. One testimony to the efficiency of bloodstone comes from Thomas Boyle, who, in 1675, writing on "The Origine and Virtues of Gems" tells us that a gentleman suffering from constant nose-bleeds was very distressed until "an ancient gentleman presented him with a bloodstone the size of a pigeon's egg, to be worn round the neck, and upon the use of this stone he not only cured himself, but stopped haemorrhage in a neighbour".

Marbodus thought that the bloodstone should be set in silver. Chinese tradition, however, states that a gold setting is more efficacious.

Because of its red colouring bloodstone is believed to help in all disorders of the blood, including leukaemia and haemophilia. It stimulates the flow of energy and has good effects when placed over the kidneys, liver, intestines and bowels if they are operating slug-gishly. It is the stone of the First Chakra at the base of the spine, the source of all energy in the chakra system. In Kabbalistic numerology it is given the number twelve.

Carbuncle

The carbuncle is referred to in so many old texts that it cannot be left out of the list although, in truth, the name refers to a garnet, or ruby or any deep red stone. It protects the wearer from fascination, night-mares, poison, plague and incontinence. It is a stone of Scorpio. As one would expect of a red, or blood-coloured stone, it is reputed to stimulate the heart and also brings determination and health. It protects children from drowning and soldiers from being killed in war. Carbuncles protect the wearer from extravagance and from being bewitched, and bring the possessor increased energy, confidence and determination as well as popularity and good health. When hung around the neck a carbuncle will cure sore throats and indigestion. In Africa and the East it was believed to prevent soldiers being wounded in battle. It is the gem of St. Andrew the Apostle, and of Amriel or Ambriel the guardian angel of the month of May, the chief of the officers of the night's twelfth hour and a ruler of Gemini. His name is inscribed on a Hebrew amulet to protect the wearer from evil.

Cairngorm

The cairngorm is a light brown or yellowish variety of smoky quartz and its name comes from the Cairngorm mountains of Scotland where it is found. Whether or not the Scots' connection has anything to do with it, the cairngorm is supposed to assist the wearer to be shrewd and discriminating and to respond to everything that occurs both tactfully and decisively. Cairngorm brooches were very much in vogue in the nineteenth century.

Carnelian

While carnelian is usually blood red in colour, there are many other varieties that range in hue from yellow to brown. The three main varieties are: blood red or burned brick; honey coloured; and brown. The colouring is caused by the presence of iron oxide.

In the fifteenth century the name Carnelian was thought to have been derived from the Latin *carneolus* which had its root in the word *carnem* meaning flesh. It is in fact a corruption of the original name cornelian which was derived from the medieval Latin word *cornum*, meaning the cornel-berry or cornelian cherry.

Modern astrologers have ignored the carnelian and no month has acquired it as a birthstone. Even the indefatigable and frequently dubious Aleister Crowley has omitted it from his Table of Correspondences, but Appolonius of Tyana tells us it is the gem appropriate to Thursday, and another authority gives it as the stone for Virgo and the month of August, whose guardian angel is Hamatiel, one of the rulers of the order of virtues whose personal gemstone is the diamond.

The carnelian was considered to possess magical powers, possibly because, like other chalcedonies, if rubbed briskly in a dark room it can be seen to give off sparks. Carnelian, like agate, was used for talismans by both Arabs and Persians. The Assyrians and Babylonian placed great importance upon cylinder seals which were made from various gemstones and other materials. Those made of carnelian, together with jasper, assured the possessor that he would never be denied the protection of his god.

Because of its blood colour, the carnelian was carved by the Egyptians into the heart-shaped Ab amulet mentioned in the preceding chapter.

Like red agate, Carnelian was also believed to symbolize the blood of Isis. The Persians, at a later period, also buried carnelian with their dead; they considered it to be a symbol of the new flesh which would come into being at the moment of rebirth.

Carnelians were enormously popular in older times for signet rings. H.B. Walter's catalogue of the engraved gems and cameos, Greek, Roman and Etruscan, in the British Museum (1926) lists two thousand six hundred items half of which are carnelian or sard. The Sumerians discovered an ingenious way of decorating carnelian. They would draw a design on the surface of the cut stone with a soda solution and then heat it; the soda design then penetrated the stone and the design became permanent. They also would immerse the stone completely in an alkali, probably soda, solution and etch a design into it with copper nitrate solution.

Mohammed is believed to have worn a carnelian ring, for he considered that anyone who wore carnelian would always be happy, blessed and fortunate in friendship. Indeed, carnelian is a most positive stone. Like all red stones it has been thought to help in preventing or limiting bleeding; it has indeed been termed a "blood-stone" and it is supposed to prevent the blood rising to the head, consequently, it may prevent apoplexy. It also prevents excessive or painful menstruation, and corrects other menstrual disorders. There is still a strong folk belief that toothpicks made of carnelian will prevent the gums from bleeding. It also cures pimples, blotches and sores upon the skin.

Carnelian has always been associated with protection. As recently as the early years of this century Jews, Arabs, Turks and Greeks wore carnelian amulets as a defence against the Evil Eye. Carnelians remove lethargy, ease the mind and promote feelings of self-worth, friendship, and courage. Place carnelian on the pelvic area to cure impotence and infertility. Like all red stones it increases energy. It helps those people who suffer from absence of mind and muddled thinking. It is a stone of the Second Chakra, the sexual organs. It enables one to communicate therefore with the goddess as Venus and to acquire the energies of the sun.

Cat's Eye
This chrysoberyl is also called cymophane and is a stone of Cancer. It ranges in colour from a dark olive green to the more popular honey-yellow. The stone has a white band of light that moves when the stone is moved and causes the "eye" to blink.

The cat's eye protects the wearer from being bewitched and ensures wealth and long life. It is a protection against death and if a woman drinks milk in which a cat's eye has been washed, she can make love without fear of becoming pregnant. (It is not clear how long the effect lasts!) The Assyrians believed the cat's eye could confer invisibility. If hung around the neck it will relieve asthma and cure croup in babies. It promotes strength of mind and ensures success in games of chance and all business speculations.

Chalcedony
Chalcedony is basically compact silica. Minute crystals of quartz combine with minute pores containing saline solutions or water and there are many impurities which give it a wide range of colours. Indeed, the range of colours and their various disposition as spots, blotches and bands, and the differing degrees of transparency, have

resulted in names being given to particular chalcedony types. The stones termed chalcedonies are: agate of several kinds, onyx, sardonynx, carnelian, sard, prase, chrysoprase, plasma, heliotrope (or bloodstone) and Jasper. (see below)

Although it is not a gemstone, flint is a form of chalcedony and so is chert. Chalcedonies are porous and are therefore easy to dye. Some stones have been created by this process. Chalcedony that has been stained green has been called emeraldine and blue-stained chalcedony blue moonstone.

The name Chalcedony was once believed to derive from Chalcedony, a city in Asia Minor, but this is now doubted. Its appearance as Carcedonius in the Vulgate Old Testament has suggested to some that it may have taken its name from Carthage. The true chalcedony is regarded as by many as being grey, but for commercial purposes some United States authorities have given the name only to blue stones.

Almost colourless or white chalcedony has been described as chalcedony moonstone; it is found on beaches all over the world. It is sometimes passed off as moonstone proper, which it is not (see moonstone).

All forms of chalcedony were popular for making seals in ancient times. These were used to print images on tablets and to seal up boxes of valuables, and tombs and in Egypt, sarcophagi. Each type of chalcedony was believed to have certain spiritual or magical and protective powers. Figures of animals, birds and gods, and even incidents from myths were engraved upon them. From the destruction of Nineveh (612 BC) to 350 BC chalcedony was in great favour for making cone shaped seals rather than the earlier cylindrical ones. Wallis Budge tells us that "on these were cut symbols of the gods Shamash, Sin, Adad, Marduk and Nabu; mythical beasts and winged demons; men standing by the sacred three above which is the symbol of the god Asshur; scenes from the Gilgamesh legend; man-headed goat-fish, man-headed birds, cock, crescent, hunting scenes, etc." Chalcedony is a stone of Aries and of Mercury and is credited with being able to clear the mind, clarify thought and even cure insanity. It eases the passage of gallstones and helps to reduce fever. Like many talismans, it protects the wearer from the Evil Eye. When blue it is regarded as having the same qualities as sapphire. If engraved with the figure of a man on a horse holding a pike and galloping, it protects travellers, which any stone associated with Mercury should do. White chalcedony increases the flow of milk in nursing mothers. It also assists the wearer to become popular, to be victorious and to drive away nightmares. It protects in times of political and social upheaval.

Chrysocolla
Chrysocolla is blue or bluish-green and opaque. The name is an English transcription of a Greek work meaning gold-solder. It is found in copper mines and is therefore a stone of Venus. It has the power to disperse fears and ameliorate guilt; it cures or eases any disorder or blockage of the throat and is, indeed, a stone of the Fifth, the throat Chakra. It assists the wearer in the expressing of his or her emotions and increases intuitive and intellectual perceptiveness, enabling creative and intuitive ideas to be given practical application.

Chrysolite
Chrysolite is a stone of the Sun and of Leo. As a talisman it brings the wearer wisdom and prudence and, if engraved with the figure of an ass, it protects the wearer from gout. It is the birthstone of September whose Guardian Angel is Thoriel or Zuriel, a ruler of Libra, who is able to cure stupidity. Chrysolite is also the gemstone of St. Bartholomew, whose month is May.

Chrysoprase
Chrysoprase is a fine grained, somewhat translucent, compact quartz. It is apple green in colour, sometimes vivid and sometimes pale. Astrologers appear to have paid little or no attention to the chrysoprase, but in one Jewish tradition it is named as a stone of December along with turquoise and malachite.

The name chrysoprase is derived from a Greek word meaning golden-green. The stone symbolizes joy and gaiety and the ancients believed that it would bring grace and love to the possessor. It protects its wearer from bad dreams, dispels anxieties and keeps away demons. Albertus Magnus stated that Alexander the Great wore a chrysoprase amulet. It is the gemstone of St. Jude, the Apostle and patron of lost causes.

Chrysoprase was one of the gemstones used for amulets by the gnostics between 250 BC and 400 AD.

If a piece of chrysoprase is placed in the mouth it will cause invisibility according to medieval belief; for this reason or some other it was thought to help thieves escape punishment. It also brings artists inspiration. Those people born under the signs of Virgo and Pisces should not wear chrysoprase.

Citrine

Citrine is a yellow crystalline quartz and is so called because the French word for lemon is *citron*. As a talisman it helps the wearer find emotional stability and steadiness. It helps to ease digestive troubles and disorders of the kidney, bladder and bowels. It creates a general protective field around the wearer and helps neurotic and hypersensitive people to cope. Others also find it valuable when dealing with practical matters of family or business. It unblocks the Third Chakra, the navel.

Coral

Coral has always had talismanic significance and has been considered as signifying a variety of spiritual powers. It was, in Egyptian times, associated with Isis. In Roman times it was dedicated to Venus, and it has also been associated with Mars and Libra. Some regard it as the birthstone of Taurus and Scorpio and it is generally believed to have a particularly strong relationship with mothers and children. Women wore coral to prevent sterility, and, of course, babies were given rings of coral to assist them in teething. Necklaces of coral were also popular as they protected children from all evil powers as well as preventing or curing colic convulsions, whooping cough and the inflammation caused by teething. The general belief in coral as a protection against the Evil Eye is shown in its wide use for rosary beads and in Italy carved coral pendants are common. Coral is worn as a protection for swimmers, which is understandable as coral is a creation of the sea; it also will help the wearer to communicate with the spirits of seas, rivers and lakes. Wearing coral beautifies the skin and keeps away impurities of the liver and blood. It also protects the wearer from venereal disease even while it is helpful in attracting lovers. This last function is peculiar to red coral.

White coral, like white chalcedony, improves the milk supply of nursing mothers. It protects against thunderstorms, lightning and hail and is a good luck talisman worn by many ballet dancers. Red coral, if engraved with a man carrying a sword, stops haemorrhages, promotes emotional attachments and is a defence against the plague. All coral except brown coral is believed to cure cholera. When tied to a ship's mast, coral prevents shipwrecks and drives away storms. Tied to fruit trees it ensures a good harvest. Coral is said to change colour in the presence of poison or when illness is imminent. All corals save brown are beneficial in effect. Brown coral, however, attracts evil forces.

Diamond
The Diamond is a stone of Aries, Scorpio and Mars and diamonds have been regarded with awe for centuries.

It was in India and Borneo that diamonds are believed to have first been discovered. As diamonds were originally presented to rulers and monarchs, they have long since been revered and associated with wealth, kingship and strength, medicinal and magical powers. They are involved in many myths and legends, and were held sacred by Indians who consecrated them to the God Indra (the incarnation of storms, thunder, and lightning). "Black Diamonds" (hematite) shaped like the head of a snake were attributed to Yama the God of Death. (Various coloured crystals were dedicated to Vishnu, God of the Heavens.) There are many famous diamonds with long and sometimes lurid histories and one thinks immediately of the Hope Diamond, the Koh-i-Noor, and the Regent Diamond. These, however, do not concern us, except in as much as their chequered careers echo the belief that a stolen diamond brings evil fortune to the thief.

Diamonds were considered unlucky in Europe until the sixteenth century, but since that time they have been highly regarded and thought to bring good fortune of all kinds, the finer the stone the greater the fortune. Diamonds are associated with love and marriage and symbolize courage for men and pride for women. They have also been associated with masculine energy and are considered by some to be the "King Stone". In Crowley's kabbalistic Table of Correspondences, the diamond is linked with God, the state of Union with God, Elixir Vitae, Ambergris, Zeus, Wotan, Jupiter Brahma, Ptah and hidden intelligence among other things, as well as the Soul and the Jewish Messiah. Diamonds aid in mastery and symbolize fortitude, invincibility and perfection. It is said that Alexander wore diamonds into battle. While powdered diamonds were used to poison princes and popes, diamonds had the power of removing the effects of poison if dipped into the venomous potion. In the past, brown diamonds from India were thought to be male stones and diamonds from Arabia female. Male diamonds aided in female fertility and ensured that the child was born healthy and whole. Female diamonds prevented bones from breaking in a fall and were much more beneficial if received as a gift rather than purchased.

Diamonds defend the wearer from all forms of evil and promote sincerity, loyalty, affection and candour. Worn on the left arm a diamond will keep off wild beasts and demons, promote courage and give its wearer victory in battle. Worn as a pendant it protects against the Evil Eye and the plague. The diamond is an antidote to all poisons and also prevents nightmares. It strengthens both body and mind and water into which it has been dipped preserves the drinker from gout and apoplexy. A necklace of green-tinted diamonds eases childbirth. If set in steel a diamond is a protection against insanity when worn on the left arm. In general, however, diamonds set in steel should be avoided. Diamonds should always be worn on the left side of the body. Sir John Maundeville explained the reason and wrote: "A man should carry a diamond on his left side, for it is the greater virtue than on the right side; for the strength of their growing is towards the North, that is the left side of the world and the left part of a man when he turns his face to the East." Care should be taken in how diamonds are used. Very large stones are believed to cause mental distress in the wearer and cuff links and buttons made of diamonds are believed to bring ill fortune or even death. Diamonds, moreover, should always be given and never bought or sold. Stolen diamonds bring great misfortune to the thief. Diamonds that have been cut into square or triangular shapes make people quarrelsome and cause mental distress, although diamonds of other shapes, especially those with six corners, bring good fortune and improve the strength and vitality of the wearer in old age. The diamond is the birthstone of April whose Guardian Angel is Ashmodei, otherwise known as Ashmedai, Asmodee, Asmadai, Asmodeus, Chammaday and Sydonay. He is, according to Gustav Davidson's astonishing *A Dictionary of Angels*,[10] a messenger of God, but having opposed Solomon with sixty six of his own legions is regarded by rabbinical scholars as an evil spirit. Best known in the West

---

10. For further information on anything about angels see: Gustav Davidson: *A Dictionary of Angels Including the Fallen Angels.* Collier-MacMillan, 1967.

by the name Asmodeus, he is credited (or debited) with controlling all gambling and with being a demon of impurity. He has appeared in much fiction, notably Le Sage's *The Devil on Two Sticks* and James Branch Cabell's *The Devil's Own Son*. In some legends he is also credited with being the inventor of dancing, music and drama. In Solomonic legends he is named variously as Saturn, Narcolf or Morolf.

The diamond is also the gemstone of the Guardian Angel Hamatiel, a ruler of the order of virtues. The diamond has, indeed, a most various reputation.

Recently, it has been suggested that the blue light from the spectrum that is emitted from this stone has the potential to alleviate, if not cure glaucoma. Evidently, this has something to do with the carbon content of diamonds, for glaucoma is said by some to be the result of a deficiency of carbon.

Simply contemplating the stone's beauty, rather than its material significance, is said to be enough to tune the soul. Furthermore, the colours emitted from a diamond were once thought to symbolize confined glories which would ultimately bring prosperity to the wearer. In Kabbalistic numerology the diamond is number thirteen.

Emerald

The emerald is a stone of Venus and Cancer and the birthstone of the month of May which is, of course, the month dedicated to the Goddess, the name deriving from the Scandinavian Maia. It is the gemstone of the angel Muriel who rules Cancer and is one of the officers of the third hour of the day. It is said that, if properly invoked from the South, he can provide the applicant with a magic carpet. It is also the gemstone of the Apostles John and James.

The Chaldeans believed the emerald to be a key to help them to the Goddess and that the emerald could be used to channel her power. The emerald can indeed be used to invoke the Goddess in several personae, and especially Ceres for it is the colour green, of growth. Cancer is ruled by the Mother Goddess and so the emerald is a suitable talisman for mothers and in the past pregnant women were advised to wear emerald pendants. It is of great value in protecting the eyes and in improving sight. Hippocrates would bathe the eyes of a sufferer with water in which an emerald had been steeped and Pliny maintained that simply looking at an emerald when one's eyes are weary from much study would refresh the sight. In Islam the emerald is believed to preserve good eyesight, especially if a verse from the Koran has been engraved upon it.

Emeralds engraved with starlings help the eyesight also. In the nineteenth century, Persian travellers would bind an emerald on the left arm with green string to protect them from evil. Emeralds are so powerful a protection against evil that serpents are said to be blinded by a mere glimpse of the stone.

Emeralds promote fidelity, especially in love relationships, though some astrologers maintain that this is only so if the wearers are born under Cancer. Indeed, according to some authorities, emeralds should only be worn by those born in that period (June 22-July 22). Being associated with Cancer, ruled by the Goddess Venus and also associated with Isis, emeralds make excellent protective talismans for fishermen and sailors. Emeralds not only improve the physical eyesight but also spiritual vision and memory, enabling the wearer to foresee the future and recall the past with impressive clarity. This also means that emeralds are useful in helping people to find what has been lost and also help the wearer to discover secrets. The emerald is a calming influence; it reduces tension, stimulates open mindedness, promotes eloquence and brings the wearer both wealth and strength. Gazing at emeralds will cure constipation and improve the appetite. Emeralds worn as rings grow hot when they are near poison and lose their colour in the presence of treachery. The emerald is associated with the Fourth and Seventh Chakras, those of the Heart and the Crown of the Head respectively. In Crowley's Table of Correspondences the emerald is paralleled with the rose, the Lynx, the Messiah, Venus, Aphrodite, Freya, Hanuman, and the Egyptian Goddess, Hathor, one of the oldest Mother Goddesses. In Kabbalistic numerology the emerald is given the number fourteen.

Feldspar

Feldspar is a stone of Cancer and when worn around the neck was believed by the Egyptians to give protection from sunstroke, headaches and nosebleeds during the night.

Fluorite

Fluorite, also called fluor and fluorspar, is violet or purple and streaked in different shades of these colours. Known as Blue John in England, where it was excavated from the Blue John mines of Derbyshire, it has been used not only for large vases and other decorative objects, but also for rings, pendants, earrings. G.F. Herbert Smith[11] partly explains why it should be regarded as having talismanic power when he states: "A remarkable property of fluor is the capacity that some greenish-blue pieces have of appearing green by transmitted light and blue by reflected light. Many specimens, too, will glow with a lovely violet light, which is constant in tint whatever be their colour when excited by ultra-violet rays or others of short-wave length. This phenomenon is consequently known as fluorescence.

As a talismanic stone Blue John calms the nerves, as do the majority of blue stones, and helps in the curing of mental disturbance. It helps the wearer to think, to meditate, even while in a whirl of activity. It cleans and clarifies the aura when it is laid on the third eye, for it belongs to that Chakra. Some call Blue John or Fluorite the "Stone of Genius" or "Genius Stone" because it clarifies the mind so effectively.

Garnet

The Garnet is the birthstone of January and Aquarius (January 21-February 19) according to one authority. Another states that it is that of Virgo, but should be avoided by those born under Taurus. (It has also been accredited to Saturn.) It has been called "Cape Ruby" because of the wine-red colour of most stones, though some are pink and some have a yellow tinge. An Italian name for the garnet is *pietra della vedonanza*, meaning "the widows' stone" because Italian widows tend to wear garnet necklaces. This may be because the garnets are believed to promote loyalty and devotion and increase energy, health and good humour. They prevent the wearer from poison and the plague and lightning. They prevent bad dreams and diseases of the skin and change colour when danger threatens. If a garnet is engraved with a lion it will prevent epidemics and protect travellers.

In Ancient Greece and Rome garnets were often engraved with portraits of emperors, possibly to express loyalty rather than for talismanic purposes. Because of its colour the garnet protects the wearer from wounds and purifies the blood. Like the diamond, a stolen garnet carries a curse with it until it is returned to its owner. It cures depression, increases sexual energy, and positive thinking, enlivens the imagination and helps to achieve success in commercial ventures.

---

11. G.F. Herbert Smith: Op. Cit.

It relates to the Second Chakra, that of the sexual organs, and in Kabbalistic numerology it is numbered eight.

Haematite (See Bloodstone)

Heliotrope (See Bloodstone)

Hyacinth (See Zircon)

Jacinth or Nephrite (See Zircon)

Jade
Jade is the birthstone of Virgo according to some authorities and unlucky for people born under Sagittarius or Gemini. Others state that it is closely related to Venus in Libra. It has a long history of talismanic use stretching back to the fourth millennium BC. Chinese businessmen would hold jade in their hands while performing a transaction, though usually jade talismans were worn at the throat or on the breast. Jade was carved into the shape of storks or bats to bring the wearer longevity. The Chinese considered jade to possess the five cardinal virtues of Courage, Justice, Charity, Modesty and Wisdom. They regarded it as symbolizing the finest qualities of humankind: benevolence, the understanding of signs and symbols, virtuous actions, purity, innocence and, because when made into a gong or bell it produces a very clear and sweet note, musical ability.

Perhaps because of its colour, green jade is regarded as curing eye disorders both in China and in Peru. It is used in both China and New Zealand for carved ritual amulets and implements. In New Zealand it is shaped into ceremonial clubs and axes and also figures of the deities and spirits which are worn as pendants. Jade is regarded in many cultures as a bringer of rain and as a charm against intestinal disorders in both the Far East and Latin America, as well as the Europe of the Middle Ages. White jade cures kidney disease, helps the wearer to pass kidney stones, assists women in childbirth and drives away wild beasts. Green jade drives away wild beasts. Black jade brings the wearer increased strength. All jade prevents epilepsy and averts accidents and injuries. It brings good fortune to gamblers and is supposed to be especially lucky for people involved in horse racing.

Green jade, as a ring or bracelet or pendant, eases tension and promotes comfortable sleep. Gardeners should possess jade to help them succeed.

Jasper

Jasper is a compact quartz which, like chrysoprase, is made up of very small grains. It differs from chrysoprase by its perfect opacity and deep colour. Nevertheless it is so varied in kind and quality that in the past it has been given many different names. Jasper contains as much as twenty percent foreign material, most frequently clay and iron oxide, and it is these impurities that are responsible for the variety of colours that jaspers exhibit; red, yellow, brown, dark green; some stones are heavily patterned or marked.

The name jasper is derived from the Greek *Iaspis*. Jasper is the stone of Aries and of March, as well as Pluto though some authorities say that bloodstone is the stone in question. This appears to be because red jasper is often called bloodstone. Jasper is also the stone of the tribe of Benjamin in Jewish tradition. Another Jewish tradition gives jasper as the stone of Pisces, whose ruling angel is Barchiel also known as Barachiel, Barbiel, Barakiel, Barkiel and Barquiel, the "lightning of God", who is also the ruler of February and is invoked by gamblers for assistance. In kabbalistic numerology it is allocated to the number seven along with turquoise and associated with Sagittarius, though this only applies to red jasper; pink jasper is associated with the number two, whose zodiacal sign is Virgo. Jasper has been associated with the sign of Leo and in the Middle Ages it was believed that the image of a lion carved into a piece of jasper could cure fevers and dispel poison. Others state that jasper is beneficial for people born under the signs of Virgo and Sagittarius. Still others give jasper to the sign of Aries and the month of March which belongs to Mars, though this may be because red jasper is a bloodstone. In one tradition jasper is regarded as the gem of the Apostle Peter.

Jasper, especially green jasper, was a favourite medium for stone carvers and the makers of signet rings and talismans. Pliny the Elder reports that he once saw a nine inch jasper statuette of the Emperor Nero wearing a cuirass and fully armed. He states that jasper is often transparent which suggests that he is not talking about jasper at all. He reports on a blue jasper from Persia called Aerizusa because it is the colour of the sky but commentators believe this to be a sapphirine variety of chalcedony.

An ancient lapidary states that "As many colours as she hathe, as many vertues god hath put in hire." It also states that if jasper was worn to battle, one's enemies would be overcome. Jasper is also credited with staunching blood though this may be a reference to bloodstone or heliotrope as the stone is described as "deep greene and when is polyshid, she hathe rede dropes". Aristotle and Pliny both believed that jasper could cure wasting fevers and dispel poison. Red jasper has the power to stop excessive bleeding of all kinds, including menstrual, and to ease childbirth. This may be not only because of its red colouring but also because it is associated with the blood of Isis, a Mother Goddess. When it is engraved with the image of a hawk or an eagle holding a serpent in its beak it is said to be most powerful as a protection against the Evil Eye. Some authorities state that the image should be of a kite tearing at a serpent. This would be in the form of a ring.

Red jasper rings have been found in considerable numbers in Egyptian tombs, all without inscriptions, and all with gaps in them. As rings of red glass and red faience were also found it seems likely that these were the "bloodstone rings that protected soldiers and lessened bleeding in either men or women."

Jasper was also widely believed to ease labour pains if it was placed on the body. It was regarded as an effective astringent and used as a cure for epilepsy. Like many other stones it was thought to protect one from witchcraft.

According to some, jasper represents joy and happiness. It increases sensitivity and insight and gives security. Green jasper is thought to promote the understanding of others and is said to help in solving emotional problems.

Jet

Jet is a birthstone of January and of Capricorn; being black, it is also a stone of Saturn. It has been used for talismans for many centuries. A piece of jet held in the hand helps to ease childbirth. It protects people from devils, poison, witchcraft, snakebite. A beetle carved out of jet was worn by Italians as a protection against the Evil Eye and the Manu Cornuta talisman is frequently made of jet. The Sardinian Pinnadellu, another talisman against the Evil Eye, is also made of jet. The colour is important here; the blackness is used to protect against spiritual darkness. In India and in Egypt small discs of jet have been discovered and they probably served the same functions. Jet became worn as a token of mourning in Victorian times and jet beads or beadwork upon clothing of all kinds was common. Whether or not this use of jet derived entirely from the association of black with mourning or whether it was used talismanically to protect the wearer against death's darkness is hard to determine. Some say that jet should not be worn by people born under the signs of Aries or Libra, but this, like so many similar bans, is hard to understand and the more so when one considers the general multiplicity of views and opinions in this area.

Lapis Lazuli
Lapis lazuli is the birthstone of September and of those born under Libra. Being a blue stone, it was considered a sacred stone of Isis, Venus and the Virgin Mary. The Mesopotamians used lapis to create their cylinder seals, which were considered to have talismanic and protective powers; many discovered in Ur of the Chaldees are to be seen in the British Museum. The Sumerians believed that anyone wearing a lapis talisman carried the actual presence of God. Lapis was used by the Egyptians in the carving of many talismans and especially the scarab. The mask of Tutankhamun is made of lapis and gold. The Pharaohs, by custom, used to marry their sisters and lapis was long considered as a talisman to be worn by anyone traumatized by an incestuous relationship. Lapis is indeed credited with calming psychological and psychic disturbances and is valuable when the wearer is anticipating stress. It will not, however, function if it is put on during stress or emotional excitement; it must be put on during calm periods. Lapis, as it is a gem of the Mother Goddess, can prevent miscarriages and lapis talismans were frequent in use in Macedonia at the end of the nineteenth century. Lapis increases the psychic power of the person who wears it and is a strong psychic protector. It can also be used in healing. If a lapis is held in one hand and the other hand is laid upon the afflicted part of the sufferer, then the lapis will help you send healing thoughts. Lapis is also supposed to bring material wealth, but it is mostly revered for possessing the wisdom of the gods and for increasing the wearer's psychic abilities, insight and powers of judgement. Because of its stabilizing powers it helps in the healing of all kinds of inflammation in the throat and lungs; it is associated with the Sixth Chakra, the third eye. Some say it should not be worn by those

born under Cancer or Capricorn, though it is difficult to see why this should be so. Crowley's Table of Correspondences links lapis lazuli with Jupiter and Pluto, Saffron, Cocaine, Brahma, Indra, Zeus, Amoun-Ra; it is indeed a most royal gem.

Lodestone

Otherwise known as magnetite, the lodestone is a birthstone of Scorpio and November. Just as amber and other stones have been revered because of their electricity, so the lodestone has been regarded as magical because of its magnetic powers and its ability always to point to true north. It was thought to relieve pain in the feet and hands and to get rid of depression as well as assist women in labour. When placed on the neck it protects the wearer from being bewitched and improves the memory. In the Middle Ages it was set into wedding rings because it attracts and holds the hearts of others and thus made the marriage successful; this maybe is why it is highly regarded by prostitutes. Mexicans carry lodestones in their belts to ensure success and in India it brings its wearer wealth and good health as well as protection against the Evil Eye. Because the lodestone is regarded as having life, as being a creature, in Mexico it is put in a bowl of water on a Friday so that it may drink and, after it has dried out in the sun, is fed iron filings. It is believed that knives made of lodestone, or magnetized, deliver wounds that are invariably fatal. Lodestones must not be worn during a thunderstorm because they attract lightning and they have no healing power during a rainstorm. The lodestone is a protective talisman for sailors and can cure the gout if bound to the sufferer's foot.

Combined with coral in a necklace it eases childbirth. When combined with silver it sharpens the eyesight; when set in gold it brings strength to the heart. It loses its powers if placed next to diamonds or garlic, but it regains its strength when provided with iron filings or dipped in the blood of a goat. It brings the wearer health, vitality and the love of both gods and men.

Malachite

The malachite is a birthstone of those born in January and under Capricorn and it is in tune with Venus. It has many healing properties. In Italy it is known as *pietro del pavone* and has the reputation of curing eye diseases. Malachite amulets were common in Europe as ways of making teething painless. It also protects the wearer from rheumatism, cholera and colic, as well as lightning. It promotes constancy of affection and sound sleep and, when engraved with the symbol of the sun, prevents melancholy. It is, not surprisingly, a protection against the Evil Eye.

Moonstone

The moonstone is also called selenite, after Selena, one of the names of the Goddess as Moon Goddess. Supposedly it changes colours as the phases of the moon change, or according to the psychic health of the wearer. It has been credited with many powers and uses. According to Camillo Leonardo in *The Mirror of Stones* (1502), it helps to reconcile lovers and heal those suffering from tuberculosis (consumption) when the moon is waxing; when the moon is on the wane if held in the mouth it will enable the wearer to foretell the future and come to correct decisions about the business ahead. The moonstone is a birthstone of Cancer and it protects the wearer from diseases to which Cancer people are prone such as dropsy. It is also good for kidney disorders and protects travellers, especially those whose journeys require them to cross water. Being so very much part of the moon's power the moonstone also affects vegetation and moonstones should be hung on trees to ensure a good yield of fruit. Moonstones help nervous people calm their fears, especially if there are fears of the darkness and the unknown, and prevents epilepsy. Though a birthstone of Cancer and a stone of Scorpio, the moonstone is also associated with the first truly summer month of June, probably because of the moon's association with growing things. Moonstones are often worn by people who use their psychic energies and psychic powers of channelling for healing purposes.

In Crowley's Table of Correspondences the moonstone is seen as corresponding to Almond, Mugwort, Hazel, Diana, Artemis, Hecate Hathor among others. It is a great help in dealing with problems of menstruation and digestion. It helps to develop psychic sensitivity and brings the wearer into a peaceful state of mind. It also improves access to the subconscious and is associated with the Fourth Chakra, that of the heart.

Obsidian

Obsidian is not commonly regarded as a gem or semi-precious stone, but it does have talismanic properties. It is associated with Saturn, probably because of its glossy black colouring and is often used to make knife handles or even complete knives for magical purposes. Obsidian has also been used by occultists to make magical wands. Saturn was a god of agriculture for the Romans both at home and in North Africa. His feast, the Saturnalia was held December 17-19 and it involved the giving of presents of candles, so that it was, effectively, the midwinter feast of lights which is still notably present in Sweden in the Festival of Lights. Thus obsidian, which is also made into sickles and knives for agricultural use, is a talisman to give the wearer confidence and strength and productivity. Being black it may also be assumed that it is a talisman to protect against the dark and the unknown and its mirror-like gloss makes it an admirable defence against the Evil Eye.

Obsidian brings the intestines and the stomach into balance and strengthens the wearer immeasurably. Obsidian talismans should be worn by the faint-hearted, shy and easily-manipulated, to give them confidence and to prevent them being exhausted by the emotional or psychological demands of others. Obsidian is a stone of the Root Chakra, the Chakra at the base of the spine.

Onyx

Most astrological authorities do not ascribe a particular planet or sign of the zodiac to the onyx, though it is in general thought to favour those born under the signs of Cancer, Leo and Capricorn. It does appear in Aleister Crowley's Table of Correspondences where it is associated with Saturn and other writers have made the same connection.

Onyx could well be listed as yet another kind of agate, that most versatile of stones. It is indeed a kind of chalcedony in which the bands of colour are straight and parallel. One authority states that in the true onyx these bands are black and white, but others state with equal firmness that only contrasting colours are required. For all that, there are totally black onyxes which are not deprived of the name which comes from a Greek word meaning "nail", perhaps because of the regular pattern of the ridges on the human finger nail and perhaps because of the way in which the colour of the skin can be seen through the transparent nail. It may also derive from the Latin word for a veined gem. Onyx may be considered a kind of riband agate, for the onyx proper is a riband agate in which milk white bands alternate with others of contrasting colour or colours. If these bands are red it may be called carnelian-onyx; if they are brown it may be termed sardonynx; and if the bands are pale the name is chalcedony-onyx. Of all these terms only sardonynx is in general use and usually given the dignity of being regarded as a distinct stone with its own characteristics and influences. It appears in Crowley's Table of Correspondences where it is associated with: Indigo, Ash, Cypress, Yew, Saturn, a sickle, Words of Malediction and Death, Crocodile, Brahma, Sebec, Mako and the perfumes assa foetida, scammony, sulphur (all unpleasant odours). Crowley gives the onyx a very bad press..

Crowley was not alone in this. In Arabic the word onyx means sadness. In China it was believed to bring nightmares, doubts, discords and lawsuits. It can also create distance between lovers and bring them to separation. It is held to cause friends to fall out and even to induce premature childbirth.

In Jewish traditional lore the onyx is the stone for July and the tribe of Zebukun; it is also the stone for Aquarius and its angel is the Angel Gabriel, the angel of mercy, vengeance, death, revelation, annunciation and resurrection. It was the Angel Gabriel who dictated the Koran to Mohammed and he is therefore regarded by Mohammedans as the Angel of Truth. In kabbalistic numerology the white onyx is associated with the number eight whose zodiacal sign is Capricorn, and the black onyx is associated with the number eighteen whose sign of the zodiac is Cancer. Onyx appears in the Bible in the Genesis 2: 12 where we are told that the river flowing out of Eden before the fall split into four, the first branches, the first being Pison "which compasseth the whole land of Havilah, where there is gold; and the gold of that land is good: there is bdellium and the onyx stone." This was most probably written about 500 BC and the onyx was most likely from the Saana district of Arabia. The New English Bible gives us carnelian instead of onyx.

In the Book of Job we are given a hint of how highly the onyx was regarded, for in the 28th chapter we are told that wisdom "cannot be valued with the gold of Ophir, with the precious onyx or the sapphire". Again the New English Bible replaces onyx with carnelian (and sapphire with lapis lazuli).

The Greeks and Romans also wore onyx rings. Aristophanes in his play *The Clouds* first produced in 423 BC has Socrates referring to idle men and listing among them "lazy, long-haired, onyx-ring wearers". This mixed reputation did not prevent the Romans from carving onyx into drinking vessels and vases, some of which were very elaborate. Onyx has also been used for making boxes and was used very often in the nineteenth century for lamp bases or statuettes for the tops of ornamental occasional tables and in this century for ash-trays and cigarette boxes. Kaiser Wilhelm II of Germany wore an onyx ring handed down from his grandfather Wilhelm I; the stone was reddish-white and engraved with a design of the German eagle with a crown above it, a most talismanic design.

It may be, of course, that those who chose to treat onyx with such confidence had decided to believe not the dark version of its powers but the other, more pleasing version. Onyx is said to provide self-control and if placed near a woman in labour it will lessen the intensity of her labour pains and ease delivery. The onyx cools passions and especially sexual ones which may be regarded as a positive or a negative quality. It helps its wearer to achieve marital happiness.

Onyxes are used for the creation of cameos, the white band being used for the figure and the other colour or colours for the ground. The black onyx is quite simply an onyx that is entirely black, having been cut from the stone in such a way as to omit any lighter colour. Black onyxes are considered particularly powerful, especially in protecting the wearer from the Evil Eye. In India and Persia black onyxes are worn for this reason.

Opal

The Opal is associated with both Scorpio and Libra and particularly with Venus in Libra. Some also regard it as belonging to the moon and as the birthstone of Taurus. Because it has so many colours some have thought it possesses the virtues of all the stones whose colours are to be seen in its depths—the amethyst, the emerald, the garnet and the carbuncle or ruby in particular. It was called the Eye Stone or Opthalmius in the fourteenth century because it was thought to improve eyesight and heal the eyes, as well as improve memory and induce clarity of mind. In India it is believed that an opal passed over the forehead will clear the brain and improve memory. Almost all talismans supposed to help eyesight are also believed to help both intellectual and spiritual perception. The opal enables its wearer to see into the future, but if this ability is used selfishly it will result in misfortune, especially in love which may be why it is thought unwise to use it in engagement rings. Some people have given the opal a bad reputation, stating it to be unlucky; it has been suggested that this originated with Sir Walter Scott's Anne of Gierstein who had a large opal and was, to say the least, unfortunate. The opal is supposed to become more or less brilliant according to the wearer's situation; if dull it warns of coming difficulties; if bright it augurs success. The opal is regarded as a sacred stone in many parts of the East and believed to contain the Spirit of Truth. Mexican fire opals, which are deep in colour and vivid with flashes like flames, are considered very powerful, but the black opal is generally considered to be the most effective bringer of good fortune. The fire opal in Crowley's Table of Correspondences is associated with Mercury, Truthfulness, Hermes, Odin, Loki, Hanuman, Anubis and Thoth. In kabbalistic numerology it is given the number three.

Pearl

While the pearl is not a stone at all, it is nevertheless treated like a precious or semi-precious stone and has talismanic properties and so it belongs here. Pearls, probably because of their origin in the ocean, are associated with the Moon and in Crowley's Table of Correspondences they are associated quite predictably with Neptune, Fish, Dolphin, Poseidon, the Moon, and with the casting of illusions and bewitching. Powdered pearls have been used as medicine, but this does not concern us. As talismans they reinforce moral purity and have symbolized the Unicorn and Christ. The pearl represents and provides peace, wisdom and tranquillity and was consecrated to Isis in Roman times. Because it looks somewhat like a tear and is caused by irritation and suffering, the pearl may also bring sadness, particularly to couples who are in love. Some say even married couples should not wear pearls; certainly pearls should not form part of an engagement ring. This seems rather to run counter to the pearl's activity as a provider of tranquillity or wisdom.

Prase

Prase is a leek-green, translucent compact quartz of a slightly greasy lustre.

The astrologers have paid no attention to prase, but, like all green stones, it must be considered a stone of Venus.

Prase was once called mother-of-emerald because it was thought to have been the rock from which emeralds originate. It has been said that prase enables artists to focus on a number of projects at the same time without becoming disorganized.

Peridot

Peridot is a deep green chrysolite and it is a stone of Leo and of August, being filled with the energy and vibrations of the sun. For this reason it should be set in gold. It is a very positive stone; worn in a bracelet on the left arm, (and almost all talismanic bracelets should be worn on the left arm,) it protects against the Evil Eye; it helps with diseases of the liver and cures dropsy; it banishes envious thoughts, melancholy and delusions and fear of actual or spiritual darkness. Carried in the pocket it may cause a change in the life-style of the owner and it will bring him or her money.

In Crowley's Table of Correspondences the peridot is paralleled with the snowdrop, white lily narcissus, Ceres, Adonis and Isis as a virgin.

Pumice

Pumice helps to ease labour pains and ensures a satisfactory birth, according to country lore.

Quartz

Quartz in this context should also be called quartz crystal, rock crystal, or even just crystal. There are three main varieties--clear quartz, rose quartz and smoky quartz which, if yellow, is named cairngorm and has already been discussed. Clear rock quartz which we mean whenever we use the word crystal has been used as a substitute for diamonds in the past. The word crystal derives from the Greek *krystallos* meaning ice, for it was thought that it was ice in a permanent state; crystallization is, indeed, similar to freezing. Crystal is, not unexpectedly, associated with Aquarius the water carrier, and also with the moon. In Australia and Guinea it is thought to be able to bring rain; the Romans considered it a talisman to cure fever. Crystal has been associated with both healing and divination for centuries. It aids in clarity of mind and improves the wearer's powers of observation. It has strong vibrations that increase ones psychic energies in acts of healing. Indeed, it increases all one's psychic powers, enables one to focus clearly in meditation and assists in communication with spirits of the natural world and other discarnate entities. If in a pyramid shape it should be held with the point palm-inwards and then placed on/or near the Chakra which needs to be unblocked or on the site of the disorder. This is one view. Another is that one should use a long crystal -like a finger and point it at the place you wish to cure. Crystal has a powerful effect on the Solar Plexus, Third Eye, and Crown of the Head Chakras.

Rose quartz revitalizes the skin and helps to cure disorders of heart, lungs, liver and kidneys. It releases suppressed emotions, including those caused by traumas or cruelty or unloving attitudes in childhood. It is associated with the Heart Chakra and helps one to like oneself. It works particularly well in double harness with amethyst and enables one to keep one's heart and head, one's emotional and one's intellectual energies in balance.

Smoky quartz should be carried when one is suffering from stress as it eases tension. It increases physical energy and strengthens the heart. It adds to one's sense of pride in oneself and is therefore of great value to people suffering from fatigue or depression. It enables one to abandon attitudes and feelings that are no longer needed for one's development and it gets rid of negative attitudes that have been repressed. It is associated with the First Chakra at the base of the spine and therefore provides energy.

Rhodochrosite
Rhodochrosite derives its name from a Greek word meaning rose-coloured, though, in fact, it often includes yellow and brown. It has another name, Dialogite, which comes from a Greek word for doubt, which seems inappropriate as it is a very positive stone from the talismanic point of view. It belongs to the Fourth Chakra, the heart and might almost be said to be a path-clearer, for it tidies away obstructions in the lung, the digestive system, kidneys and spleen and cures constipation. It assists in bringing visionary light down to the psyche by way of the Crown Chakra and protects against hallucinations, delusions and nightmares. It acts as a bridge between the three upper and the four lower Chakras thus clearing the path for strong energy flow.

Ruby

The Ruby is variously regarded as the birthstone of July and December and is associated with Cancer, late Capricorn, Taurus and Mars. As has already been pointed out, some stones called carbuncles may be rubies. The ruby is the gemstone of the angel Malchediel or Machidiel, the angel governing March. According to Gustav Davidson this angel can provide the one who invokes him properly and fixes a time and place with the "maiden of his desire". Machidiel also is the ruler of Aries. As might be expected of any brilliant red stone, it heals disorders of the heart, mitigates bleeding, heals wounds, and counteracts anaemia and other wasting diseases. It protects its owner's house from storm damage. It makes men invulnerable in battles, heals quarrels, mitigates the fury of lust, promotes love and friendship. It increases beauty in women and protects the wearer from witchcraft and from both the plague and starvation. It changes colour in the presence of poison or danger. It prevents bad dreams and illness of the spleen and liver. The variety of ruby known as spinel gives protection against hail and storm. Crowley's Table of Correspondences links the Ruby with Mars, the Sword, all pungent odours, the horse, bear and wolf, Pan, Priapus and Horus, all of which have associations with blood if one accepts that the horse is a warhorse and the pungent odours are somewhat violent. In kabbalistic numerology it is given the number eighteen.

Sapphire

Ancient opinions of the Sapphire are rather difficult to judge for it seems that almost any blue stone was liable to be given the name, including most notably, lapis lazuli and turquoise. The various authorities disagree about the sapphire's place in the astrological scheme of things. Today it is generally regarded as being the birthstone of April and associated with Taurus. Another authority adds Capricorn and in the past it has been associated with Venus, Gemini, Mercury, Saturn and Jupiter. Yet others say that the Sapphire is ruled by either Jupiter or Mercury and may be used to call up Neptune.

The sapphire is the gemstone of the angel Verchiel who is the ruler of Leo and of July according to one authority; another makes him the governor of the sun, who is elsewhere regarded as the angel Nakiel or Nachiel who, in kabbalistic thinking, becomes the intelligence of the sun when it enters Leo. It is also the gemstone of Saint Paul. The Jewish

Tables of the Law were once believed to have been made of sapphire though later translators have decided that lapis lazuli is more probable. The sapphire has a long history of use in religious devotions. The Buddhists think it gives Spiritual Light, Peace and Happiness and promotes the desire to pray. In the twelfth century Pope Innocent III decided it was the right stone for Bishop's rings because of its virtues. These were defined by St. Jerome who wrote "It procures favours with princes, pacifies enemies, frees from enchantment and obtains freedom from captivity". The importance attached to the sapphire may be partly explained by the reference to it in Exodus 24 as "the body of heaven in its clearness." Be that as it may, in the Middle Ages it was credited with enabling the wearer to uncover treachery and fraud, preserve chastity and resist black magic–all characteristic of clear stones. Predictably, it is also credited with inducing sincerity, tranquillity, fidelity, wisdom, truthfulness; of course it protects the wearer against the Evil Eye. It is of use in curing disorders of the eye, ulcers, and rheumatism—all of which can be regarded as disorders obstructing the path of the sufferer.

The lighter blue sapphire is considered female and able to prevent attacks of fear and anxiety. The darker sapphire is considered male. Some sapphires are cloudy and show six rays of light; these are called star sapphires and are powerful love charms. Because of their six rays they are associated with the hexagram that is known as the Seal of Solomon and which is discussed elsewhere. Some people feel that the sapphire should be engraved with the image of a ram. Crowley ignores the ordinary sapphire in his Table of Correspondences but associates the star sapphire with the Virgin Mary, Juno, Cybele, Hecate, Silver, Belladonna, Demeter, Rhea, Isis and Thoth; the emphasis is clearly upon the Goddess.

Sard

Sard is associated with Mars and Aries. It is an opaque chalcedony that ranges in colour from brown to reddish brown and consequently is sometimes confused with carnelian. It is believed to protect the wearer from snake bites and to help women in labour to have a comfortable delivery. It is also said to comfort those who are without a home or family and to remind the wearers of their family loyalties and commitments. It has been used to invoke the presence of Minerva. The name sard derives from a Greek word meaning reddish brown. In kabbalistic numerology it is given the number two.

Sardonynx

Sardonynx is yet another variety of agate with alternating reddish brown (or sard) bands and white bands. This is one description. Others give the sardonynx as composed of red and white bands or being reddish brown on a white background. Whatever its exact appearance it has been regarded as important from the time of Pliny (428-347 BC) to the present day. Astrologists have given the sardonynx to Mercury and Virgo, and also to Leo. In Jewish tradition it is regarded as the stone of August and the tribe of Reuben. It is the gemstone of the Apostle, James the Less. It has been used very frequently for the creation of cameos of all kinds. A common symbol carved into sardonynx has been the quail and this is supposed to confer invisibility upon the wearer, or at the very least render him or her unnoticeable.

Sardonynx improves vitality and brings fame. It protects the wearer from infectious diseases and the bites of snakes and insects, especially scorpions. Worn around the neck it will bring friendship, happiness in marriage and a successful outcome to legal business. It will strengthen self-control, especially in those prone to dissipation, and protect the wearer from witchcraft. When engraved with an eagle or the figures of Mars or Hercules it makes the wearer courageous. It also eases the pains of childbirth. It should be set in gold. In kabbalistic numerology it is given the number nineteen.

Serpentine

This stone is probably so called because its speckled green colour reminds one of the skin of a serpent. Because of its appearance it is thought to protect the wearer from the bites of snakes and insects. Again, because of the association of the snake with poison it is believed that a serpentine goblet will sweat if the drink within it is poisoned, but will improve the taste and potency of any non-toxic liquid it holds, especially medicine. It also helps to stabilize the milk flow of nursing mothers.

Stalagmites

Stalagmites are clearly not precious stones, but if portions of stalagmites or small ones taken from the floors of caves are carried in small bags, they will protect the wearer from the Evil Eye and witchcraft. It is probable that the reason for this is that the earth has "grown" these objects and so they are sacred to the Earth Mother.

Topaz

Topaz is a gemstone of Asmodeus whom we have already discussed in the note on diamonds; it is also the gemstone of Saint Matthew and nowadays is generally regarded as a birthstone of November and Sagittarius. By others it is given variously to Mars and Saturn. The topaz is to be found in several colours; white, yellow and pink are those most used for jewellery and regarded as gems; the green and black topazes are in less favour. In Brazil the white topaz is sometimes referred to as the slave's diamond because it is particularly hard, clear and unflawed. A yellow variety found in Ceylon is worn to preserve the wearer's health, prevent sudden death and improve wisdom and caution. The Romans wore the topaz to protect them from the ill effects of air pollution, as well as from the dangers of travel, scalds and burns and also to stave off disorders of the chest and bowels. In the Middle Ages it was worn on a bracelet—on the left arm, of course--to avert the Evil Eye. It was also regarded as able to cure asthma, haemorrhoids, gout, insomnia, liver disorder and prevent both lunacy and sudden death. It can also control anger, greed and lust. Some state that it helps to improve the eyesight, stops bleeding and strengthens the heart. To be most effective it should be engraved with the image of a falcon. If worn on the breast it will prevent thirst. Worn on the left hand, it improves the wearer's intelligence and courage and protects from melancholy. It prevents the wearer from feeling envy and assists in the curing of liver disorders. The yellow topaz ensures health and prevents sudden death. It makes the wearer cautious and wise and helps the traveller avert danger. It calms anger, prevents sensual overindulgence and brings wealth, happiness and the admiration of those in authority. It should not be worn by those born under the signs of Pisces and Virgo. It is associated with the Third Chakra, the navel, and in kabbalistic numerology is given the number four.

Tourmaline

Tourmaline belongs to Leo and inspires the mind and brings friendship and good fortune. It strengthens the nerves, the heart and the immune system and inspires creativity. It is associated with the Heart Chakra.

139

Turquoise

The turquoise is regarded as being the birthstone of December by the Goldsmiths of Great Britain, but others consider it the birthstone of Taurus and, because of its blue colour, see it also as belonging to Venus. Still others have given the stone to July and to Saturn and Mercury. Turquoise has been considered a protective stone for centuries. The Arabs call it "the lucky stone", *fayruz*, and it is popular also in parts of Africa. It is used for necklaces, rings, bracelets, brooches, pendants and, in New Mexico, Mexico and Arizona also for belt buckles and watch bands. The Buddhists revere it because there is a story in which a monster was defeated by the Buddha with the aid of a turquoise. The turquoise warns its wearer of approaching danger by changing from blue to green, though it should be pointed out that age will cause a turquoise to make this change also, as will washing it with soap. It also changes colour and grows moist in the presence of poison. It is used for inscribed talismans in Islam and it protects the wearer from eye disease, malaria, blindness and the bites of snakes, scorpions and other insects. It is a powerful talisman against evil and brings the wearer courage and promotes success in all endeavours. It makes horses sure-footed and protects horsemen from falling and resultant injuries and is called the horseman's talisman in some Eastern countries. In Iran, turquoise beads are attached to the tails of horses, camels and mules. In the Middle Ages it was believed to heal quarrels, prevent headaches, defeat enemies and renew friendships. It is also a stone of good fortune for lovers and married couples.

American Indian medicine men use turquoise in their charms and hunters place turquoise on their bows to achieve perfect aim. Turquoise also protects animals from the danger of drinking water when over-exerted. Valued by the Egyptians it was placed in their tombs; in fact the earliest turquoises were found in a tomb and date back to 5,500 BC. The name derives from Turkey as the first turquoises were found there and for a while it was called the Turkey Stone. In kabbalistic numerology its number is seven.

Zircon

Zircon is also known as jacinth and hyacinth. The hyacinth-jacinth is deep orange or bright red and the name hyacinth derives from Greek legend as we have noted when discussing the hyacinth flower. The

White Zircon is known as the *jargoon* and can be mistaken for a diamond. Other varieties which are in different varieties of grey, brown, green and yellow are named zircons. The jacinth, set in a gold ring, calms the restless brain according to Barrett Camillus Leonardus who said in 1750 that it strengthens the heart, banishes stupid suspicions, prevents jealousy, protects travellers from robbers and accidental injury. Worn on the neck jacinth amulets help women in childbirth, prevent bad dreams and make for comfortable sleep. It also deals with flatulence, strengthens the limbs and rids the mind of melancholy. It protects against lightning. The jargoon has the same attributes but is less powerful. The zircon is a birthstone of Saturn and also belongs to Aquarius. It is not lucky for people born under Taurus or Scorpio.

This has been a complicated and confusing list, but in order to understand how talismanic thinking works and to show how almost every stone taken from the earth has been regarded as possessing magical properties, it was necessary to run to length. Were one to contemplate making a talisman by following the attributes laid down here, one might well become confused. Nevertheless, if one steps back a little from the detail, one soon sees that various principles are involved. Stones that are transparent and clear are regarded as helpful to both the physical and the spiritual vision. If coloured, these stones will apply particularly to matters we associate with that colour; green we associate with growth, red with blood, etc. Moreover, if a gem resembles anything, then that must be taken into account as in all practices of sympathetic magic. The key concern must be, ultimately, does this stone, this talisman, carry conviction because its symbolism is appropriate to the task it must perform? If the answer is "yes" the talisman maker may empower the particular talisman by giving its energy field the message that is required and directing its energy towards a particular end. The exact way of doing this will be discussed in a later chapter. We must at present move on to consider inscriptive talismans, many of which made use of the stones we have just surveyed.

Inscriptive Talismans

Whoso hath a copy of this in his house, no evil spirit nor evil shall vex him, nor hunger nor ague, nor any evil spirit shall annoy; but all goodness shall be where a copy of this shall be found.

From a 17th Century Inscriptive Talisman

So many talismans involve the engraving or writing of words and names of power that it is necessary to devote a separate chapter to talismans composed of inscriptions. The simplest form of inscriptive talisman is perhaps that which simply presents the name of the spiritual power whose protection one is seeking. In Mohammedanism there are ninety-nine names of God and each one has a distinct and separate meaning (see Table 6.1). In kabbalistic thought there are ten names of God which also have different significances (see Table 6.2).

Talismans make use of other names than those of God, of course. There are a great many which utilize local deities, and the names of spirits associated with different powers. It is impossible to list all these here, but we can perhaps illustrate the situation by looking at one particular group.

A large number of Saints and Martyrs have been designated as Patron Saints, and talismans bearing their names and/or emblems are considered to be protective.[1] Some saints have also been listed as appropriate powers to invoke when attempting to prevent or cure various diseases and their names can be used talismanically.

Table 6.1 The Ninety-nine Names of God (Mohammedan)

1. Ar-Rahman .... The Merciful
2. Ar-Rahim .... The Compassionate
3. Al-Makik .... The King
4. Al-Kuddus .... The Holy
5. As-Salam .... The Peace
6. Al-Mu'min .... The Faithful
7. Al-Muhaimin .... The Protector
8. Al-Aziz .... The Mighty
9. Al-Jabbar .... The Repairer
10. Al-Mutakabbir .... The Great
11. Al-Khalik .... The Creator
12. Al-Bari .... The Maker
13. Al-Musawwir .... The Fashioner
14. Al-Ghaffa .... The Forgiver
15. Al-Kahhar .... The Dominant
16. Al-Wahhab .... The Bestower
17. Al-Razzah .... The Provider
18. Al-Fattah .... The Opener
19. Al-Alim .... The Knower
20. Al-Kabiz .... The Restrainer
21. Al-Basit .... The Spreader
22. Al-Khafiz .... The Abaser
23. Ar-Rafi .... The Exalter
24. Al-Mu'izz .... The Honourer
25. Al-Muzil .... The Destroyer
26. As-Sami .... The Hearer
27. Al-Basir .... The Seer
28. Al-Hakim .... The Ruler
29. Al-Adl .... The Just
30. Al-Latif .... The Subtle
31. Al-Khabir .... The Aware

---

1. I have not attempted to list the patron saints of countries and cities as these are extremely numerous and frequently derived from dubious local traditions.

32. Al-Halim .... The Clement
33. Al-Azim .... The Grand
34. Al-Ghafur .... The Forgiving
35. Ash-Shakur .... The Grateful
36. Al-Ali .... The Exalted
37. Al-Kabir .... The Great
38. Al-Hafiz .... The Guardian
39. Al-Mukit .... The Strengthener
40. Al-Hasib .... The Reckoner
41. Al-Jalil .... The Majestic
42. Al-Karim .... The Generous
43. Ar-Rakib .... The Watcher
44. Al-Mujib .... The Approver
45. Al-Wasi .... The Comprehensive
46. Al-Hakim .... The Wise
47. Al-Wadud .... The Loving
48. Al-Majid .... The Glorious
49. Al-Bais .... The Raiser
50. Ash-Shadid .... The Witness
51. Al-Hakk .... The Truth
52. Al-Wakil .... The Advocate
53. Al-Kawi .... The Strong
54. Al-Matin .... The Firm
55. Al-Wali .... The Patron
56. Al-Hamid .... The Laudable
57. Al-Muhsi .... The Counter
58. Al-Mubdi .... The Beginner
59. Al-Mu'id .... The Restorer
60. Al-Muhyi .... The Quickener
61. Al-Mumit .... The Killer
62. Al-Hayy .... The Living
63. Al-Kaiyum .... The Subsisting
64. Al-Wajid .... The Finder
65. Al-Majid .... The Glorious
66. Al-Wahid .... The One
67. As-Samad .... The Eternal
68. Al-Kadir .... The Powerful
69. Al-Muktadir .... The Prevailing
70. Al-Mukaddim .... The Bringer Forward

71. Al-Mu'akhkhir .... The Deferrer
72. Al-Awwal .... The First
73. Al-Akhir .... The Last
74. Az-Zahir .... The Evident
75. Al-Batin .... The Hidden
76. Al-Wali .... The Governor
77. Al-Muta'ali .... The Exalted
78. Al-Barr .... The Righteous
79. At-Tawwab .... The Accepter of Repentance
80. Al-Muntakim .... The Avenger
81. Al-Afuw .... The Pardoner
82. Ar-Ra'uf .... The Kind
83. Malik ul-Mulk .... The Ruler of the Kingdom
84. Dhu'l-Jalah wa'l-Ikram . The Lord of Majesty and Liberality
85. Al-Muksit .... The Equitable
86. Al-Jami .... The Collector
87. Al-Ghani .... The Independent
88. Al-Mughni .... The Enricher
89. Al-Mu'ti .... The Giver
90. Al-Mani .... The Withholder
91. Az-Zarr .... The Distresser
92. An-Nafi .... The Profiter
93. An-Nur .... The Light
94. Al-Hadi .... The Guide
95. Al-Badi .... The Incomparable
96. Al-Baki .... The Enduring
97. Al-Warith .... The Heir
98. Ar-Rashid .... The Director
99. As-Sabur .... The Patient

Table 6.3 presents a list of saints who are generally regarded as patrons and protectors in this way. The accompanying Table 6.4 shows which saints to invoke for specific purposes.

In every instance the lives of the saints, or very frequently the nature of their deaths or martyrdom, bears a close relationship to the trades or professions they are supposed to guard and assist. There is no space to deal with them individually here, but there are many accounts of the saints available to provide the information.

By no means all inscriptive talismans are made up of names. Many are composed of connected linguistic statements and the thinking behind these differs to some extent from other aspects of talismanic thought.

The first important distinction is between pictographic writing--such as the Egyptian heiroglyphs and the Chinese ideograms--which does not in itself provide any clue to spoken languages and writing which clearly indicates pronunciation. The actual speaking aloud of a name or of words has always been regarded as potentially magical. The saying of a word aloud involves the use of the breath, which was regarded by older civilizations, and is still regarded by many so-called primitive societies, as the life force, as the spirit (*spiritus* meaning breath) of the human individual. The saying of a name gave the speaker power over the person, force or object which bore that name, for the saying of the name brought the bearer of it distinctly to mind and therefore actually into one's presence. Of course, the name had to be pronounced with a special kind of concentration and in a special tone of voice, otherwise all conversation could become hazardous and all expressions of disagreement dangerous. From this beginning arose the stylized speech of magical statements and incantatory formulae and, ultimately, poetry. The importance of names was such that in some societies people kept one of their names secret so that nobody could pronounce it and thus gain power over them. This notion of the secret name has remained a part of magical tradition, in that members of occult societies always have names whose significance is clear only to members of the society. Many magical books--indeed most of them--have been published under pseudonyms partly because of this tradition.

Just as the saying of the name had to be in a special voice, so the writing of it for magical purposes had to be made quite different from normal writing, simply to establish that the words were being used magically.

Table 6.2 The Ten Names of God (Kabbalistic)

1. Eheia .... The Essence of Divinity
2. Jod .... Wisdom
3. Elohim .... Providence and Understanding
4. El .... Mercy, Grace, Piety, Magnificence
5. Elohim Gibor .... Judgement and Power

6. Eloha .... Glory and Beauty
7. Adonai Sabaoth ...... Justice, Triumph, Victory, Eternity
8. Elohim Sabaoth ...... Agreement and Piety
9. Sadai .... Omnipotence
10. Adonai Melech ..... Empire

Table 6.3 Patron Saints

Of Bell Founders .... Saint Agatha (Emblem: Two breasts
    on a dish)
Of Boy Scouts .... Saint George (Emblem: A red cross
    on a white ground)
Of Children .... Saint Nicholas (Emblem: Three
    Balls)
Of Circus Folk .... Saint Julian the Hospitaller
Of Cripples .... Saint Giles
Of Domestic Servants .... Saint Zita (Emblem: A bunch of
    keys)
Of Drunkards .... Saint Ambrose
Of Emigrants .... Saint Frances Cabrini
Of Farriers .... Saint Eligius (or Eloi)
Of Ferrymen .... Saint Julian the Hospitaller
Of Foreign Missionaries ... Saint Francis Xavier
Of Gardeners .... Saint Fiachra (Emblem: A Spade)
Of Gunners .... Saint Barbara (Emblem: A Tower)
Of Hunters .... Saint Hubert (Emblem: A Stag or
    Hind)
Of Innkeepers .... Saint Julian the Hospitaller
Of the Insane .... Saint Dympna of Gheel
Of Journalists .... Saint Francis de Sales
Of Leatherworkers .... Saints Crispin and Crispinian
    (Emblem: A Last)
Of Lovers .... Saint Valentine
Of Medical Doctors .... Saint Pantaleon
Of Merchants .... Saint Nicholas (Emblem: Three
    Balls)
Of Metal Workers .... Saint Eligius (or Eloi)
Of Midwives .... Saint Peter Nolesco
Of Miners .... Saint Barbara (Emblem: A Tower)

Of Musicians .... Saint Cecilia (Emblem: An Organ)
Of Nurses .... Saint Camillus de Lellis, Saint John
of God
Of Pawnbrokers .... Saint Nicholas (Emblem: Three
Balls)
Of the Poor .... Saint Giles
Of Prisoners .... Saint Leonard the Hermit
Of Sailors .... Saint Erasmus (or Elmo) (Emblem:
A Windlass)
Of Shoemakers .... Saints Crispin and Crispinian
(Emblem: A Last)
Of the Sick .... Saint Michael the Archangel
Of Smiths .... Saint Eligius (or Eloi)
Of Soldiers .... Saint George (Emblem: A Red Cross
on a white ground), and Saint
Nicholas (Emblem: Three Balls)
Of Students of the
Natural Sciences .... Saint Albert the Great
Of Trappers .... Saint Hubert (Emblem: A Stag or
Hind)
Of Travellers .... Saint Christopher
Of Workers for International
Justice and Harmony .... Saint Martin de Porres

Hence, names or words are reproduced using materials not usually used for day to day communication and sometimes upon extremely valuable materials, such as gemstones, gold and silver. The medium used may also differ from the norm—the most obvious instance of this is the use of blood as ink; this clearly establishes the intent of the words, for blood is as much a vital power as breath. Some talismanic writing has used other fluids and special inks have been constructed for magical use.

There are a number of specially contrived magical alphabets in existence, and these not only establish that the writing is magical, but also make it unintelligible to all but initiates. The most famous of these is the Enochian alphabet (see Table 6.5) which was brought to light by Dr. John Dee, the astrologer of Queen Elizabeth I. This alphabet forms part of an Enochian language obtained through the clairvoyant skills of Dee's colleague Edward Kelley. In structure the alphabet is not unlike Hebrew, for the majority of the vowel sounds have no letters and must be supplied by the reader or speaker. Another famous alphabet is that attributed to "Honorius the Theban" (see Figure 6.1) it may originate as late as the seventeenth century or as early as the thirteenth; there is no telling.

Table 6.4 Saints to Invoke

When in Desperate Difficulty .... Saint Jude
Against Disasters at Sea .... Saint Sinach Ma Dara
Against Disease in men
and animals .... Saint Blaise (Emblem: A Comb
                                                    or Two Crossed Candles)
In Emergencies .... Saint Expeditus
Against Epilepsy .... Saint Dympna of Gheel and
                                                    Saint Vitus (Emblem: A Dog or
                                                    a Rooster)
Against Eye Disease .... Saint Lucy (Emblem: Two eyes
                                                    in a dish)
Against Fire .... Saint Agatha (Emblem: Two
                                                    breasts on a dish)
Against Haemorrhoids .... Saint Fiachra (Emblem: A
                                                    Spade)
Against Headaches .... Saint Aedh
Against Insanity .... Saint Dympna of Gheel
Against Lightning .... Saint Barbara (Emblem: A
                                                    Tower)
To Discover Lost Objects .... Saint Antony (Emblem: A Bell
                                                    and a Pig)
Against all Physical Disease ...... Saint Rock (Emblem: A
                                                    Dog)
Against Syphilis .... Saint Fiachra (A Spade)
Against Toothache .... Saint Appolonia (Emblem:
                                                    Forceps gripping a tooth)

Similarly constructed is the Alphabet of the Magi (see Figure 6.2), first presented to the general public by Paul Christian in his *Histoire de la Magie* (1870).[2] The three Angelic alphabets (see Figure 6.3) presented

2. Paul Christian: The History and Practice of magic, Translated by James Kirkup and Julian Shaw, Citadel Press, 1972.

by Ambelain in his *La Kabbale Pratique* are composed of little more than reworded Hebrew letters. Nevertheless, all these alphabets served their purpose to keep one mode of writing pure of all mundane connections, therefore making it effective for magical purposes. Numbers also occur in talismans and very few secret ways of presenting numbers are to be found. Perhaps the only one that is at all well known is that provided by Francis Barrett in *The Magus* (1801) which is reproduced in Figure 6.4.

Enochian Alphabet	Symbol Title	English Equivalent	Enochian Alphabet	Symbol Title	English Equivalent
ꝟ	Pe	B	∩	Mals	P
ꝑ	Veh	C or K	℧	Ger	Q
℔	Ged	G	ꝩ	Drun	N
ꭓ	Gal	D	Γ	Pal	X
ꝗ	Orth	F	λ	Med	O
ꝗ	Un	A	ε	Don	R
ꝯ	Graph	E	ꝑ	Ceph	Z
ε	Tal	M	ꝯ	Vau	U, V, W
Ꝺ	Gon	I, Y, J	ꝯ	Fam	S
ꝺ	Na-hath	H	ꝩ	Gisa	T
ꝓ	Ur	L			

Table 6.5 The Enochian Alphabet

Magical alphabets are often used by makers of esoteric talismans, and the letters usually spell out names of power. Talismans of this kind differ very little from those esoteric talismans discussed elsewhere in this book, save in their almost total reliance upon the "spoken" word. Other talismans, however, are composed not of names only but of coherent sentences and of passages from holy books.

The use of passages from holy books as talismans extends as far back as writing itself, and indeed probably began as soon as traditional wisdom became available in written form. There are many talismans which combine both pictographic and written elements. Some of the most interesting are the cylinder seals of Babylon, Assyria and Egypt.

150

The cylinder seal was, as its name suggests, a cylindrical object frequently made of precious stone, the magical significances of which I have discussed in Chapter 5. These seals were used to seal contracts. They were rolled onto a wet clay tablet and left an impression which clearly identified the owner of the seal. Frequently, the name was accompanied by a hieroglyph or inscribed picture of a god and this meant that anyone who broke the agreement thus sealed, or who disobeyed the orders made in the document, was defying the god.

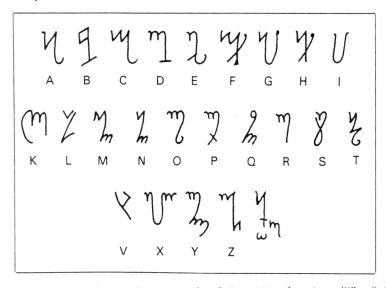

Figure 6.1 Alphabet of Honorius the Theban. Note there is no "j" or "u" in this alphabet. The "w" symbol following the "z" has no equivalent in the Roman alphabet.

Cylinder seals bearing the names of gods were also used as protective talismans and worn around the neck. In Egypt, these talismans were commonly made of bone, ivory, bronze, copper, stone or blue porcelain. The image or hieroglyph of the god was often accompanied by an invocatory prayer to that god—several of this kind of talisman portray the Sun god.

The Hebrews appear to have been among the first to use talismans that are entirely written. On their foreheads covering the third eye, they wore frontlet bands made of skins which were inscribed with religious text, such as: "Hear, O Israel: The Lord our God is one Lord; and thou shall love the Lord thy God with all thine heart, and with all thy soul and with all thy might." (Deuteronomy 6:4-5).

These talismans were called phylacteries, and were worn on the hand and on the left arm as well as the forehead. When the inscribed leather strip was hung on the doorpost of the house, it was a talisman called the Mezuzah.

Many of the inscriptions used in these talismans are clearly intended as protections against ill fortune and the Evil Eye. One is "Thou

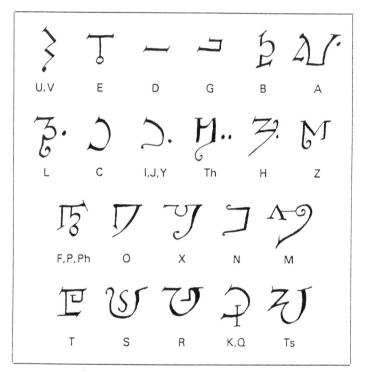

Figure 6.2 Alphabet of the Magi

shalt not be afraid for the terror by night; not for the arrow that flieth by day; not for the pestilence that walketh in darkness; nor for the destruction that waketh at noonday." The whole of Psalm 97 was written on leather and arranged in the form of a seven branched

A

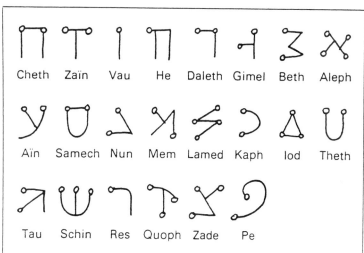

| Cheth | Zaïn | Vau | He | Daleth | Gimel | Beth | Aleph |

| Aïn | Samech | Nun | Mem | Lamed | Kaph | Iod | Theth |

| Tau | Schin | Res | Quoph | Zade | Pe |

B

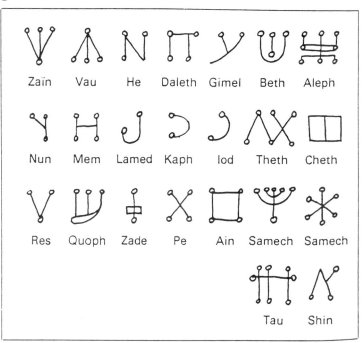

| Zaïn | Vau | He | Daleth | Gimel | Beth | Aleph |

| Nun | Mem | Lamed | Kaph | Iod | Theth | Cheth |

| Res | Quoph | Zade | Pe | Ain | Samech | Samech |

| Tau | Shin |

C

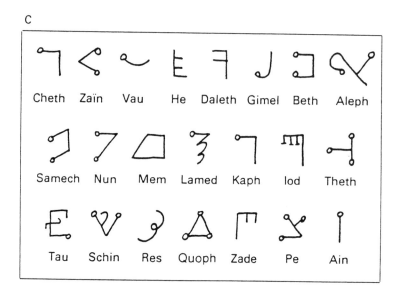

| Cheth | Zaïn | Vau | He | Daleth | Gimel | Beth | Aleph |

| Samech | Nun | Mem | Lamed | Kaph | Iod | Theth |

| Tau | Schin | Res | Quoph | Zade | Pe | Ain |

Figure 6.3 The Three Angelic Alphabets: a) The Celestial alphabet (an angelic script); b) the Malachim alphabet (an angelic script); c) the alphabet called "du passage du fleuve," or "passing the river".

candlestick. This psalm reads:

1   O praise the LORD, all ye nations: praise him all ye people
2   For his merciful kindness is great towards us: and the truth of the LORD endureth for ever.

Another favourite psalm used for talisman was Psalm 121:

1   I will lift up mine eyes unto the hills, from whence cometh my help.
2   My help cometh from the LORD, which made heaven and earth.
3   He will not suffer thy foot to be moved: he that keepeth thee will not slumber.

4   Behold, he that keepeth Israel will neither slumber nor sleep.
5   The LORD is thy keeper; the LORD is thy shade upon thy right
     hand.
6   The sun shall not smite thee by day, nor the moon by night.
7   The LORD shall preserve thee from all evil: he shall preserve
     thy soul.
8   The LORD shall preserve thy going out, and thy coming in,
     from this time forth, and even for evermore.

Some talismans included double meanings. One uses the word
"ayin", meaning both a well and an eye, in a text from Genesis which
reads: "Joseph is a fruitful bough by a well," and thus is a talisman
against the Evil Eye. The well-known blessing of Aaron (Numbers
6:24-26) was also a favourite:

The Lord bless thee, and keep thee; the Lord make his face
shine upon thee and be gracious unto thee; the Lord lift up his
countenance upon thee, and give thee peace.

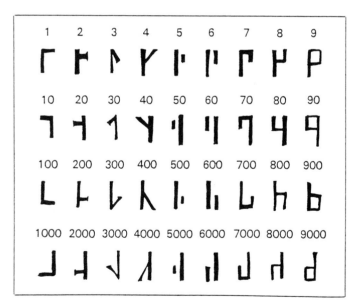

Figure 6.4 Ancient Number Symbols noted by Francis Barrett

155

Mohammedans used, and still use, the text of the Koran in the same way as the Jews use the text of their holy books. They regard the whole of the Koran as a talisman and even in the first years of the twentieth century few people from the Mohammedan countries would travel without a copy. After photolithography came into use, copies of the whole of the Koran were made measuring no more than 1 inch by 3/4 inch by 7/16 inch and enclosed in carrying cases made of metal with a ring attached to them so that they could be worn round the travellers' necks. These are also equipped with a magnifying glass so that they can be read. Some chapters and passages of the Koran are written on parchment or, recently, paper and carried in specially made containers. Some are carved on precious or semi-precious stones. The texts used are selected both to assert the general power and benevolence of the one true god and to defend the talisman wearer from demons and from the Evil Eye. Surah (Chapter) 112 is often used:

1   Say: He, Allah is One.
2   Allah the self subsisting.
3   He begetteth not, and He was not begotten.
4   And there is no one like unto Him.

Surah 2, v 256 may remind us in part of Psalm 121:

God: There is no GOD but He; the living the self subsisting;
Neither slumber nor sleep seizeth Him;
To Him belongeth whatsoever is in heaven, and on earth,
Who is he that can intercede with Him but through His good pleasure?
He knoweth that which is past, and that which is to come unto them;
And they shall not comprehend anything of His knowledge, but so far as He pleaseth;
His throne is extended over heaven and earth, and the preservation of both is no burden unto Him.
He is the High, the Mighty.

The opening prayer of the Koran, the Fatihat, is also popular:

In the name of Allah, the Merciful, the Compassionate,

1	Praise be unto Allah, the Lord of the worlds.
2	The Merciful, the Compassionate.
3	King of the Day of Judgement.
4	Thee do we worship, of Thee we entrust for help.
5	Direct us in the path which is straight.
6	The path of those on whom Thou has shown favour.
7	Not of those with whom Thou art angry. Nor those who wander.

From Surah 113 the following text is used to avert evil:

In the Name of God, the Merciful, the Compassionate,

1	Say: I fly for refuge to the Lord of the Daybreak.
2	From the evil things which He hath created.
3	And from the evil of the night when it hath come.
4	And from the evil of women who are blowers on knots.
5	And from the evil of the envious man when he hath envied.

The phrase "blowers on knots" refers to the practice of tying knots in string while reciting spells intended to do harm to others; the knots are intended to keep the evil spell secure and unbreakable, at least until they were untied. During the making of these spells, the spell maker would blow on the knots as they were being tied.

While all these passages of holy books are used as talismans proper, they are also clearly used as prayers—the prayer is being repeated all the time the talisman is worn. In some instances it can actually be read by the wearer; in others, of course, it is written or inscribed in so small a script or arranged in so complex a pattern that this is not possible.

Many societies have used passages from scripture in this way. The Buddhist monks of the Temple of the Tooth in Kandy, Ceylon, inscribe passages on dried bo leaves for talismans to be given to visitors and worshippers. Tibetan models of the Buddha made of cast metal usually have a cavity in their base which often contains written material as well as, or instead of, relics and sometimes precious stones. The Chinese have always used talismans of the written, or rather painted, kind. Indeed this kind of talisman is common in all literate societies.

157

It is as common today, moreover, as it has been. The small discs and badges inscribed with the Ten Commandments which were fashionable in the nineteenth century can still be found, and are still being made.

Many talismanic tattoos consist of passages from the Bible. Some of the most popular are "Jesus saves," and "The Lord is my Shepherd, I shall not want," and "God is my strength." Many of these are accompanied by religious pictures, which range from portraits of the Madonna and Child and Christ on the Cross, to the whole of the Last Supper. Sometimes the whole of the Lord's Prayer is used as a tattoo. This, like other written talismans we have been surveying, might be called not simply a verbal but a discursive talisman.

Not all verbal talismans are discursive in this fashion, of course. Some are simply arrangements of words or letters. One such is the Agla, which was used by Sir John Dee and was popular in the Middle Ages as a talisman against fever. The letters A G L A stand for Ate Gebir Leilam Adonai ("Thou art mighty for ever, O Lord") and these four letters were inscribed in the four quarters of a mandala on a brooch or ring.

There is a Hebrew amulet which consists of the five letters of the name Elohim, one of the names of God, arranged in a square of 25 letters. Sometimes texts are manipulated in this fashion also. The most widely known letter's square is the SATOR talisman in which the letters spell out the same words both vertically and horizontally, whether read upwards or downwards or from the right or the left:

S A T O R
A R E P O
T E N E T
O P E R A
R O T A S

The Latin sentence thus spelt out can be translated as "Arepo, the sower, holds back the works that are being done with his wheels" or, more simply, "Arepo, the sower, holds back the work with his wheels." Arepo is not a known name. It could, possibly, be a near anagram for Ore'a, an angel guard of the fourth hall of heaven, recorded in Hebrew lore. This does not seem likely. Arel, one of the angels of fire, would be more appropriate as this talisman is most commonly reported as being an implement to put out a fire. If the letters are written on a wooden plate and the plate is thrown into the fire, the fire will go out. This was so firmly believed that in Saxony, in 1742, people were ordered to have these plates to hand for fighting fires. If written in pigeon's blood on parchment and held in the left hand, the SATOR talisman will grant your wishes, according to one old manuscript. If it is hung around the neck of an animal or a human being before dawn on a Friday at an hour which has an uneven number, and if it is augmented by writing beneath it the following, then it will drive away the plague and foul air.

+ J + C + S + H S b y l S a n n e t
U S M m a t e r o n n y + S b a b e 2
S +

It may also be used to discover a witch if it is hung as before but augmented with the inscription + IN + RI + at the top and C + M +B + at the bottom. To make this work, the afflicted person should also be given a mixture of three pinches of flour and three of salt and three pinches of dust created from the timber of the house by filing wood. The witch will then appear. If you simply wish to protect yourself or your animals from witchcraft and the Evil Eye, it is sufficient to hang the basic square around the neck of the one requiring protection.

This may also be hung around the neck of a cow after it has calved, or when it has the fever. It should be hung around the neck of the animal on a Friday between twelve noon and one o'clock. This will drive away fever and ensure a good milk yield. If it is put into a leather bag together with roots of the St. John's Wort and another unidentified herb called moto and hung around your neck, witches will not be able to bear your company. In this case, the first three lines should be followed with additional words. The first line should be augmented with "+ Cross of Christ mildepos," the second with "+ Cross of Christ mesepos," and the third with "+ Cross of Christ habenepos".

In all instances, this talisman is used to stop a destructive process. It may be that the correct way to read the Latin is not as one complete sentence, but as a sentence accompanied by a magical verbal gesture. Thus: SATOR (Arepo) TENET (Opera) ROTAS. The sentence now reads: "The Sower holds back the wheels," and the two words in brackets are simply an indication of what the Sower is doing—altering the backward movement of events, of the Opera, the works, that which is being done, to the forward movement. It might also be noted that if the word Opera is written around a wheel, the counterclockwise movement of the wheel would bring the word Arepo. One might therefore like to translate the remaining words, SATOR TENET ROTAS freely as The Sower (or Creator), holds (or controls, retains mastery of), the wheels (the Wheels of Life). Another interpretation is based upon the notion that the talisman is a Christian one, for it has been found inscribed in a number of Bibles of the period 700-800 A.D.

This suggests that

SATOR AREPO TENET OPERA ROTAS

is an anagram of PATER NOSTER twice repeated, together with the letters O and A standing for Alpha and Omega, the beginning and the end, which placed together in this fashion are a symbol of Christ. Unfortunately, for this view there is only one N in the sentence. On the other hand it can be maintained that as the letter N occurs at the very centre of the square, it can be regarded as having double value. A less well known anagrammatic solution is that which suggests it is an anagram of PATER NOSTER (Our Father) SOTER(Savior) PATERA (Offering Dish), which has the virtue of being a version of God the Father, God the Son, and the Virgin Mary who was often referred to as a holy vessel. Latinists may like to attempt further solutions.

There are other equally mysterious verbal talismans made along the same lines as this one. The most well known are those of the magician Abremalin; the manuscript containing them was written in the eighteenth century, but dated 1458, and was claimed to be translated from the Hebrew. One of these is very close to the SATOR talisman and because the similarity lies in the inclusion of the two words AREPO and OPERA, it tends to support the view that these two words are not to be considered as part of the statement, but rather as an indication that "works" are being done. The square goes:

S A L O M
A R E P O
L E M E L
O P E R A
M O L A S

If we extract the three words which carry meaning we get SOLAM LEMEL MOLAS. If we are to believe that this was originally in Hebrew we can ignore the vowels, for written Hebrew does not have letters for vowel sounds. We must, however, because of the word OPERA assume that the words were originally Latin, even though written in Hebrew form. If we perform this feat of mental juggling we get SLM LML MLS, which would be read in the kind of Latin frequent in these maneuvers as SEMEL (At a word) LIMULA (squinting) MULSA (Sweet as honey). This is probably as good an interpretation as any, for the talisman is one to gain the love of a woman. If laid to her bare skin, however briefly, she will fall in love with the man concerned.

Another of Abremalin's talismans is to enable the wearer to fly like a crow. The word ROLOR is supposed to be derived from a Hebrew word ROL which means to move quickly. The other words remain doubtful:

```
R O L O R
O B U F O
L U A U L
O F U B O
R O L O R
```

This square is interesting in that two of the words are palinodes, and not just the third one, which is always necessary. Another, rather unlikely talismanic square of Abremalin is:

```
M I L O N
I R A G O
L A M A L
O G A R I
N O L I M
```

If this is written on parchment and placed on the top of your head, you will be given insight into the past, present and future. Whether or not you will be given insight as to the meaning of the words on the talisman is not clear.

The other squares of Abremalin are just as difficult to interpret as the ones we have seen and perhaps we have looked at enough of them. There are, however, other verbal talismans which are possibly even more baffling. One consists of a stick upon which the following letters have been cut or written:

+ Z + D I A + B + Z + S A
B Z + H V W F + B E R + + +

If this stick is laid on a valuable object no thief will be able to steal it. Another talisman of this kind is one against the plague. If the following is written on a new piece of parchment and buried under the house it will prevent the plague arriving:

Z + O A + B I Z + S A B + Z H G F + B F R S

A talisman against sudden shooting pains consists of the following written upon paper:

ARILL. AT. GOLL. GOTTZO.

If you wish to improve your marksmanship place the following inscription under your gun barrel:

D E W D W S H H D F S K O M W V R
V J S K N U F M U E S O Mi

When a women is suffering labour pains you can alleviate them by writing on a piece of paper:

A b h z P O b L 9 h b m g n Subratum nome nex gr.
[The Woman's Name]
+ Ecgitar + Circabato + Bessiabato + Argon + Vigaro Tanet.

This should then be placed in a bag of leather which must be sewn up with the seam on the right hand side without there being any knots or loose threads and hung on the patient during an hour with an uneven number.   If you wish to make yourself invulnerable to gun shot, carry the following words about with you:

LIGHT BEFF CLETEMATI, ADONAI CLEONA FLORIT

or the following:

SOBATH, ADONAY, ALBOA, FLORAT.

To cure or prevent cataract, hang the following verbal talisman around the neck:

GAA, SAGA, FASSAA.

I have not attempted to explain these verbal talismans because I cannot do so. It seems clear that all these letters were originally symbols for specific spiritual forces and that we have now lost the key to them. To judge from the alternative talismans against gunshot it also seems that the texts are probably garbled. It is doubtful if talismans of this kind can have any effect for those who are unable to imbue them with energy, because they would not understand the forces to which they refer. It is likely that in the Middle Ages they had considerable meaning and the letters were most carefully chosen.

Another less cryptic but possibly more ingenious form of written talisman is formed on the basis of the dwindling spell. This is a verbal spell in which a disorder is told to dwindle away by reciting an ever diminishing series of words, sounds or numbers. One might begin by saying that there were nine spirits, and then eight, and then seven, dwindling down to zero. Many of these dwindling spells were written out on paper and bound to the patient's body. It is not always easy to be sure whether talismans of this kind were read aloud or simply worn. The Hebrew talisman against both eye disease and the Evil Eye is written out in the form of a triangle with the point downwards; this, if pronounced aloud, would read Shebriri, Briri, Iri, Ri, I, and then, of course, silence. This is a true talisman, however, in that it is worn on all occasions and not simply read aloud when needed.

The most famous of all the talismans utilizing dwindling spells is, of course, the Abracadabra. This word, now used as a general word of power by illusionists when taking rabbits out of top hats or performing other feats of legerdemain, has baffled almost everyone who has attempted to find a meaning for it. Perhaps the most sensible solution to the problem was offered by Bischoff,[3] who suggested that ABRACA-

---

3. Dr. Erich Bischoff, *The Kabbalah: An Introduction to Jewish Mysticism and Secret Doctrine.* Originally published in Germany. English translation published by Samuel Weiser, Inc., York Beach, ME, 1985.

DABRA is a corruption, probably caused by oral repetition of the Chaldee words ABBADA DEDABRA which he translates as "Perish like the word." This command was directed specifically at the fever. The ABRACADABRA talisman is usually written out in this fashion:

ABRACADABRA
ABRACADABR
ABRACADAB
ABRACADA
ABRACAD
ABRACA
ABRAC
ABRA
ABR
AB
A

The same dwindling formula is used on a Hebrew talisman against fire. This consists of a hexagram on the six sides of which are written the names of God, and the spell itself written on the front and back of the parchment consists of the Hebrew for "And it (meaning the fire) dwindled," this being from the second verse of the 11th chapter of Numbers, which reads:

And the people cried unto Moses; and when Moses prayed unto the Lord the fire was quenched.

No talisman of this or any other kind can be expected to be effective if it has not been made with the right kind of concentration, or in some way blessed and imbued with energy. In *Amulets and Talismans,* Wallis Budge gives the text of a talisman together with the rules for making it--this may be consecrating talismans of the kind we have been describing. The talismanic words are:

Ab Abr Abra Abrak Abraka
Abrakal Abrakala Abrakal
Abraka Abrak Abra Abr Ab.

"And the people called unto Moses and Moses prayed to God, and the fire abated" (Numbers 6:2). "May healing come from heaven from all kinds of fever and consumption--heat to N son of N. Amen. Amen. Amen. Selah. Selah. Selah." Here is the perfect Hebrew amulet which contains (1) The magical NAME Abrakala; (2) The TEXT from the Bible; (3) The PRAYER, which is the equivalent of the pagan incantation; (4) The THREEFOLD AMEN and the THREE-FOLD SELAH. Dr. Gaster (Hastings' Encyc., vol. iii p. 455) has translated the directions for writing this amulet. The Name must be written exactly as it is written in the scroll of the Law on specially prepared parchment. It must be written with square or "Ashuri" letters so that no letter shall touch the next, i.e. there must be a free margin round each letter. It must be written in purity and whilst fasting. It must be wrapped in leather or in some soft rag, and be wrapped round with a piece of clean leather. It is to be hung on the neck of the patient without his knowing it or when he is asleep, and he is not to look at it for the next twenty-four hours. The lines for the writing must be drawn on the hairy side of the parchment and the writing is to be done on the flesh side, and in the name of the patient. The parchment must be cut and the lines drawn on it in the patient's name. When the writer dips his pen into properly prepared ink he must say: "In the Name of Shaddai who created heaven and earth. I, N, the son of N, write this Kemi'a for X, son of X, to heal him of every kind of fever." And then he must say the blessing of the Kemi'a as follows: "Blessed art Thou, O Lord our God, Who has sanctified Thy great Name and has revealed it to Thy pious ones, to show its great power and might in the language [in which it is expressed] in the writing of it, and in the utterance of the mouth. Blessed art Thou O Lord, holy King, whose great Name be exalted."[4]

When we study inscribed talismans, we see how many talismans have been made in terms of a complex system of ideas. In this chapter, we have seen them related to both Mohammedan and Jewish religious beliefs and other views. One of the oldest of systems is that presented by astrology. We will look at astrological talismans in the next chapter.

4. Sir E.A. Wallis Budge, *Amulets and Superstitions*, 1930. Re-issued as *Amulets and Talismans*, University Books, New York, 1968, pp.221-222.

Astrological Talismans

It is the stars,
The stars above us, govern our conditions.

Shakespeare
King Lear, IV.iii, 34

Modern astrology does not pay much attention to talismans. Most of the current works in the field mention them extremely briefly, if at all. Nevertheless, astrology does establish correspondences between bodily weaknesses and astral influences and it is clear that effective talismans can be made along lines proved by modern astrologers. Moreover, as we have seen, many gemstones are regarded as being ruled by the stars and therefore carrying the particular powers of those stars. Astrology is also, of course, relevant to the making of Identity Talismans. A thorough exploration of astrology from the talismanic point of view, however, would land us with a very complicated and lengthy discussion. Those who wish to explore this subject would do better to study astrology itself in depth. In the meantime, for our purposes, it is only necessary to examine the qualities and symbols associated with the twelve signs of the zodiac and the planets.

166

Signs of the Zodiac

Aries (♈) rules the head and Arians are consequently subject to headaches. Because Aries is opposite to Libra in the zodiac, and Libra rules the kidneys, the headaches may be associated with kidney disorders. Arians are adventurous, energetic and freedom-loving, but inclined to be egotistical, impatient and pugnacious. The Arian colour is fiery red; the metal is copper; the stone is the ruby or the diamond. Among the plants it is associated with the tiger lily, the honeysuckle, the geranium and the thistle, and among the trees it is associated with blackberries, hawthorn and anything that bears thorns. Its symbols are the owl and the ram.

Taurus (♉) rules the neck and throat and Taureans are prone to catch cold easily and to suffer from laryngitis. As it is opposite to Scorpio which rules the sexual organs it is possible that sexual difficulties may result in psychosomatic illnesses of the throat. Taureans are reliable, patient, strong-minded, persevering and warm-hearted, but inclined also to be stubborn, self-indulgent and conservative. The Taurean colours are pale blue, pink and dark green; the metal is copper; the stone is sapphire or topaz. It is associated with the rose, the poppy, the violet and the foxglove, and, among trees, with the ash, the apple and the cypress. Its symbol is the bull.

Gemini (♊) rules the ears, arms, hands, lungs and shoulders and Geminis are therefore likely to break arms and collarbones, and to suffer from bronchitis. As this sign is opposite Sagittarius, which rules the hips and thighs and the liver, Geminis may suffer in these areas also. Geminis are lively, versatile, intelligent and often garrulous, but sometimes cunning, over-inquisitive, hypocritical and inclined to nervous tension. Some say the Gemini colour is chestnut brown, others that it is bright yellow, but all colours are relevant; the metal is mercury; the stone is agate or tourmaline. Gemini is associated with lavender, lily-of-the-valley and orchids and with all nut-bearing trees. Its symbol is the magpie.

Leo (♌) rules the heart and the spine and Leo types are prone to heart attacks, which may be caused by defects in the circulation and by hardening arteries, as this sign is opposite to Aquarius which rules the circulation of the blood. Leo characters are generous, creative, enthusiastic, sometimes histrionic, but can become conceited, pompous and overbearing. Leo's colours are gold, orange and golden yellow; the metal is gold; the stone is ruby or cat's eye. Leo is associated with marigolds and sunflowers, and with orange trees, lemon trees and the bay and the palm. Its symbol is the lion.

Cancer (♋) rules the stomach, the intestines and women's breasts and Cancerians tend to suffer from nervous dyspepsia and from stomach ulcers. These may in part be caused by mouth and dental infections as the ruler of the mouth and teeth and of bones generally is Capricorn, which is placed opposite to Cancer in the zodiac. The Cancerian is imaginative, sensitive, sympathetic and often shrewd, but can suffer from moodiness, quickness of temper and hypersensitivity which may lead to self-pity and emotional instability. The Cancerian colours are silver and the more subtle tones of green and grey; the metal is silver; the precious stone is the pearl or amber. The plants associated with Cancer are the lotus, all wildflowering plants, and trees particularly rich in sap such as gum trees and pines. Its symbols are both the crab and the turtle.

Virgo (♍) rules the intestines and the nervous system, and, like Cancerians, Virgos are subject to indigestion and ulcers caused by nervous tension and stress. Virgos are modest, precise in thought and tidy, but tend to be hypercritical, over-conventional and fussy and to become neurotically anxious over details. The Virgo colours are dark blues, greys and browns; the metal is mercury; the stones are sardonynx and peridot. Virgo is associated with snowdrops, lilies and all small bright flowers, and nut-bearing trees. Its symbol is the Virgin.

Libra (♎) rules the kidneys, and Librans tend to suffer from kidney trouble which may be associated with nervous tensions caused by the adrenal glands ruled by Aries. The Libran is easy going, romantically inclined, idealistic and fair minded, but can be indecisive and too easily influenced by the views of others. The Libran colours are pink, pale blue and watery green; the metal is copper; the stone is sapphire or emerald. Libra is associated with all blue flowers, with the larger varieties of rose and with the ash tree. Its symbols are the scales and the elephant.

Scorpio (♏) rules the genitals and Scorpios suffer from being highly sexed, and are therefore prone to nervous frustration and emotional difficulties, which sometimes cause throat troubles as their opposite number is Taurus. Scorpions are very emotional and imaginative, as well as preserving and subtle, but can also be sly, stubborn and jealous. The Scorpio colour is vermillion or dark red; the metal is iron; the stone opal or ammoniate. Scorpio is associated with all dark red flowers, and with blackthorn and cactus. Its symbols are the wolf, lobster, beetle, as well as the scorpion.

Sagittarius (♐) rules the thighs, hips and liver and Sagittarians have a tendency to overweight. They are optimistic, adaptable, jovial, candid and sincere with a good fund of common sense, but can be tactless, boisterous, and inclined to exaggeration. Sagittarian colours are purple, dark blue and sky blue; the metal is tin; the stone is topaz or jacinth. Sagittarius is associated with tomato, asparagus, rush, dandelion, and with the mulberry, the ash, the birch and the oak. Its symbols are the horse, dog and centaur.

Capricorn (♑) rules the bones, the teeth and the knees and Capricornians are liable to suffer dental ailments and weakness of the knee joints. Capricornians are prudent, determined, ambitious and disciplined, with a good sense of humour, though this cannot always save them from becoming rigid in outlook, pessimistic and mean. The colours are black and dark grey, brown and deep green; the metal is lead; the stone turquoise or black diamond. Capricorn is associated with thistles, pansies, onions, ivy, willows, pines, elms, poplars and with cannabis. Its symbols are the ass and the goat.

Aquarius (♒) rules the circulation of the blood and the ankles and Aquarians are liable to suffer from hardening of the arteries and varicose veins, which may lead to heart disorders as Aquarius is opposite to Leo in the zodiac which rules the heart. Aquarians are friendly, loyal, idealistic and intellectually inventive, but their very originality can lead them to become eccentric and rebellious, and inclined to cherish unconventionality for its own sake. The Aquarian colour is grey or electric blue; the metal is uranium; the stone is amethyst or glass. Aquarius is associated with orchids, coconuts and with fruit trees. Its symbol are the peacock and the eagle.

Pisces (♓) rules the feet, and Pisceans are unduly affected by foot disorders. Pisceans are emotionally sensitive and intuitive, and extremely kind and sympathetic, but their sensibility can lead them to become indecisive and easily confused. The Piscean colour is sea green or sea blue; the metal is tin; the stone is moonstone or pearl. Pisces is associated with water lilies, willow trees, fig trees, and the opium poppy. Its symbol are the dolphin, fish and beetle.

The Planets

Just as the signs of the zodiac affect the human bodily functions, so do the planets, which also have traditional associations with various metals, colours and planets.

Mercury (☿) affects the brain, the nervous system and breathing. Its colour is yellow; its metal is, obviously, mercury. Its stones are opal and agate. Associated plants are lilies, narcissi, vervain, palm and the fir tree. Its creatures are the swallow and the ape.

Venus (♀) affects the kidneys and like Libra which it rules it also affects the throat and especially the parathyroid glands, which control the calcium level in the body and therefore have to do with the health of the bones. Its colour is green; its metal is copper; its stones are the turquoise and emerald. Associated plants are the aster, rose, clover, daisy, myrtle and verbena. Its creatures are the sparrow, dove and swan.

Sun (☉) The Sun, like Leo, affects the heart and the spine, and also the thymus, which lies behind the sternum at the very centre of the body, and which is largely responsible for enabling the body to fight off diseases caused by bacteria. Its colour is gold, which is also its metal; its stone is crysoleth. Associated plants are the vine, the sunflower, the marigold and the laurel. Its creatures are the lion and the sparrow hawk.

Jupiter (♃) like Sagittarius rules the liver and also the pituitary glands which control the body's rate of growth and its production of hormones. Its colour is blue; its metal is tin; its precious stones are amethyst and lapis lazuli. Its creature is the eagle.

Moon (☽) The moon affects many parts of the body including the breasts and the whole of the digestive system, including the pancreas, the liver and the bile ducts. Its colour is silver, which is also its metal. Its stones are crystal, pearl and moonstone.

Associated plants are the iris, almond, hazel, mugwort and ranunculus. Its creature is the dog.

Pluto (♀) affects the reproductive system, and the body's capacity to produce cells.

Mars (♂) affects the sex glands in both men and women and also the muscles. Its colour is red; its metal is iron; its stone is ruby. Associated plants are the briar, buttercup, verbena and wormwood. Its creatures are the horse, bear and wolf.

Neptune (♆) orders the nervous system in general, and especially the thalamus which is responsible for the efficiency with which the nerve endings in the body transmit their messages to the brain.

Uranus (♅) affects the circulation and the pineal body, or "third eye," which is situated in the centre of the forehead and whose function appears to be entirely perceptive, but perceptive of stimuli which remain unnoticed by other parts of the body.

Saturn (♄) affects the skin, the teeth, the bones and the gall bladder as well as the frontal part of the pituitary glands. Its colour is black and its metal is lead. Its stones are star sapphire and pearl. Associated plants are the monkshood, cypress and opium poppy.

Table 7.1 Signs of the Zodiac and Angelic Rulership

Sign	Governed by	Angel of
Aries	Malahidiel	March
Taurus	Asmodel	April
Gemini	Ambiel	May
Cancer	Muriel	June
Leo	Verchiel	July
Virgo	Hamaliel	August

Sign	Governed by	Angel of
Libra	Uriel	September
Scorpio	Barbiel	October
Sagittarius	Advachiel	November
Capricorn	Hanael	December
Aquarius	Cambiel	January
Pisces	Barchie	February

All but one of these angels have been described already, under the notes on gemstones thus: Malahidiel or Malchediel / Bloodstone and Ruby; Asmodel or Asmodeus / Diamond; Ambiel or Ambriel / Carbuncle; Muriel / Emerald (though the month is given as May; Verchiel /Sapphire); Hamaliel or Hamatiel / Diamond; Uriel or Zuriel/Chrysolite; Barbiel / Agate; Advachiel or Adnachiel / Amethyst; Hanael or Humiel / Beryl; Barchiel or Barakiel / Agate. The one angel not noted is Cambiel who is the ruler of Aquarius.

Table 7.2 Governors of the Seven Planets

Planet	Angel or Governor
Sun	Raphael
Venus	Anael
Mercury	Michael
Moon	Gabriel
Saturn	Zaphiel
Jupiter	Zadkiel
Mars	Camael

Of these governors of the planets we have already mentioned only Gabriel under the heading of onyx. Raphael has so many attributes that it is impossible to list them all, but from the talismanic rather than theological point of view he must be seen as primarily a healer, his task according to the Zohar, being to heal the earth. He personally brought Solomon the ring of the pentalpha so that with it he could make demons help him complete the building of the temple. He looks after the winds of evening and the Tree of Life, and is the angel of knowledge and science. He is one of the seven angels round the throne of God.

Anael is one of the seven Angels of Creation and also known by the names of Haniel, Hamiel, Onoel and, interestingly enough, Ariel. He is credited with looking after all matters of sexual love, and, is the chief of the angels for Friday, the day of Venus. Michael is generally regarded as the greatest and most powerful of angels by members of not only the Christian but also the Jewish and Islamic faiths. He is a very active angel and was involved in many successful battles as when he destroyed the hosts of Sennacherib. In general he is regarded as an embodiment of the Holy Ghost, and the leader of the angels of light against the hosts of darkness. He crops up in ancient Hebridean healing spells as a kind of substitute for the God of the Old Religion, and a deity of power. In 1950, Pope Pius XII gave St. Michael to the policemen as their patron saint.

Zaphiel, known as the wrath of god, is the angel of storms, hurricanes and destruction. Some authorities regard him more as a demon than an angel. This dark character clearly fits well with Saturn.

Zadkiel is one of the seven angels around the throne of God and is an angel of mercy, charity and righteousness.

The information given here is taken from many sources and some authorities are inevitably in disagreement. This is especially the case with the associated colours, metals and plants, for astrology has developed over a long period and its theories have consequently changed over the centuries. Nevertheless in talismanic magic it is always the intent which is the most important part of the operation, and does not matter a great deal if some of the symbols one uses are somewhat approximate. I have tried, however, in making my list to take a consensus and also to exclude associations which, for various reasons, seem to me to be somewhat dubious.

Although we have now listed the main functions and qualities of the signs and planets of the zodiac, we have not arrived at anything like a complete picture of the symbolism attached to them or of the traditional views of their powers--and many authorities will inevitably be in disagreement with the correspondences. Indeed, kabbalists and other occultists and mystics have given names to the powers in the planets, and also signs. Consequently, an absolutely comprehensive "character" of any one planet or sign of the zodiac could occupy many volumes. Nevertheless, anyone wishing to make an astrological talisman might well decide that he could do so with more conviction if he had a named spirit to associate with it. Table 7.1 provides a list of the angels associated with the signs of the zodiac, while Table 7.2 presents the angels associated with the planets. The old astrologers and occultists took account of only seven planets; Uranus, Neptune and Pluto were then unknown.

We can now design a simple talisman making use of all this information in a fairly straightforward fashion. In so doing we are not running counter to the views of occultists who have drawn up elaborate methods of making talismans according to kabbalistic thought; we are using exactly the same principles but in a simpler manner.

Let us assume that we wish to create a talisman to protect us against being susceptible to colds and bronchitis. Those born under Taurus and Gemini are particularly prone to these disorders. Mercury governs respiration. We therefore need a talisman which shows, in simple symbolic terms, Mercury controlling Gemini and Taurus. Because Mercury's metal is itself mercury, of which no talisman can be made, we substitute a metal which looks like it, and the usual substitute is tin, though an alloy of silver, tin and mercury would be the ideal prescription. We can take a circle of tin, however, quite easily from our garbage can, and even though the alloy used in canning is not tin, it is generally known and therefore responded to as such. The colour of Mercury is yellow; a yellow circle should be painted on a circle cut from tin. In the top half of the circle, the sign of Mercury should be painted also in yellow and then, below it, in a much smaller size to show subjection, the sign for Gemini in yellow also (for yellow is a Gemini colour), and the sign for Taurus should be painted in pale blue. On the back of the piece of tin should be written the name of the angel of Mercury, Michael.

In order to consecrate the talisman and make it operative we should then hold it in the smoke of a fire made of the leaves and stalks of the plants with which it is associated--narcissi and lilies. If the season of the year makes this difficult, it would be just as sensible to hold it in the smoke of any incense or fire which pleases the nostrils and eases the lungs, since as we do this we must concentrate our minds upon the act of deep clean breathing, upon clarity and purity of air, upon all images which we associate with health in the respiratory system. The talisman should then be put in a silken bag (silk being traditionally regarded as an insulator against a field of energy dissipating itself) and it should be worn around the neck of the person for whom it is intended, and whose name must have been in our minds all the time while making the talisman. It need not be kept in the bag of silk when it is being worn, but at other times it should be wrapped up and protected in this fashion.

This is a very simple talisman to make and other talismans for physical and psychological disorders can easily be made in the same way. The important thing is for the talisman maker to be able to understand fully why each part of the talisman is made in the fashion it is, and what all the parts of it refer to. If materials prove impossible to find or to afford for a sun talisman, gold foil or even gold paper will do, for the message is of primary importance and the material merely a vehicle for the message. On the other hand, it must be pointed out that metal retains an energy field better than any other material. Still, there are many talisman makers who consider that a well drawn talisman, lettered and painted with care, will operate with total success even if it is made of cardboard. Indeed, many effective talismans have been made this way.

I have already pointed out the importance of the act of consecration. I must underline it here. The symbols used, even on our simple Mercury talisman for bronchitis, are all symbols of multiple powers. Mercury does not only affect the respiratory system, for example, and Gemini rules more than the chest. Similarly, Michael is an angel associated with much more than the planet Mercury. Mercury itself, of course, is regarded as a planet which can bless financial interests and businesses. The act of empowering, therefore, is most important, for it defines the task the talisman is to perform. Chapter 9 addresses the whole business of empowering and consecration in greater detail.

Those who have studied the making of talismans have also pointed out that the talisman that makes use of a particular planet should be made on the day of the week which is ruled by the planet, and others have gone further and suggested that before any talisman is made a full study of the position of the relevant planet in the heavens should be made. It appears to me, however, that only two considerations are of such importance as to be regarded as essential. Firstly, all talismans should be made during the waxing of the moon, and never during its waning, and secondly, one should pick the right day of the week. The days ruled by the planets areas follows:

Sunday ... Sun
Monday ... Moon

Tuesday ... Mars
Wednesday ... Mercury
Thursday ... Jupiter
Friday ... Venus
Saturday... Saturn

This scheme leaves the new planets out in the cold; there are no days of the week for Pluto, Neptune, and Uranus. This problem is easily solved: talismans calling on the power of these planetary powers should be made on Sunday, since the Sun is the symbol of universal and all encompassing power.

Talismans of this kind are easy to make and their symbolism is not particularly complicated. There are, however, other astrological talismans which are much more sophisticated. These are based upon the mystical and philosophical system of the Jewish Kabbalah, upon which most kinds of ceremonial magic in the Western world also depend. Understanding of the Kabbalah, indeed, enables one to make many kinds of talisman, including some which we have not yet discussed.

Kabbalistic Talismans

*Now there is a traditional correspondence, which modern
experiment has shown to be fairly reliable. There is a certain
natural connexion between certain letters, words, numbers,
gestures, shapes, perfumes, and so on, so that any idea or (as
we might call it) "spirit", may be composed or called forth by
the use of those things which are harmonious with it, and
express particular parts of its nature.*

Aleister Crowley[1]

The basic contention of the Kabbalah is that the whole of the
universe is a unity and that everything in creation is related to
everything else. Moreover, everything that exists can be related to the
planets and the signs of the zodiac, to the letters of the Hebrew
alphabet, to precious stones, living creatures, flowers and plants and
to the gods and spiritual powers of all faiths. It is the most complete and
the most elaborately worked out system of correspondences in the
world.

The easiest way to approach this mystical system is by way of the
Tree of the Sephiroth (see Figure 8.1). This is a diagram of the forces

---

1. Aleister Crowley, *Magic in Theory and Practice*, first published for subscibers only, in
Paris in 1929. Re-issued under the title *Crowley: Magik*, edited by John Symonds and
Kenneth Grant, Routledge and Kegan Paul, London, 1973, and Samuel Weiser, Inc., York
Beach, ME, 1973, p. 143

which animate and control the cosmos and the life of mankind and of each individual human being. The cosmos and mankind and the individual are all regarded as being created from the origin of all things by an evolutionary process.

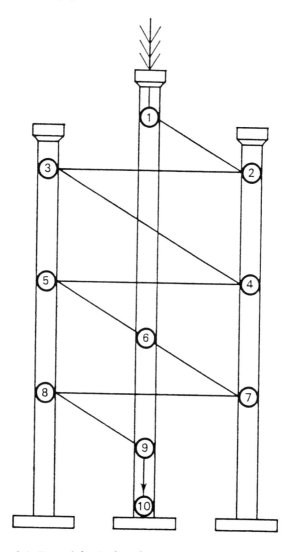

Figure 8.1 Tree of the Sephiroth

This can be shown as a descent down a ladder, or down a tree, from the ineffable to the material world of here and now. The individual and mankind must, having descended into the world we know, attempt to return up the ladder or tree and achieve unity with the spirit that is the essence of all things. This great power is unknowable by man on earth, just as the secret name of God is unknown in Mohammedan thinking. It is placed at the very top of the diagram of the tree of the Sephiroth and given the name of the Sephirah Kether (Sephiroth being the plural of Sephirah). From Kether the power flows onwards to create the second Sephirah, Chokmah, where what had previously been a force without direction, an unknowable and all-encompassing absolute, takes on direction. Chokmah has been named Wisdom and Jehovah, the first graspable idea--Kether is simply called the Crown. The force now moves from Chokmah to Binah, or Understanding, and the simple power of wisdom takes on form, as it were, and becomes what has also been called the Sanctifying Intelligence, the Great Sea and the Mother. It is Binah which causes the second stage of evolution to begin by creating the fourth Sephirah, Chesed. Chesed, although called Mercy, Love and Majesty is, like Chokmah, a Sephirah of force without form; it is the fifth Sephirah, Geburah, which gives form to the energy of Chesed, just as Binah gave form to the energy of Chokmah. Chesed and Geburah, even though the latter derives from the former, are in some ways opposite; Chesed standing for Obedience, Law, Order, Majesty, Love, and Geburah for Power, Justice and violent energy. Chesed is Jupiter, and Geburah Mars. These forces are resolved and balanced in the sixth Sephirah, Tiphareth, which provides a vision of the harmony of things, and which is associated with the very limit of human apprehension of spiritual truth, and therefore with the crucifixion of Christ. Tiphareth is indeed the highest spiritual state which a man may reach and it is also therefore symbolized by the Sun, by a king, a child, a sacrificed god.

We have now, in the "downward flow" of the force of life, reached the spiritual experience of man, though not yet his sensual experience. The four remaining Sephiroth are those available to human experience and are called the Four Lower Sephiroth. The seventh Sephirah, Netzach, is called Victory, and symbolized by a beautiful naked woman. It is a vision of beauty in triumph and only one stage "down" from the complete harmony of Tiphareth. If this force is used positively it presents the virtues of unselfishness and love; if it is perverted it

179

presents lust and greed. It can also be regarded as the Sephirah in which the individual experiences intuitively and psychically; in this it is opposed to the eighth Sephirah, Hod, which is the Sephirah associated with human reason and intelligence, and one of whose symbols is Mercury, the messenger. It represents truthfulness and, therefore, if misused, falsehood. The ninth Sephirah, Yesod, brings the two previous ones into harmony and is called The Foundation, for we have now reached, on the downward path, the Sephirah which is the basis of human experience, and also the first step on the upward path to illumination. Yesod combines both great strength and independence of judgement with a certain fluidity and restlessness. It is the stuff of life as experienced by the whole human being, the intellectual, sensual, and spiritual creature. It may be the stuff of that energy we see in auras or as the result of Kirlian photography. It is indeed the place of magical powers and also of magical confusions.

The tenth and last Sephirah on the downward evolutionary path is Malkuth, the Kingdom, which is life itself, sensual and intellectual existence. It is the earth we know. It is regarded as the end of the "fall" from Kether. It is also, however, the condition from which each of us starts to move towards Tephireth, towards "God", towards illumination, returning upwards on either the middle path from Malkuth through Yesod to Tephiroth, the path of meditation and illumination, or by a more indirect route through Hod or through Netzach.

This evolutionary process is to be seen firstly as an account of the creation and evolution of the universe we know, or think we know. Secondly, it must be seen as the creation of each individual. It must be seen, too, as a map of all the powers, knowable and unknowable, affecting us, for Malkuth is affected by all the previous Sephiroth. It must be seen as a map of the route towards social, personal, even national, development, and evolution "back" up the Tree. The Tree, indeed, is a map that applies not only to man, but also to all other forms of life, known to us or only guessed at.

It now becomes clear that since the Tree is a map of everything that is, then everything that is must have its place on the Tree, and must fit perfectly into the pattern and into the qualities that the Sephiroth embody and the powers of which they are composed. This is the case according to Kabbalists. All the gods and named spirits, all the archangels and angels of all religions have their place on the Tree. All the religious systems--and especially Christianity, Judaism, Hebraism, the Greek Mysteries and the Egyptian religion--fit the pattern. Indeed, even the world of so called inanimate matter can be seen in relationship to this extraordinary design.

This being the case, the "correspondences" we have so far been observing between metals, planets, precious stones, plants and so forth can be regarded as part of one all-comprehensive system of thought and belief, one pattern. The system of correspondences was worked out most fully by Aleister Crowley and can be found in his book *777 and Other Qabalistic Writings* of which we have already made use, and where it occupies, together with the necessary commentaries and appendices, 155 pages. We obviously cannot repeat all this information here. We can, however, point out that once this system is recognized it causes the whole of daily experiences to be regarded as an interplay of forces which have their place in a cosmic structure and which all have powerful significance.

The kabbalistic system does not explain everything, of course, and many talismans have only an oblique relationship to it. It does, however, enable us to see where, in the system of things, talismanic power may rest. It is in the energy of Yesod, the Sephirah of the Moon, that we find on our diagram that balance of strength and fluidity, that energy field, which is the stuff of life and which is to be seen as the energy field of talismanic magic of all kinds. Even the "found" talisman and those of countrylore can be fitted into places upon the Tree. As everything in existence, spiritual or material, has a place in its system, the Kabbalah is inevitably extremely complex, and its complexity has multiplied over the centuries so that it is liable to take a student many years to learn all its various aspects. In this book, however, we do not need to explore more than some basic ideas, in order to understand the principles upon which kabbalistic talismans are made.

Firstly, it is necessary to understand that kabbalism includes astrology and the kabbalistic talismans are therefore often based upon the need to call upon planetary powers. The planets, according to the kabbalists, are not simple forces. They include both Intelligences and Spirits--sometimes called Demons. The Intelligences are wholly beneficial; the spirits are pure power which may be used for good or for bad purposes. As a consequence of this, some occult practitioners have made use of the kabbalah for selfish and destructive ends, calling upon the powers in their dark rather than their beneficial aspects.

Secondly, we must understand that in kabbalism every letter in the

Hebrew alphabet, and there are twenty-two of them, has a numerical value (see Table 8.1). Thus it is possible to write words as numbers and numbers as words. Not only do the letters have numerical value, however, they also have symbolic significance, so that a name or a word can have an esoteric meaning in addition to its ordinary one. The Hebrew letter *Beth* (the equivalent of our B), for example, signifies ambition, intellectual activity and science, has a numerical value 2, and corresponds to the first trump of the Tarot, the Magician (or Juggler) which in its turn symbolizes the beginnings of conscious life in the child, and the path between Kether and Binah on the Tree of the Sephiroth. It also corresponds with the Egyptian gods Thoth and Cynocephalus, Hermes (also Mercury), the swallow, ibis and ape, vervain, marjolane, herb mercury, opal, agate, the perfumes sandal, mace, storax and the colour yellow. Because it corresponds with the planet Mercury, it also corresponds with all the symbols associated with the planet. The word "Beth" also means "House".

Because the letters themselves, one by one, provide the inner meaning of the words, any combination of the same letters has the same inner meaning. Consequently, by juggling the letters around, making anagrams, one can gain further insights into the word's total significance. Moreover, in such a rearrangement, the numerical value of the word remains unaltered and this is considered important. Another way of discovering the inner meaning of words and their correspondences depends entirely upon making use of their numerical equivalents. This is called Gematria. The method is to convert the letters of the word into numbers, add them together, and then discover another word whose letters, when changed into numbers, add up to the same figure. This has been used by many scholars of the kabbalah in studying scripture. Richard Cavendish provides a number of interesting examples of this use. He tells us:

> When Abraham was on the plains of Mamre, Genesis says "and lo three men stood by him". The Hebrew words for 'and lo three men' add to 701. The words for 'these are Michael, Gabriel and Raphael' also add to 701, so it was deduced that the three men were really the three archangels. 'Shiloh shall come' means 'the Messiah' shall come, because Shiloh and Messiah both add to 358.....The ladder which Jacob saw reaching from

earth to heaven is Sinai, because both sulam (ladder) and Sinai total 130; the law revealed from Sinai is the ladder from heaven to earth. A striking example of a genuine use of the type of code in the Old Testament comes from the Book of Daniel in which the identity of the Seleucid king Antiochus IV Epiphanes is cloaked under the name Nebuchadnezzar, probably because the Hebrew letters of both names add to 423.[2]

Gematria is not used simply to interpret scripture. It can be used "in reverse" as it were, in order to interpret numbers. Thus, Cavenish tells us, "the number 13 means 'love of unity', because the words for 'love' and 'unity' both total 13." A surprisingly accurate discovery of gematria is that a normal pregnancy should last exactly 271 days because the letters of the word for pregnancy (herayon) add up to 271.

The most famous problem in gematria is, of course, that of the Great Beast whose number is 666, which appears in Revelations. There have been many solutions to this problem. A scholar called Peter Bungus once said that it referred to Martin Luther; Luther responded by saying it referred to the number of years in which the church had been ruled by Popes. Other people have, with rather suspect ingenuity, identified the beast as Napoleon, Caligula and Nero.[3] Aleister Crowley decided that it referred to himself. Perhaps the most ingenious, and possibly the most intellectually acceptable, is the interpretation of Robert Graves who does not use Gematria but another Kabbalistic method of interpretation and word transformation called Notarikon.

Notarikon consists of making either a phrase or a new word by putting together the first or the last letters of the original phrase, or of taking the constituent letters of a word or phrase and using them as the initial or final letters of a new statement. Graves used Notarikon on 666 by suggesting that, the latin for 666 being DCLXVI, it could be expanded to read Domitius Caesar Legatos Xti Violenter Inerfecit, or "Domitius Caesar violently killed the envoys of Christ." Domitius was the original name of Nero. Other examples of Notarikon are the translation of ICTHUS, fish, into Lesos CHristos THeous Uios Soter, "Jesus Christ, the Son of God, the Savior," which we have already

2. Richard Cavendish *The Black Arts*, Pan Books, Picador edition, 1977, pp. 135-136.
3. See Robert Graves, *The White Goddess*, Faber and Faber, London, 1948, pp. 340-346.

noted. Richard Cavendish tells us:

The first word of the Bible--berashith, 'in the beginning'--has been subjected to innumerable twisting and turnings. If each of its letters are taken as the initial letters of a word, one result is 'In the beginning the Elohim (God) saw that Israel would accept the law'. Another is 'Ye shall worship my first-born, my first, whose name is Jesus', one of six examples of Notarikon which persuaded a seventeenth century Jewish cabalist to turn Christian.[4]

Gematria and Notarikon are often combined in these ingenious exercises. Sometimes, also, another method of transliteration is used called Temura. This is described most clearly by Aleister Crowley in *777 and Other Qabalistic Writings*:

Temura is permutation. According to certain rules, one letter is substituted for another letter preceding or following it in the alphabet and thus from one word another word of totally different orthography may be formed. Thus the alphabet is bent exactly in half, in the middle, and one half is put over the other, and then by changing alternately the first letter or the first two letters at the beginning of the second line, twenty-two commutations are produced. These are called the "Tables of the Combinations of TzIRVP, Tziruph." For example's ake, I will give the method called ALBTh, Albath. Thus:

11 10 9 8 7 6 5 4 3 2 1
K I T Ch Z V H D G B A
M N S O P Tz Q R Sh Th L

Each method takes its name from the first two pairs composing it, the system of pairs of letters being the groundwork of the whole, as either letter of a pair is substituted for the other

---

4. Richard Cavendish *The Black Arts*, Pan Books, Picador edition, 1977, pp. 135-136.

Hebrew Symbol	Name of Letter	English Equivalent	Meaning of Letter	Numerical Equivalent
א	Aleph	A	Ox	1
ב	Beth	B	House	2
ג	Gimel	G	Camel	3
ד	Daleth	D	Door	4
ה	He	H or E	Window	5
ו	Vau	U, V, W	Nail	6
ז	Zain	Z	Sword	7
ח	Cheth	Ch	Fence	8
ט	Teth	T	Serpent	9
י	Yod	Y + J	Hand	10
כ	Kaph	K	Palm	20 or 500
ל	Lamed	L	Ox Goad	30
מ	Mem	M	Water	40 or 600
נ	Nun	N	Fish	50 or 700
ס	Samekh	S	Prop	60
ע	Ayin	O	Eye	70
פ	Pe	O	Mouth	80 or 800
צ	Tzaddi	Tz	Fishhook	90 or 900
ק	Quoph	soft K	Back of Head	100
ר	Resh	R	Head	200
ש	Shin	Sh	Tooth	300
ת	Tau	soft T	Egyptian Tau	400

Table 8.1 The Hebrew Alphabet: Some Correspondences

letter. Thus, by ALbath, from RVCh, Ruach, is formed DTzO, Detzau.[5]

This looks more difficult than it is unless we realize that we are dealing with the Hebrew alphabet of 22 letters and that Hebrew reads from right to left. It then becomes one of the simplest of substitution codes. There are as many methods of Temura as there are letters in the letter. Thus, by ALbath, from RVCh, Ruach, is formed DTzO, Detzau.[5] Hebrew alphabet. The others are ABGTh (which means that the two pairs on the right are written as G A). The others are AGDTh, ADBG, AHBD, AVBH, AZBV, AChBZ, ATPCh, AIBT, AKBI, ALBK, AMBL, ANGM, ASBN, AOBS, APBO, ATzBP, AQSTz, AREQ, AShBR, and AThBsh. There are, for some reason, two others, ABGD and ALBM.

There are several other methods of Temura, none of them particularly complicated and all of them familiar to anyone interested in simple kinds of codes.

Much of this may seem irrelevant to the consideration of talismans, but talismans frequently make use of words of power and these words of power have often been formulated through the use of Gematria, Notarikon, or Temura. Moreover, many of the names of angels, spirits and intelligences have been constructed in a similar manner. Consequently, if one wished to find the name of, or a name for, the spirit of a particular place or even object, one might choose to do so using these methods. As an illustration let us take the name OTTAWA. Using Crowley's method of transliteration, which is generally regarded as the most authoritative, we get the Hebrew letters Ayin (70), Teth (9), Aleph(1), Vau (6), Aleph (1). Some gematrists might omit the vowels because in orthodox gematria they are not taken into account, in which case we would get only Teth (9) and Vau (6). Thus we have now to find a name that adds up to either 87 or 15.. The number 87 could provide the three letters Gimel (3), Pel (80), Daleth (4), which translates as GPD and, by Notarikon, could read as "God Preserve Democracy." The number 15 could result in Beth (2), Gimel (3), Yodh (10), which transliterate as BGY and could result in the word "Bogey".

This may be facetious, but if one wishes to create a talisman which uses words found specially for it, and which correspond exactly to the

5. Aleister Crowley, *777 and Other Quabalistic Writings,* Samuel Weiser , Inc., York Beach, ME, 1973, p.3

work the talisman is to perform, then the methods here provided will do the job. Ideally, of course, the whole of the operation should be conducted in Hebrew, as all the kabbalistic systems are based upon the language. Nevertheless, there is good precedent for adjusting the system to work with another alphabet. Modern western numerology has developed a most effective and sophisticated system of divination from the methods used by the Greeks and Hebrews, and though this need not concern us here as it is rarely used in the making of talismans, it does suggest that when we are dealing with concepts that belong essentially in languages using the Roman alphabet, some form of adaptation might be in order. Modern numerologists use the following table of numerical equivalents:

A:1, B:2, C:3, D:4, E:5, F:6, G:7, H:8, I:9, J:1,
K:11, L:3, M:4, N:5, O:6, P:7, Q:8, R:9, S:1, T:1
U:3, V:22, W:5, X:6, Y:7, Z:8.

This would give us 15 as the numerical equivalent of Ottawa, and, by Gematria, we could produce the word Tome or Ties and a number of others. In dealing with the Roman alphabet in this way, however, we must realize that it has never been deliberately organized into a system of multiple correspondences as has Hebrew, and that therefore our experiments are likely to have limited results. The Hebrew system is indeed very complex. Just as the letters have significance in themselves so do the numbers and many talismans are made entirely from numbers. The numbers basic to all forms of numerological thinking are those from 1 to 9, for these are the basis of all later numbers, and all have importance. In the Arabic alphabet, for example, the first letter of the alphabet is 1 and its significance is God. Other correspondences are 2: male and female, heaven and earth, light and dark, sun and moon, winter and summer, and indeed all pairs of this kind. "Four" stands for the four archangels, elements, and seasons and explains why these talismans are always squares and not rectangles. "Seven" is particularly powerful, for it alludes to the seven heavens, planets, and hells, and the Seven Seals and the seven stages in the life of man as well as the seven prophets, Moses, Jesus, David, Solomon, Jacob, Adam and Muhammad, who preside over the seven days of the week respectively.

The basic principle of talismans using numbers appears to be that the numbers, when given letter equivalents, should spell out a name of power, or, when added together, result in the numerical equivalent of a name of power or a passage of scripture. In Arab talismans it is frequent for the name chosen to be one of the ninety-nine names of God which we have already listed. Sometimes four or more names of God are chosen, according to the particular attributes of God that the talisman maker wishes to bring into mind. The sheer ingenuity of these talismans is clearly regarded as magical in itself. The amount of intellectual labour and cunning required to construct them is regarded as proof of a corresponding amount of passion, faith and magical energy.

One talisman using the numbers 1 to 9 is of great antiquity. Although nowadays known as the Table of Saturn (see Figure 8.2), it is supposed to have been discovered by the Chinese Emperor Yaou inscribed on the back of a huge tortoise which appeared on the banks of the Yellow River in 2348 BC after a great flood. This talisman takes the form of a Zahlenquadrat, or magic square, in which the numbers of the vertical columns and the horizontal columns add up to the same number (15), which is also the sum of the numbers read diagonally. The table is called the eightfold path or Patao by the Chinese because there are eight squares surrounding the central square which is the number for man himself, five, which is related to the five senses.

The Zahlenquadrat is the basis of all kabbalistic planetary talismans, where it is called a Kamea. The numbers are directly related to the numerical equivalent of the names of the intelligence and/or spirit of the planet, or to some other significant name. The sigil, or seal, of the planet's intelligence and spirit is made by drawing lines within the numerical squares that spell out, numerically, the correct names. The actual sign of the planet itself is basically an abstract design so contrived as to pass through all the numbers in the squares.[6]

The talisman made according to this system should have the Kamea on one side of it and the sign of the planet and the sigil (sign) of its intelligence on the other. The sigil of its spirit (or demon) may be added for extra power, but the demon's sigil should never be used without

6. This information is gathered together from a large number of different sources, including works by Eliphas Levi, A.E. Waite, Israel Regardie and *The Key of Solomon* by Mathers. One of the more complete accounts can be found in Israel Regardie's *The Golden Dawn*, Llewellyn Publications, St. Paul, MN, 1971. This does not, however, include the Hebrew. This can be found in E.A. Wallis Budge's *Amulets and Talismans*.

the sigil of the intelligence to control it. In addition to this one may add to the talisman the names which are associated with the planet, those of its angels and archangels, and, indeed, any other names considered relevant. These talismans should be worn as pendants, though they can also be used as brooches, belt buckles, or rings provided that the necessary attachments do not touch the actual designs.

There are differing views of the powers of these planetary talismans and some of the names are transliterated from the Hebrew in different ways by different occultists. The following, however, gives as full a picture, including variants, as seems necessary.

Saturn

Saturn's Spirit is Agiel (45), and the Demon is Zaziel (45). The numbers in the Kamea add up, in total, to 45 which is not only the number of both the spirit and the demon but also that of the full length tetragrammation, the name of God, which can be written as YWD HA WAW HA (see Figure 8.3). The shortest form of the Tetragrammation is YH (abbreviated from YHWH) which has the numerical equivalent

ד	ט	ב		4	9	2
ג	ה	ז		3	5	7
ח	א	ו		8	1	6

Figure 8.2 Table of Saturn

of 15 (Y, Yod, being 10, and H, He, being 5), and all the horizontal and vertical columns in the Kamea add up to 15 as do the diagonals. This is the oldest recorded Kamea and appears to have been in use in Sumerian times and in ancient India. This Kamea should be made of lead, which is the metal of Saturn and be made on a Sunday.

Some commentators state that this talisman will bring greater ability in business and politics and help the wearer to shoulder heavier responsibilities and duties. Others point to the medical associations of the planet, which we have already discussed, and state that the talisman protects against being killed as a consequence of poison or conspiracy. It is also a protection for women in childbirth.

ר	ט	ב
ג	ה	ז
ח	א	ו

4	9	2
3	5	7
8	1	6

Seal of the Planet   Spirit: Zazel   Intelligence: Agiel

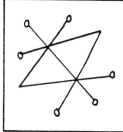

Figure 8.3 Kamea of Saturn

ד	די	הי	א
ט	ז	ו	בי
ה	אי	י	ח
יו	ב	ג	גי

4	14	15	1
9	7	6	12
5	11	10	8
16	2	3	13

Seal of the Planet   Spirit: Hismael   Intelligence: Yophiel

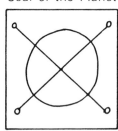 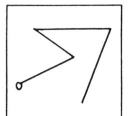 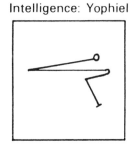

Figure 8.4 Kamea of Jupiter

Jupiter

Jupiter's Intelligence is Yophiel (136) and the Demon is Hasmael (or Hismael) (136). The sum of all the numbers in the square is 136. When the numbers in the vertical and horizon talcolumns and the two diagonals are added the result is 34 which is the numerical equivalent of the Hebrew word for tin (see Figure 8.4). This talisman should be made of tin and on Thursday. According to some authorities it can also be made on coral as a protection against witchcraft.

This talisman is a protective talisman for travellers, and a help in legal and commercial negotiations. It causes sympathy in others and banishes anxiety and also protects against accidents.

Mars

Mars' Intelligence is Graphiel (325) and the Demon is Barsabel (or Bartzabel) (325). All the numbers add up to 325, and the vertical and horizontal columns and the diagonals add up to 65 which is the numerical equivalent of ADNY or ADONAY, one of the names of God. (see Figure 8.5). The talisman should be made of iron and on a Thursday. It protects against enemies and assists the wearer in matters connected with machinery. It also increases the wearer's strength and physical courage.

א'	וכ	ᴋ	כ	ג
ז	ב'	הכ	ח	י'
ᴋ'	ה	ג'	אכ	ט
'	ה'	א	ד'	בכ
גכ	ו	ט'	ב	ה'

11	24	7	20	3
4	12	25	8	16
17	5	13	21	9
10	18	1	14	22
23	6	19	2	15

Seal of the Planet   Spirit: Bartzabel   Intelligence: Graphiel

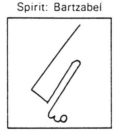
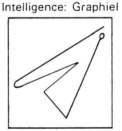

Figure 8.5 Kamea of Mars

Sun

The Sun's Intelligence is Nakiel (or Nakhiel) (111) and the Demon is Sorath (666). The overall total of the figures is 666, and the vertical and horizontal columns and the diagonals add up to 111 as shown in

191

Figure 8.6. Six hundred and sixty-six is, of course, the powerful number of the "Great Beast" of Revelations. The number 111, however, a triple unity, is even more powerful. The talisman should be made of gold and on a Sunday. It strengthens the wearer's confidence and powers of leadership.

ו	לב	ג	לז	לה	א
ז	איִ	כז	כח	ח	ל
יט	יד	יז	הי	כג	כד
יח	כ	כב	אכ	זי	ןי
הכ	וכי	י	ט	וכ	בי
לו	ה	לג	ד	כ	אל

6	32	3	34	35	1
7	11	27	28	8	30
19	14	16	15	23	24
18	20	22	21	17	13
25	29	10	9	26	12
36	5	33	4	2	31

Seal of the Planet*   Spirit: SORATH   Intelligence: Nakhiel

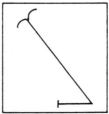
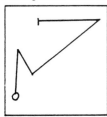

Figure 8.6 Kamea of the Sun (Sol). Note that the Sun is called a "planet" by many astrologers. The term was coined because it was easier to say the "ten planets" when referring to the celestial bodies, rather than the correct "eight planets and two luminaries." Astrologers know, however, that both the Sun and the Moon are not planets.

Venus

The Intelligence of Venus is Hagiel (49), and the Demon is Kedemel (175). There is an additional intelligence in the form of a choir of angels named the Beni Seraphim. The numbers in the squares represent Hagiel by running for 1 to 9. The columns horizontally, vertically and diagonally add up to 175 which is not only the number of Kedemel but also the number of the Hebrew (Sodh-Mny) for "Secret council of the goddess Meny," Meny being a name for Venus. The total for all the numbers is 1,225 which is the number of the Beni Seraphim, which are the highest order of angels, and angels of love, light and fire. There are four seraphim according to Michael, Seraphiel, Johoel, and Metatron. Satan is supposed to have been their leader before his fall. This talisman should be made of copper and on a Friday. It preserves marital happiness and can transform dislike to affection. It protects women from cancer and everyone from poison. It also helps with all social relationships and in money matters. (See Figure 8.7)

כב	חר	יר	חא	י	לה	ד
ה	כבג	חר רי	חב	איע	כב	
ל	ו	כבטמ	חי	רל	יר	
יר	אל	ר	הכב	מבג	ריע	לר
לה	רי	בל	א	וכ	חר	כ
אכב	על	ה	גל	ב	רהכב	חר
מ ו	הי	מ	ע	בל	ג	חכב

22	47	16	41	10	35	4
5	23	48	17	42	11	29
30	6	24	49	18	36	12
13	31	7	25	43	19	37
38	14	32	1	26	44	20
21	39	8	33	2	27	45
46	15	40	9	34	3	28

Seal of the Planet   Spirit: Kedemel   Intelligence: Hagiel

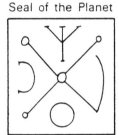 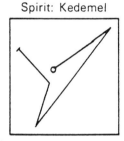 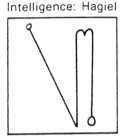

Figure 8.7 Kamea of Venus

Mercury

Mercury's Intelligence is Tiriel (260) and the Demon is Taphthar-tharath (2080). The horizontal, vertical and diagonal columns add up to 260 which is the number of Tiriel and also the number of the consonants in the Hebrew for "Star of Living Silver" (kokab kesef hayyim). All the numbers add up to 2,080. The talisman (see Figure 8.8) should be made of tin and on a Wednesday though it can also be made of aluminum, silver, or platinum. It helps in all matters to do with commerce, and if buried under the threshold of a shop, or even placed above the door, it will attract customers. It preserves its wearers from madness and epilepsy and from death by murder. If placed beneath the pillow at night it can bring prophetic dreams. It is also good as protection while travelling.

ח	נח	נט	ה	ד	סב	סג	א
מט	יה	יד	נב	נג	יא	י	נו
מא	כג	כב	מד	מה	יט	יח	מח
לב	לד	לה	כט	כח	לח	לט	כה
מ	כו	כז	לז	לו	ל	לא	לג
יז	מז	מו	כ	כא	מג	מב	כד
ט	נה	נד	יב	יג	נא	נ	יו
סד	ב	ג	סא	ס	ו	ז	נז

8	58	59	5	4	62	63	1
49	15	14	52	53	11	10	56
41	23	22	44	45	19	18	48
32	34	35	29	28	38	39	25
40	26	27	37	36	30	31	33
17	47	46	20	21	43	42	24
9	55	54	12	13	51	50	16
64	2	3	61	60	6	7	57

Seal of the Planet Spirit: Taphthartharath Intelligence: Ririel

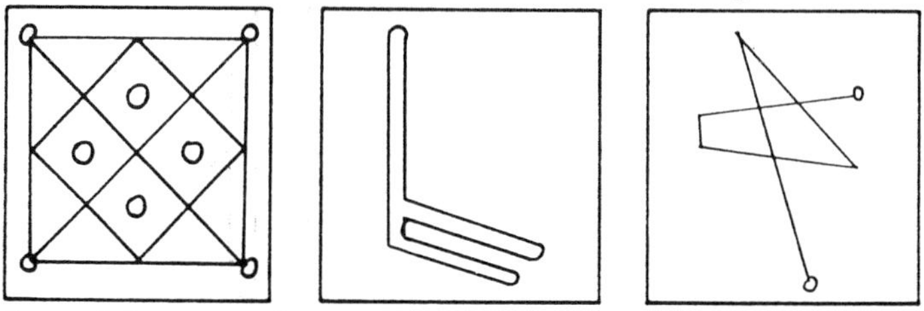

Figure 8.8 Kamea of Mercury

Moon

The Moon's Intelligence (see Figure 8.9) is Malka Betharshesim (or Malcah Betarshisim ve-ad ruachoth ha-schedralim) (3321), and the Demon is Hasmoday (or Chasmodai) (369). The Demons of the moon have a demon of their own named Shedbarshemoth Sharthathan (or Shad Barshemoth Hschartathan) (3321). The numbers in the horizontal and vertical columns and diagonally add up to 369, which is the number not only of Hasmoday but also of the consonants in the Hebrew for "golden horn" (keren ha-zahab). All the figures add up to 3,321. It should be made of silver and on a Monday. This talisman helps in all domestic matters and in anything to do with plant growth and the care of animals.

All these talismans should not only be made on the appropriate day, but at a time when the moon is waxing, and at an hour ruled by the planet when the moon is in good aspect to it. One authority suggests that the appropriate hours in all cases are from midday to 1 P.M., from 7 to 9 P.M., from 2 to 3 A.M. and from 9 to 10 A.M. the next day. This seems, on the face of it, to be a little too easy.

ה	גד	יא	סכא	אכבא	ע	כג	עשׁטׁ	חר
מ	ידי	ו	סאכבכ	עעא	ל	עשׁ	חל	ו
יה	הגה	כג	עבגאל	פ	לשׁ	ר	סד
נו	סד	סד	פאבל	פ	נז	ח	סם	חם	יי
כהה	הסה	עלע	גל	מאמא	ט	סמ	סי	כי
סו	בלד	עדמד	א	ג	יח	גח	כו
להה	עה	מג	ב גנא	י	גנ	כי	סרו
עו	מד	ג	גבי	אי	ס	יט	סח	טי	בל
מה	גנ	יב	סאא	כ	סכ	נח	סעי

37	78	29	70	21	62	13	54	5
6	38	79	30	71	22	63	14	46
47	7	39	80	31	72	23	55	15
16	48	8	40	81	32	64	24	56
57	17	49	9	41	73	33	65	25
26	58	18	50	1	42	74	34	66
67	27	59	10	51	2	43	75	35
36	68	19	60	11	52	3	44	76
77	28	69	20	61	12	53	4	45

Seal of the Planet

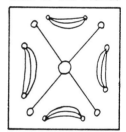

Spirit: Chashmod

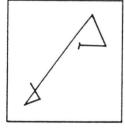

Spirit of the Spirits
of the Moon:
Shad Barschemoth
Schartathan

Intelligence of the Intelligences of the Moon:
Malcha Betarshisîm Ve-ad Ruachoth Ha-Schechalim

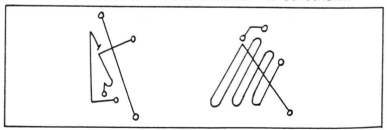

Figure 8.9 Kamea of the Moon (Luna).

The talismans described here are not the only planetary talismans prescribed by tradition, though they are the most complicated and intellectually interesting. Another series of seven is described in considerable detail by Elphas Levi in his *Rituel de la Haute Magie* (1856).[7]

The basic pattern of these talismans is a circle of metal on one side of which is engraved a pentagram, a five pointed star made of two triangles, with two points at the bottom and one at the top. To place it or think of it upside down with the two "horns" at the top is to court disaster. This pentagram should be accompanied by the signs of the planets, preferably not the conventional ones but others; these being for the sun a circle, the moon a crescent, (pointing to the left), Mars a sword, Venus a G, Jupiter a crown, Mercury a caduceus and Saturn a scythe. These should be placed outside the pentagram design itself, except for the sign that applies to the particular planet involved. On the reverse side of the talisman the shield of Solomon or six pointed star composed of two triangles should be engraved.

It is this reverse side which makes the talisman particular to a given planet. The emblem of the planet should be engraved in the centre of the design: for the Sun a human figure, for the Moon a chalice, for Mercury a dog's head, for Jupiter an eagle's head, for Mars a lion's head, for Venus a dove's head, for Saturn the head of either a goat or a bull. The names of the seven angels of the planet should be added and written in Hebrew, or Arabic, or one of the kabbalistic and magical alphabets which have been created for such purposes. There is some disagreement over which angels govern which planet, but the consensus appears to be that Raphael governs the Sun; Aniel, Venus; Michael, Mercury; Gabriel, the Moon; Zaphiel, Saturn; Zadkiel, Jupiter; and Camael, Mars. The metals used for these talismans are the same as for the others I have described.

It is not, of course, enough to construct these talismans. They have to be imbued with power, to be consecrated.

---

7. This title, translated into English by A.E. Waite, and called *Transcendental Magic: Its Doctrine and Ritual*, is published in the UK by Rider & Co., and in the USA by Samuel Weiser, Inc.

The Empowering of Talismans

*The virtue of consecrations chiefly consists in two things, viz,
the power of the person consecrating, and the virtue of the
prayer by which the consecration is made.*
*For in the person consecrating, there is required firmness
constancy and holiness of life; and that the consecrator himself
shall, with a firm and indubitable faith, believe the virtue,
power, and effect thereof.*

Francis Barrett
The Magus

In the making of talismans, we face three tasks. We must make, or
find, or buy, an object proper to our purpose. We must purify it by
cleansing it of all associations and transfer energies that we do not wish
it to possess. And we must give it the power and intent we wish to have
by means of some kind of blessing, consecration, or other form of
empowering. The subject of purification, and empowering is of such
importance that we will deal with it here as a separate chapter. The
principle behind consecration or empowering is simple. The talisman
maker must place within the potential talisman a powerful message
that will continue to emit its signal, rather like a radio wave. The
talisman must also, however, because of its appearance, its traditional
symbolism, its generally accepted virtue, or its religious associations,
carry conviction to the wearer. Thus it would be stupid to give a

talisman of a spider to an arachnophobe, or a Hand of Fatima to a Christian.

Before the empowering takes place, however, the potential talisman must be purified; its existing energy field must be cleansed, though, of course, only in terms of its particular message, not of the energy itself. An object owned by anyone for a long time picks up the energy field and the emotional experiences of that person and this may well get in the way of a new message being given it. Of course, in some instances, knowledge of a previous owner may lead one to feel that the talisman is already on the right track--in which case purification may not be necessary. A lot of psychic sensitivity and intuition is needed here. It is not sufficiently realized that a stone taken from the earth may have an unfortunate energy field because of happenings upon that spot or even the presence of earth elementals.

Most empowering rituals are referred to as consecrations in existing texts. This is a term I dislike as it suggests that the empowering consists, necessarily, in the dedication of the potential talisman to some deity or spirit, and this is not true in all cases; indeed it may be true only of a minority of talismans made within a particular religious tradition. Both Empowerings and Purifications have been put forward as requiring complex rituals, such as those used by Eliphas Levi, but complexity is not always necessary.

There are numerous ways to purify a talisman. It can be done by blessing it in the name of the powers that carry most conviction to you, while symbolically washing it. In other words, one may imitate baptism, which is, of course, itself a purification rite. Or you may hold the talisman up to the four quarters of the heaven and invoke purification by the four elements. You may choose simply to place it over incense which will, you feel, banish all previous associations it may have. Or you may lay it out in the garden under a glass dome on a night of the full moon, asking the moonlight to purify it. Indeed, as long as whatever you do has strong connections with ideas of washing clean, or making bright with light, or banishing by means of fire and smoke, or making whole by subjecting it to an expression of cosmic unity, you cannot go far wrong. If the potential talisman is small enough it can be easily cleansed by burying it in rock salt or sea salt for forty eight hours. This has succeeded in cleansing many talismans that were having ill effects upon the wearers.

After purification comes the empowering. This can take many

forms. There are elaborate rituals available as we shall see, and you may like to use one of these or even create one of your own, or you may take other routes to your goal. One such is to place your talisman for a time in a box with objects that are already charged with the correct energy or that are symbolic of it. If you have created a talisman to bring wealth, for example, you might place it in a box with gold and silver coins or other symbols of money. This is using the principle of energy transference, or of psychic contagion. If this is not possible, then you can follow the principle of morning and evening concentration to charge the talisman as you would charge a battery. To do this, take the talismanic object and hold it in your hand and concentrate upon its protective qualities. Hold it for as long as you can keep up the concentration. Then place it in a wrapping of silk or in a special place reserved for it. Do not treat it casually. Charge it again at the next opportunity. It is a good thing to do this early in the morning, for after sleep the deep mind is always sensitized. Late at night when the deep mind is ready for dreams is also a suitable time. If this can also be done at the time of the waxing moon or the night of a full moon, so much the better.[1]

On the whole, however, the empowering that is the most effective will be one which causes the talisman maker to make a special effort and to do something which he would not normally do. By putting on special clothes, or using incantations, or by taking the talisman to a mountain top or to a particular place, or putting it at the feet of certain statute, the talisman maker is expressing in physical terms the concentrated power of his intent, and the physical acts he performs remind him continually of the intent. It is hard to lay down any general code of practice for empowering talismans, as each talisman maker must have his or her own particular and individual one, but here are some suggestions:

1. Do not wear much clothing. The talisman should be bathed in as much of your energy field as possible. If total nudity embarrasses you, then wear a simple white shift or a pair of pajamas--anything in which you feel physically comfortable and unconstricted.

---

1. It's important to mention that you should not let anyone but yourself handle this object, unless it is a person whom you wholly trust and whose blessing would re-inforce its power. Here one must be cery careful. A person may love you deeply and be willing to go along with your "fantasies," but inwardly be entirely skeptical. It is, on the whole, best to keep these things to yourself.

2. Perform your consecration in a tidy room. In a tidy room everything is in its allotted place and therefore the many energy fields are not fighting each other, or even more important, are not felt to be fighting each other by the talisman maker. Whatever tensions occur in the room should be related directly to the act of empowering and be a positive part of that act. If the room can be bare except for what is needed for the act of consecration so much the better. A totally bare room, however, may in some instances inhibit as much as it helps.

3. If you are using a table of any kind make sure that it is clean and decent and anything on it, should be associated with your consecration. Flowers of whatever you feel to be a sympathetic colour may assist you, as may other objects which you feel to have a talismanic power supporting your own intent. Such symbolic objects as sea shells, coloured stones and candles can be used. White candles are preferred, but here again you should go by your own individual reading of colour symbolism. Don't use muddy colours and avoid mixed ones unless they are radiant and vibrant. A bowl of water may help some, and a container of salt and oil may also help. Again we are here subject to the vagaries of the individual sensibility. The table must not, however, be cluttered. I do not believe that many people can carry out an act of empowering successfully if the table looks like a cross between a curio shop and harvest festival.

4. You may, if you like, use music as an accompaniment. This is less to support your empowering positively than to block out noises from elsewhere. The music should therefore be relatively unemphatic unless, of course, you have a piece of music that means so much to you personally and has for you such power that it can help you to do the work.

5. Obviously, if you are not alone, whoever is with you must take part in the empowering wholeheartedly, either by joining in whatever words you use, or by handing you what you need. It is best, however, to do the work alone, unless you companion or companions are totally at one with you and fully understand and sympathize with what you are doing.

6. If at all possible, do not use the room again for any other purpose

until the day following, and leave the talisman in the room after it has been empowered. It may be left in its protective silk wrapping of whatever colour is appropriate, or in its special box, or it may be left out on the table. But it should not be taken away and used until the night is over.

7. Finally, when the empowering is finished and you leave the room, remove your clothing (if you were wearing any) straight away and put it aside for the next occasion or into the laundry. If you were naked you should put on some clothing in order to signify the end of your task.

These are very general principles and the individual talisman maker will find that he or she prefers to work in a different way, making use of particular symbols on the table or altar, addressing a particular deity, or the Goddess by a particular name. The basic rule is, of course, "If it feels right, do it" and if, when you have finished your ceremony, however complicated or however simple it may be, you feel that the message has been planted, the energy given, then you have done your task. The main difficulty, at first, is learning to concentrate wholly upon your intent and not allowing negative or disruptive images to confuse or blur the thrust of your energy. It is all too easy in creating a healing talisman to concentrate upon the disorder rather than its absence, and thus to negate the whole process. Sometimes, too, one's own emotions get in the way.

All the above presumes that the concentration of the talisman is a quite separate operation from the making, or buying, or finding of it. If you do in fact manufacture the talisman, then it may be difficult to do so in the same room as you empower it, or with the same accompaniment. I foresee trouble if you attempt to pour molten lead into a mould while unprotected by clothing, for example. Nevertheless, while making your kamea or your pentagram or your mandala, do wear some special article of clothing, and do it with careful regard to the environment in which you are working, and, of course, concentrate upon your intent the whole of the time you are working. In this way you will build intent into the object before the time for empowering comes and it will be that much more effective.

Eliphas Levi has written extensively about the consecration of talismans and has made the whole operation very complicated indeed.

He states that first of all the talisman maker is required to have an altar upon which is a tripod of sacred fire, and the altar and the tripod must be garlanded. Before the altar must be a carpet of a specific kind and the magician must wear robes of a particular colour together with various crowns, bracelets and rings. The altar must also be perfumed. The details are as follows:

Sunday. The operation should take place between midnight and eight a.m. or from three p.m. to ten p.m. The robe must be purple with bracelets and a crown of gold. The garlands must be of laurel, heliotrope and sunflowers, and the perfumes must be cinnamon, saffron, red sandalwood and strong incense. The magician must wear a gold ring and stand on a carpet made of lion skin, and there must also--it is not clear whether on the altar or in his hand-- be fans made of the feathers of sparrows. This is the day to make talismans of the sun.

Monday. No time for the operation is given, but the robe must be white with silver embroidery, and decorated with a collar or three layers made of pearls, crystals and selenite. He must wear a crown covered in a piece of yellow silk on which the Hebrew monogram of Gabriel is embroidered in silver. The perfumes to be used are white sandalwood, camphor, amber, aloes and pulverized seed of cucumber, and the garlands must be of mugwort, moonwort and yellow ranunculus. This is the day to make moon talismans.

Tuesday. The robes must be the colour of flame or rust or blood, and belted with steel. Steel bracelets should be worn. The crown must have gold bound round it and the ring must be of steel with an amethyst in it. The garlands must be of absinth and rue. No perfumes are mentioned, for some reason. This is the day to make a talisman of Mars and a day, too, to make a talisman to assist in vengeance.

Wednesday. The robes must be green or variously coloured, and the magician should wear a necklace made of pearls which are enclosed together with Mercury in glass beads. The jewel for the day is agate. The perfumes must be benzoin, mace and storax, and the garlands should be of narcissus, lily, herb-mercury, fumitory and marjoram. This is the day for making the talisman of Mercury.

Thursday. The robes should be scarlet and the magician should wear upon his forehead a brass plaque engraved with the sign for the spirit of Jupiter and the words GIARAR, BETHOR, SAMGADIEL.[2] The magician should wear an emerald or a sapphire in a ring. The perfumes for the day are ambergris, incense, balm, grain of paradise, macis and saffron, and the garlands must be made of oak, poplar, pomegranate and fig leaves. This is the day to make the talisman of Jupiter.

Friday. The robes must be coloured sky blue and the room should be decorated with hangings of green and of rose. The ornaments should be of highly polished copper, and the magician should wear a turquoise ring. The crown and the belt clasps should be of lapis lazuli and beryl. The fans must be made of swans' feathers, and the talisman maker should wear a copper pendant engraved with the name Anael, who is one of the seven angels of creation and who has particular charge over Venus, and also the words AVEENA VADELILITH.[3] Friday, is, of course, the day for making talismans of Venus.

Saturday. The robes must be black or very dark brown, and embroidered in black and orange silk. A lamina of lead engraved with the sign of Saturn and the words ALMALEC, APHIEL, ZARAHIEL must be worn around the neck. The ring should bear black onyx on which the double head of Janus should be engraved during the hours dominated by Saturn. The required perfumes are diagridium, scammony, alum, sulfur and assafoetida, and the garlands should be made of ash, cypress and hellebore. This is, of course, the day to make the talisman of Saturn.

In 1870, fifteen years after the appearance of Eliphas Levi's *Transcendental Magic*, Paul Christian published his *History and Practice of Magic* and in his book he included all but one of the above planetary talismans according to Levi's formulae with one or two errors. He changed the consecration process, however. He made no mention of

2. I am unable to track down Giarar and Samgadiel, but Bethoris a ruling angel of Jupiter.
3. This phrase is intended to banish Lilith, who is regarded as being the evil angel of Friday, and one of the most powerful of all evil powers, and to welcome the spirit of Venus. The first word AVEENA is a conflation of the two words AVE (Hail, or Welcome) and VENUS., and the second is made up of the two words VADE (Go, and Begone!) and LILITH. This kind of conflation and distortion is common in talismanic practice.

altars, vestments, rings, hangings and fans. He stated simply that the talisman should be held over the smoke of a fire made in an earthenware pot, the fire being composed of materials appropriate to the nature of each planet. For this perfuming he makes use of most of the materials listed Eliphas Levi. He states that the talisman of Saturn should be perfumed with the result of alum, assafoetida, scampony and sulfur being burned in a fire of cypress, ash and black hellebore. The talisman for Jupiter requires frankincense, ambergris, balsam, cardamon, saffron, and mace to be burned on a fire of oak, poplar, fig and pomegranate wood. The talisman of Mars he treats more perfunctorily, merely subjecting it to the smell of desiccated absinth (sic) and rue. The talisman of the Sun needs a recipe of cinnamon, frankincense, saffron, red sandalwood, burned with laurel and the dried stalks of heliotrope. The talisman of Venus requires a simpler procedure. It is simply held in the fumes of a fire of olive wood in which violets and roses are burned. The talisman of Mercury requires benzoin, mace and storax to be burned on a fire of dried lily and narcissus stalks, marjoram and fumitory. The talisman of the Moon requires the perfume of white sandalwood, camphor, aloes, amber and pounded cucumber seeds burned on a fire of dried stalks of artemisia, selenotrope and ranunculus.

In all these cases, the earthenware vessel should not have been used previously and should be broken and buried afterwards. The talisman should, according to Paul Christian, be placed in silk sachets and hung around the neck, the colours of the sachets to be of the following: Saturn, black; Jupiter, sky-blue; Mars, red;Sun, pale yellow; Venus, green or pink; Mercury, purple; Moon, white.

A.E. Waite's *The Occult Sciences* (published in 1923) follows the method of consecration devised by Paul Christian, but adds to it his own description of the actual ritual of consecration given by Eliphas Levi. To go into detail here of the elaborate ceremonial ritual of Levi would take us too far from our purpose, which is to survey the talismans themselves.

Now it is time to look back at what we have seen of esoteric talismans and their making and to comment upon it all. Firstly it seems clear that while the kameas are laborious to construct they are not absurdly so and that the planetary talismans of Levi, Christian, and Waite are not particularly difficult to make either. The consecrating of the talismans appears to be the difficult part and if anyone attempted to follow the rituals of Eliphas Levi in full he would need a fat bank account to purchase even the basic materials for his clothes and equipment. He would also need a very well stocked cupboard of herbs and perfumes and an equally well stocked garden. Indeed, it's clear that these requirements present the talisman maker with instances that may be insuperable. That some of them are intended to present difficulties is obvious. How can one possibly construct a necklace of glass beads with Mercury and pearls within them? And who, on a day in winter, will be able to find the materials for most of the garlands? Can talismans only be made in the summer then, or when the appropriate plants are in bloom? Moreover as we read through the recipes both of Levi and Christian we find that they are not consistent. Some refer to hangings and some not; some speak of fans and some not. What exactly, we may reasonably ask ourselves, is going on?

Both the occultists and magicians of the 19th century were very much affected by the fashion of the times, and each, as a writer, found himself expected to present mysteries and haunting obscurities rather than clarification. Many occultists found that if they were obscure enough they could attract pupils who wished for explanations and it looks sometimes as if a great many of the writers of occult works of this period made their work obscurantist and sensationalist for entirely commercial reasons. On the other hand it is a principle of all kinds of magic, whether low magic or ceremonial ritual and kabbalistic magic, that some matters must be kept secret, or at least disguised, from persons who are not psychologically or intellectually able to make use of them in a proper fashion. It is this which lies behind the same uses of Gematria and Notarikon. The clue is, however, always left for those who have studied sufficiently, though it may be buried in a complexity of false indications. Thus it seems to me that the principle behind the use of perfumes and garlands (or fires) in the Levi/Christian/Waite consecration rituals is simply that a perfume which is traditionally appropriate, and garlands which are traditionally appropriate, should be used to reinforce the talisman maker's psychic concentration upon the matter at hand. The same thing applies to the description of the vestments and the jewellery. These accoutrements are simply ways of directing the mind and psyche of the maker into the right track and improving concentration and the ability to visualize what must be visualized in order to energize the talismanic object. Similarly, while it makes perfect sense to make a talisman when the moon is waxing and when the appropriate planet is at full strength in the heavens, it is absurd to become so precise about this as to make it impossible to create a talisman for a given purpose on more than a very few days in the year and at uncomfortable hours of the day or night. Moreover, while again it is sensible to make the talismans of metal, it is not practical to make them always of the absolutely correct metal. The efficient talisman maker can, by means of his own concentrated imagination, "transform" gilt into gold, or leaden colour into lead, for the intensity is factual in the kind of psychic operation we are discussing.

When we come to the actual verbal magic of the ritual we have no real difficulties, for the words are clear enough and the gestures simple. It is this which is at the heart of the matter, for the ritual is a lucid and definite way of producing the required concentration and of excluding from the mind all intrusive elements. The survey of esoteric talismans, with all its complex names and alphabetical games, does indeed reduce itself to relative simplicity once the principles are observed. It does not really matter if in lettering the name of an angel you make a small spelling mistake, or even if you put down only one of the several available names, as long as you yourself know exactly what your intent is--and as long as you do not create a symbol so opposite to your intent that even that intent cannot prevent the deep mind from misunderstanding what you are doing.

The words used will, obviously, differ a great deal according to the talisman maker's particular beliefs. If one were to present a general pattern it would probably go something like this:

> "........." (name of deity of power), in your name and by your power and through your power I send this message, this command, into this ....(stone, gem, ring, object). Bring your wearer health and strength; bring your wearer clear pure blood....(etc., etc., repeated until it is felt that the message has been delivered), this in the power of.......(name of power or deity).

Everyone will alter this in some fashion. Gestures may be added; and an altar may be used. Candles and mirrors are often part of the ritual. We will return to this subject again later, but in the meantime, it is necessary to ask a question we have evaded by means of generalizations so far in this book: What is the nature of talismanic power and how does it function?

The Nature and Use of
Talismanic Power

*Therefore, he that works in magic must be of a constant belief,
be credulous, and not at all doubt of the obtaining of the effect;
for as a firm and strong belief doth work wonderful things,
although it be in false works--so distrust and doubting doth
dissipate and break the virtue of the mind of the worker, which
is the medium betwixt both extremes; whence it happens that
he is frustrated of the desired influence of the superiors, which
could not be enjoined and united to our labours without a firm
and solid virtue of our mind.*

Francis Barrett
The Magus

Before we move on to discuss the nature of talismanic power and
explore the ways in which talismans can be constructed for particular
purposes, it might be as well to look at another kind of talisman, one
that appears to have been empowered from the very start.

There is one kind of talisman which cannot be put on a list because
each talisman is unique and its properties depend upon its unique
character. This is a found object which appears to have no particular
symbolic character but which so fascinates the finder that it is believed
to have power. A great many stone talismans are of this kind. Precious
and semi-precious stones, of course, are almost all regarded as talismans, but they are not true found talismans. The found stone's power

appears to be given it by the wearer who is often also the finder. It may therefore be thought that it is entirely personal and useless to other people. This is not necessarily the case. The great investigator of gypsy lore, C.G. Leland, tells a story of having found an attractive black pebble that was greatly coveted by the gypsies he met. They also coveted three patterned sea shells, one of which had marking on it that could be read as NAV which, in Romany, means "the name". The gypsies told him that they had a talisman for curing seriously ill children which consisted of three Maria Theresa silver dollars hung around the neck under the child's clothes. The Maria Theresa dollar was accepted as having talismanic power not only by the European gypsies, according to Leland, but also by members of many African tribes.

Found talismans are usually regarded as lucky charms or bringers of good fortune, rather than as having specific properties unless the shape of the found object is extremely suggestive. Stones which resemble perfect spheres or eggs are very much in demand, so much so that many people are now busy manufacturing stone eggs as curios for fashionable stores. Whether made of common or of semi-precious stones, they are regarded as having talismanic properties. It is said that the actress, Carole Lombard, used to carry a smooth round pebble to bring her good fortune. Oddly shaped roots and vegetables turned up by the spade or found in the garden are also regarded as lucky. Potatoes that are shaped like animals or human beings are treasured. There is almost no area of phenomena in which the odd and apparently unique is not regarded as having talismanic power. This is particularly the case with coins. The Turnbull family of Northumberland (England) possessed, until the third decade of the nineteenth century, a famous Black Penny, which had a raised rim and was a little smaller than the current penny, and this was used to protect and heal cattle. It was dipped into a stream that ran from north to south and then water from the stream was given to the cattle. Another coin that was used to heal and protect cattle in this manner was the silver piece belonging to the Lockerby family in Dumfriesshire (Scotland). The "Lockerby Water" was even sold as medicine in the 1840s. Yet another strange coin was the Lee Penny. This was actually a *groat* of Edward I with a dark red stone set in its reverse side and it was used to cure haemorrhage and rabies as well as diseases in cattle. It was once even used to attempt to stop the spread of plague in Newcastle (England). In 1638 Sir James Lockhart of Lee was tried for witchcraft by the Synod of Glasgow because of his using this talisman. He was, however, judged not guilty because "the custome is onlie to cast the stene in sumewater, and given the deseasit cattil thereof to drink, and qt thesam is dene wtout vsing onie words, such as charmers and sorcerers vse in thair unlawfull practicsess..."

Those who acquire oddities such as these may not think to use them talismanically, or even think of them as talismans anymore than do the big game hunters who collect trophies, but they do regard them with awe, with pleasure and with affection and consider them to be lucky. The luck, the good fortune, has of course been part of them from the moment of discovery. On picking up the pebble, the coin, the strange potato, the finder tells himself "this is a bit of luck," "this is good fortune" and, by some quirk of the mind the object itself is regarded as actually being, or possessing, the good fortune it has brought. It has been imprinted by the delight and awe felt at its finding. I must emphasize here that only objects so odd as to appear unique are usually felt to be talismanic in this way. While finding a hundred dollar bill would be indeed good fortune, the bill itself would be regarded as a talisman by only a very few people. Found coins are probably only talismanic if out of date, foreign, rare, twisted or bent.

While those of us addicted to beachcombing or who walk invariably with our eyes to the ground may still acquire talismans without having to pay for them, most of us now find our talismans in shops. Indeed, apart from antique shops and junkshops in which traditional manufactured talismans can always be discovered, there are curio shops and "tourist traps" which are happy to provide anyone with "good luck charms". Many of these are somewhat bogus. The four-leaved clover, or shamrock, which is a potent protector and whose four leaves symbolize fame, wealth, success in love and health, when purchased in the form of a brooch is as likely to have been made in Japan as in Ireland. Nevertheless, the power lies at least partly in the belief of the buyer, and if the buyer sees this object with the awe and delight of the talisman finder it may well be for him the fortunate talisman he needs.

I have spoken several times of the power of belief, but have so far not attempted to define the exact nature of the belief. At first blush one might think it is a simple thing; one simply believes that the found object has talismanic power and therefore by believing this one provides the power oneself. This is not the whole of the story, however.

One does not believe in a talisman in the way in which one believes that one and one make two, or that hitting a drum with a drumstick will make a noise, or even that the day following Sunday is Monday. These beliefs are born of experience and habit and they are beliefs in an unchanging and inevitable pattern of cause and effect. Belief that a found object is a talisman, however, derives from a sudden feeling of a sympathetic connection with it. The feeling is often expressed that the object was simply "waiting for me" as if it were long lost friend, or as if an appointment had been made. The object was waiting for us, it belongs to us, it is there by appointment with us, as the sword in the stone awaited the boy that was to become King Arthur of the Round Table.

This feeling is often very strong indeed and is sometimes also connected with a particular time in one's life. It is not unusual for someone to find something which either symbolically or in practical terms exactly fits the need of the moment. This has been called, first by Horace Walpole, the spirit of Serendipity--the faculty of discovering something by happy chance. It may not however be wholly chance. Almost all collectors of objets d'art, rare books, coins and postage stamps have experienced the power of Serendipity too often to believe it to operate at random. Many have "known" that a given bookshop actually has a rare book they need; sometimes they even have an accurate intuition of the authorship of the book. Assiduous collectors, indeed, know that at those periods when they are most inclined to build up their collection these serendipitous events occur more frequently than when they have let their interest lapse for a time. The history of all collectors in all fields is crammed with stories about these discoveries. One book collector I know was once browsing idly in a second-hand bookshop when he became convinced that there was a book he particularly wanted somewhere in the shop. He looked along the shelves and could find nothing of interest. And then, as if directed by some strange command, he put out his hand and pulled out a grubby brown paper envelope and discovered inside it one of the three scarce pamphlets he had been longing for in order to complete his collection. It seemed almost as if the psyche had sent out a kind of radar to enable discovery to take place.

This is, I believe, exactly what happens. When a collector makes a discovery, or when a person finds an object that he immediately knows to be personal talisman, it is because the psyche has felt a need and responded to it. It is easy to see how the collector's find satisfies a need. It is not so easy in the instance of the talisman, for the talisman finder may not know consciously that the need exists, and it may even be that the discovery defines the need.

Found Talismans as Pendulums

The nature of the talisman, once it has been found, is not always immediately clear. The finder is only sure of the sympathetic connection; but what, exactly, is the pebble's power as a talisman? What, exactly, does this bent silver coin signify? Usually the finder simply feels that there is good fortune in it. Sometimes, however, the conviction that the talisman is not only a bringer of good fortune but a container of wisdom leads the owner to use it as an oracle. Many owners of "lucky" coins toss them heads or tails to help them make decisions.

A similar use is made of found talismans in pendant form. To accomplish this, the truth seeker should hold the pendant by the chain, preferably by the ring clasp, so that there is no inhibition of movement in the chain. After deciding what kinds of pendular movement mean yes, no, and no answer, the individual steadies his or her arm on a table to keep it absolutely still, and asks questions. If the pendulum is a success it will soon begin to swing either left to right or forwards and backwards, or in a circle or ellipse clockwise or counter-clockwise. It does this apparently of its own volition, for the hand suspending it is absolutely rigid, or feels and appears to be so. Pendulums have been used in finding lost people or hidden treasure. Held above a map of the area to be explored, they will describe a circle, the centre of which is the place sought.

In working with a pendulum in this fashion one must try to be absolutely free of all prejudice as to the answers that are likely or desirable, for it is possible by sheer will power, and without physical movement of any kind, to change the pendulum's direction. The pendulum, indeed, appears to operate in response to unseen and undetectable impulses from the user. These may be akin to electrical impulses, for the most effective and lively pendulums are made of materials that are good conductors of electricity or that can themselves, like amber, retain and emit an electrical charge. It seems likely that the answers are, in fact, provided unconsciously by the user. These answers may, however, contain information he did not know he possessed; they are provided by intuitive and telepathic processes well below the level of consciousness.

In glancing at the use of talismans as pendulums I may seem to digress from my main subject. The talismanic pendulum, however, does tell us something about talismans. Firstly, it suggests that talismans can act as an expression and transmitter of intuitive powers and perceptions of which we are unconscious. Secondly, it suggests that it is the human psyche which energizes the talisman in many cases, for the pendulum does not work unless it is held up by a human hand; if it is hung from an inanimate object it does not move. Thirdly, because of the way in which the user's belief about it can alter its movement, it indicates that its powers may be partially controlled by our view of its symbolic meaning. It is, indeed, important to understand the symbolism of the talisman one finds and possesses--the finder of a talismanic object needs to know something about traditional talismanic symbolism. He needs to be able to interpret at least something of the message he is receiving, to understand something of the nature of the sympathetic connection he feels. This connection may exist in terms of entirely personal obsessions, but may relate to traditional talismanic thinking of an intuitive nature. On the other hand the symbolism may only be explicable in terms of one of the occult systems whole symbols appear to speak directly to the deep mind and which have done so effectively for hundreds of years.

Talismanic Power

There is much disagreement about the nature of talismanic power and about the importance of total accuracy in naming the forces that one desires to provide that power. Some authorities emphasize the importance of following elaborate rituals exactly to the letter: they believe that the angels, intelligences and spirits have the same kind of reality as human beings, and must therefore be invoked and bound by exactly the correct name, and even that the name should be written in a language they can comprehend (this usually being taken to be Hebrew, or one of the magical alphabets). There is another view which states that the angels, intelligences and powers of the cosmos are also the angels, intelligences and powers within us. In this view, man is indeed a microcosm and by calling upon the name Raphael or Ophiel, or Aniel, we are summoning powers up from our own deep mind and giving them, for the purposes of acting upon external reality, an external form. This form is pictured in letters, formed in sound, and given body by the physical accompaniments of perfume and the use of the four elements air, water, earth and fire. If this is the case, then the intent of the magician is to be much more in control of the situation than others would have us believe. Many commentators maintain that all the occult systems are quite simply externalizations in terms of names, numbers and signs of entirely inward powers. Whatever we make in talismanic art, or what we perform in magic, alchemy, or any other occult system we are simply looking into ourselves as in a mirror and seeing, gradually, more and more of the nature of man.

Whatever view one takes it seems clear that talisman making can be as complex and mind-boggling and as embedded in ritual and ceremony as one wishes it to be. It is also possible that the more complex the procedure becomes, the less it is likely to succeed for the more doubts and hesitations that are felt by the talisman maker the less forceful will his concentration be. Nevertheless, there are certainly some people who find that it is only by means of lengthy preparation and long rituals that they can achieve the psychic "high" necessary to magical performance. They cannot, as it were, perform King Lear in modern dress on an empty stage.

Whether or not elaborate rituals of consecration are involved, the orthodox practical kabbalist would maintain that only by invoking the correct powers and calling them into one's service can a talisman be created. The powers are those spiritual forces which animate and direct us; but they are also forces we ourselves animate and direct. When we make up a name for an intuition, for an idea, for a spiritual hypothesis, we ourselves give the other, the energy, a form in our minds and by treating that form as if it had power we give it power. We do indeed create the powers we use, though we may prefer to regard ourselves as invoking already existing powers. To some extent, of course, we do. When we invoke the name of a power whose name has been used before by others we are moving along a well trodden path and one which our deep minds find no difficulty in travelling. Moreover if we invoke, for example, the power of Venus, we already have a vision of that power; we have indeed been helped to it by many artists, writers and visionaries. We may still be conjuring up powers that are part of our own deepest selves, but we are doing so with the assistance of our conscious minds that have a vocabulary of terms and a whole series of myths and religious beliefs and legends that enable us to give form to those powers and to name them in a fashion convincing to us both consciously and subconsciously.

If this is the case then it may not be necessary for those who wish to create talismans to go through all the elaborate rituals set down by Eliphas Levi and the kabbalists. One may indeed reach the conclusion that the catch-22 which applies to so many esoteric works on the Kabbalah can be answered by another statement: "Only if you know it do you need to use it, and if you truly need to use it you need not know it". The passionate concentration of true need will create or conjure up or form the power that is required, however few or many of the great names are used. Ultimately, it may be that great learning is its own destruction. There is certainly no end to kabbalistic research, for the seeking out of correspondences, the creation of formulae both ritualistic and numerological and the construction of new rituals that take into account new discoveries on the plane of the material world and in psychology, can take a lifetime and more. On the other hand, what is truly important about the Kabbalah is the way in which it presents a pattern that can be of use in strengthening our understanding of the importance of spiritual and psychic energy in our lives and in the cosmos.

This said we may reflect that we are saying nothing which the Kabbalah does not itself imply, for in the Tree of the Sephiroth it is clear that knowledge can be both power and paralysis, just as imagination can be both vision and delusion. The word delusion comes in appropriately here, for as we discuss these matters we must be aware that, to many people, talismanic power is a delusion. Here the answer is that given by all the leading writers on talismanic thought from Paracelsus to the present day: Faith is the key. Belief in power creates power, and is indeed the heart of that power. If you believe in a power, your belief cannot be a delusion. It may or may not be a strong enough power to perform in the way you desire, but it is nevertheless a power and no falsehood.

We are, however, here faced with the problem of who is doing the believing and who the doubting. If all around me think I am an idiot and the talisman worthless, is that doubt going to affect the power? If we believe that we are dealing in energy fields, the answer must be "Very possibly." This is one reason why many talismans are kept secret, are wrapped in silk, are kept away from contact with other objects that have other energy fields. it is one reason for all the mumbo jumbo and obscurantism of magical practices, for if you cannot understand what I am saying you cannot really doubt it except in an extremely vague and ineffectual fashion. Some objects which have powerful energy fields from some people do not appear to have any energy at all to others. The clairvoyant who can, by holding an object belonging to a person, tell you all about that person and even his whereabouts is someone who can both sense energy fields and interpret forms from them. Another person holding the same object will not be aware of feeling anything. The energy may be there, but ineffective. This is a well-known phenomenon in the history of "bad luck" charms and objects; they affect one person powerfully and another not at all, or not to an extent that can be noted.

Within the field of magic itself this problem is endemic, for, with all the various correspondences to choose from, and all the names of power, it is inevitable that one practical magician is liable to doubt the efficacy of another's chosen ritual. This is yet another reason why groups of occultists have always operated in terms of a steady progression of rituals and initiations which are, to some extent, peculiar to their own society. It is also a reason why the "Book of Shadows" (the term for the book in which societies write down their rituals) is never shown to anyone outside the group. Indeed, initiates are forbidden to show their rituals to outsiders. This secrecy has naturally resulted in a lot of confusion. Only recently have we been permitted to read of many rituals; the authors have decided either that the ban was outdated, or that it is nowadays more important to create a general understanding of kabbalistic magic than to protect the work of a particular society. Nevertheless, it is notable that many of the most significant rituals remain secret.

It may be thought that in discussing kabbalistic societies we are getting too far away from the kind of talismans that are generally accepted by and used by people who have no interest in the Kabbalah or in other esoteric doctrines. What about those country talismans discussed earlier, and what about I.D. talismans? Surely these are another matter.

This may or may not be the case. Obviously the found talisman is not necessarily felt to belong to a mystical system, and rabbits' feet and horseshoes do seem to belong to different categories. And yet, if we see these other talismans in the way that we regard the more esoteric ones, not as being powerful because of what they are, but because they have powerful associations and correspondences with many other talismans and are, as it were, simply focal points for an enormous energy field, we will find ourselves able to believe in them more strongly and therefore able to give them more power. Let us take the case of the pretty red stone we find on the beach and feel to be "lucky". We now know that this red stone corresponds to the enormous energy force of Mars, of the Sephirah Geburah, and carries with it, therefore, the names of the Archangel Khamael and the symbol of a chariot-borne warrior, as well as many other correspondences.

It does not matter very much whether or not we are able to be intellectually precise about these correspondences. Indeed we may, quite reasonably, decide that the red stone could correspond not with Mars, but with Scorpio, or with Aries, as Scorpio and Aries are both associated with red. We may, observing the round shape of our pebble, associate it also with the Sun and therefore with Leo and the Sephirah Tephireth. The important thing, indeed, is not that we need to attempt a kind of academic precision, but that we need to be aware of our talisman as being at the centre of a great deal of energy and as being the expression and vehicle of it.

It is, of course, true that some talismanic objects have been given their particular energy field and their direction by historical accident, or by their explicit symbolism. It would be flying in the face of sense to attempt to see the armoured strength of Mars in the open Hand of Fatima, for example. Some talismans, too, have been imbued with their energy field and their direction by circumstances so that a charming little object may turn out to have the darkest and most destructive energies. Indeed, any object of powerful emotions or intimately associated with the life of a person is likely to acquire an energy field that may or may not accord with its apparent symbolism, as we have already seen.

This being the case, we are faced with the problem of testing a talisman to discover whether or not it does have a powerful energy field and in what direction this energy field sends its force. In the absence of a clairvoyant who can give the answer by holding the object in his or her hand, we are obliged to check the talisman out by other methods. We must first of all be clear what questions we want answered. Firstly, "Is there a strong energy field here?" Secondly, "What form does it take and what character does it have?"

There are a number of ways of testing the talisman, but perhaps the most effective and the least confusing is that of using a pendulum. We discussed, briefly, the use of talismanic pendulums earlier, but some repetition will do no harm.

In order to use a pendulum to determine talismanic power or energy, the talisman should be placed beneath the pendulum and the person holding the pendulum should so rest his or her arm that no accidental movement can be made. If the talisman is "live" the pendulum will begin to swing and will soon swing very rapidly indeed. The person holding the pendulum must, however, make his or her mind a total blank if this test is to work correctly, for it is quite easy, without making any movement at all, to direct the pendulum to move, or to stay still, or to change direction. If the pendulum does indicate the presence of energy, then questions requiring yes or no answers can be asked of it. What the pendulum is doing, of course, is picking up from the operator's deep mind information about the talisman that the conscious mind does not possess and cannot acquire by any other method.

We now have in front of us a talisman and we have discovered that it has an energy field and we have questioned it about its purpose and power. Our deep mind has responded to it and established a relationship with it. It may be a very elaborate talisman, a golden kamea, a god carved in ivory, a ring inscribed with a name of power, or it may be simply a found pebble, a stone with a hole in it, or a piece of bone. It may be an inscription on paper or parchment or cardboard; it may be a pendant, a buckle, a statue, or even a knife. Whatever form it has, it has an energy field, and if the energy field has been increased and directed for a purpose (either by accident or intent) it is a talisman and it will affect the lives of those who come into contact with it.

All this, of course, applies to found talismans and not to talismans which we make for ourselves. Nevertheless, we may choose to make our talisman of an already existing object or use an existing object in its composition. If we do this, we must remember that any object which has for a long time been in close physical contact with a human being is affected by the energy field of that human being to such an extent that clairvoyants are able to tell the nature and character of the owner. In making talismans we must take this into account. We may be able to use this transferred energy positively, or we may have to somehow negate it.

We now realize that, as in all magic, it is hard to provide any talisman for oneself but a protective one. It is a widely-held view (although not always universally accepted) that in talismanic as in verbal magic it is forbidden to bless oneself. One may only defend oneself. Some workers of talismanic magic have made talismans intended to bring them personal power or to serve entirely selfish ends. Such acts, however, appear to cause disturbances in the deep mind and frequently end up having negative and destructive affects.

How can you make a protective talisman for yourself? You can buy or make one of the traditionally protective talismans already discussed. If you do so, however, you must, in order to bolster your belief in its efficiency, treat it with great care, keep it clean and polished, give it its own silk wrapper or box--in other words, treat it with reverence. You must also, everytime you touch it or see it, assert its protective power and express both confidence and gratitude. This will considerably build up its power and ensure that it does not decrease. Protective talismans worn around the neck under the clothing should be caressed frequently--this assists in transferring additional energy.

Traditional talismans may not be available to you. You may not be able to find them in stores or you may not have the materials, the skill or the time to make them. In this situation it is best to sit down quietly and work out exactly what has caused you to feel that you need protection. Let us assume that you feel threatened by the ill-will and malice of some of the people around you. You do not wish to hurt anyone who does not intend harm to you; you may even wish to bless those who think kindly of you. What, therefore, is the image you need to create? It is, surely, that of a magical mirror, which will reflect back to the transmitter of "bad vibrations" those same bad vibrations and will also transmit back the good vibrations of your friends. Having got this far it simply becomes a matter of deciding what kind of mirror and where to put it. I suggest a two-sided polished surface which is concave on one side and convex on the other. It should be two-sided so that if it gets turned around it does not lose its power. The concave side concentrates the image received and sends the force back multiplied, and the convex side diffuses the image it receives and makes it harmless. Mirrors, or rather polished metal, of this kind are not hard to discover. The bowls of some dessert spoons are just such a shape, as are some fishing lures. This protective talisman should be worn as a pendant, but kept out of sight beneath the clothing.

The purification and consecration of this kind of talisman is simple enough. The image itself is so closely related to its function that it is hardly necessary to do more than think of it performing its duty for it to be effective.

The principle followed here is that of creating a talisman from something that has an appearance which is a metaphor of its psychic function. It would make perfect sense to create a generally protective talisman from anything which looked like a shield, or indeed was a model of one. Here, however, because a shield has an ineffective side it would be best to pin it to yourself as a brooch rather than let it hang free. There are many brooches designed to resemble shields, of course, and it must be remembered that the I.D. talismanic badges worn on the pockets of blazers are very often heraldic shields. It is only necessary to think of the talisman working to set it working. But it should, ideally, be concealed. Just as your own deep mind can recognize and respond to the symbolism so can the deep minds of others and a protective talisman can be circumvented if it becomes known.

Another kind of talisman that you may make is a magical square. To make your own square simply take the numerological equivalents of the letters in the name you wish to use, according to the system of present day Western numerology. Thus the name Venus using modern Western numerology, would read:

$$22 + 5 + 5 + 3 + 3 = 38$$

This is at least the case if we do not reduce the numbers to single digits. If we do this, however, the 22 becomes 4 and the sum reads:

$$4 + 5 + 5 + 3 + 3 = 20$$

If we use either of these two sequences as the top and the borders of a square and then fill in the other numbers so that each horizontal and vertical column adds up to either 20 or 38 we arrive at:

4	5	5	3	3		22	5	5	3	3
5	4	3	5	3	or	5	22	3	5	3
5	3	4	3	5		5	3	22	3	5
3	5	3	4	5		3	5	3	22	5
3	3	5	5	3		3	3	5	5	22

In this square the numerical equivalent of the initial letter of Venus is repeated along one diagonal while the other diagonal spells out the name of Venus as do all the sides of the square.

If you wish to embody a text in a magical square the same procedure can be followed. Let us suppose the talisman is one to bring love and affection. Your text might be the words Love Is Come. The numerical equivalent of this is:

$$3 + 6 + 22 + 5 + 9 + 1 + 3 + 6 + 4 + 5 = 64$$

and the square can be constructed as before, or you may choose to construct your square without using the numerical equivalents of the letters, but simply in terms of the number 64. Sixty-four is a square of eight, so you might pick on a square with eight spaces on each side. Thus your top line could be:

$$4 \quad 5 \quad 6 \quad 7 \quad 9 \quad 10 \quad 11 \quad 12$$

and this line would be used as the borders of the square and the other spaces filled in so that all the horizontal and vertical columns also add up to 64.

If the number 22 is reduced to 4 then we face a different square, and a sum of 44 instead of 64, though, as 44, if further reduced results in 8, a square of eight spaces on each side, and a key figure of 8 squared-- that is, 64 would also be appropriate. In this particular square, at least as I have chosen to organize it, the actual figure 8, which is the key, does not appear. It could, of course, be made to appear quite easily by making the line read:

$$3 \quad 4 \quad 5 \quad 8 \quad 9 \quad 10 \quad 11 \quad 12$$

but I feel myself that the other sequence seems more interesting. The advantage of making this kind of talisman is that in the making of it you are obliged to concentrate upon the problem it presents and therefore you put a good deal of psychic energy into it. Moreover, as many words could provide the same numerical arrangement, if you do not choose to create a square that actually spells out the name or the text in numbers, you can be assured that the purpose of the talisman will remain hidden from all but a perceptive and ingenious few.[1] Not all protective talismans need to be kept hidden. Those whose protective intention is not obvious may be worn in full view. Thus one may wear a belt buckle, pendant or ring that has been imbued with protective power quite openly. Many people are particularly attached to rings and you will often see a man or a woman abstractedly twisting a ring on his or her finger, and, in some cases, this will be a conscious protective gesture.

Making generally protective talismans for other people is not very different from making them for oneself. The only real difference is that a decision must be made as to whether or not you tell the recipient that it has talismanic power. This can be a difficult decision to make, for if the recipient is told it is a talisman and is sceptical about such matters he or she could easily reduce its power considerably, or even negate it. Moreover, here we are facing the tiresome way in which human relationships change; the talisman we give carries with it something of ourselves and if the individual to whom it is given decides that we are untrustworthy, the talisman may well lose its power or even reverse its intent. This is something of which most people are aware, however, and many people will not wear gifts received from people they no longer like.

In talking of gift talismans we are approaching the subject of the talisman intended to operate not as a protective device but as a magical spell, with a quite specific intent. This is the problem of the "loaded" gift. The simplest example is the talismanic object we give someone with the intent to keep that person's affection and interest. Such talismans are most effective if they have been worn on the body of the giver for a fairly long period and have thus collected a good deal of that person's energy field. Rings are most often used in this way. Talismans of this kind may be regarded as little more than remembrances. The talisman maker can imbue this gift with the attributes of a radio station for it can be given the intent to make it transmit messages to the deep mind of the recipient. Thus one might give a ring to someone and then, when they are far away, use it to transmit love, or, regrettably, hate. More specific messages such as "Turn on the TV set" or "Have a drink

---

1. In present day society, a talisman can remain hidden if placed in a jacket, skirt or trouser pocket. Some women may wish to carry one in a special compartment of a purse. The important thing to remember is that the talisman must be touched frequently by the owner in order to increse its vibrations.

on me" only work if the recipient is sensitive telepathically, though they certainly do work. This kind of "loaded" gift is, of course, only a step away from a gift intended to have a specific effect--to arouse desire for the giver or to cause harm. In these instances, whether the intention is benevolent or malicious, it is wise not to permit the talismanic nature of the gift to be recognized by the recipient, as most people are quicker to detect and resent manipulation of this kind than we sometimes think. Here, of course, we are touching on the "black magic" used by many societies, in which an illness-bringing talisman is buried secretly under the threshold of a person's door, or placed under a bed, or in the chimney. That this kind of talisman can be potent has been shown by many incidents recorded by travellers and anthropologists who have spent time in tribal societies.

Talismans of this "loaded" kind do demand from the maker an enormous amount of concentration of the will and the talisman maker may feel it necessary to create, with great precision, an empowering ritual to reinforce his intent. Talismans of this kind that are created from scratch may backfire on the maker, if their presence and their nature are discovered. This is shown in many folk tales--for example, when the young princess takes off the talismanic ring, or removes the chain from her neck, she not only breaks the spell upon her but also destroys the witch who cast it.

We have not, in earlier chapters, discussed the talismanic gift intended to do other than protect the wearer. The reason for this omission is simple: the majority of talismans intended to command and bind those to whom they are given, or in whose houses they are hidden, are made with such an elaborate accompaniment of verbal magic that the talisman itself is no more than a vehicle for the message it is ordered to carry. It may even be an object which we would never think of as talismanic at all. When such is the case, the object does not lend itself to being listed in the ranks of talismans *per se*. And yet it may have talismanic power.

Many people are aware of the talismanic power and intent of gifts which do not appear to be talismans in any usual sense of the term. The man who gives his girlfriend a nightgown, or the girl who gives her male friend pajamas, is quite likely to do so with talismanic intent. This is generally recognized in that one does not give gifts of clothing of such intimate nature unless one feels that the recipient already accepts one as a close friend at the very least. If you intend to send any type of talismanic gift with particular intent, you should strengthen the power of the gift by using some of the traditional symbolism already discussed in this book. Clearly colour symbolism is relevant here.

You can, of course, make talismans in terms of your own personal symbolism, using the basic designs of the hexagram, the pentagram and the mandala. Anyone can inscribe upon, around and within these forms all the signs and names that are felt to be most appropriate and most potent, using the techniques of Gematria, Notarikon or Temura. A personal alphabet to spell out the names and system of symbols can be constructed. This might, perhaps, lead you to create ideograms not dissimilar to those of the Chinese--a symbol for fatherhood might be a formalized picture of a tree with spreading branches. An image of pregnancy could be a circle with another smaller circle inside it and close to one edge. A symbol for the healing power could be a formalized picture of a hand in whose palm was a circle to represent the Sun and its powerful energy. Most people will prefer using traditional symbols, but there is no absolute necessity to do so. It is the significance of the symbol to the talisman maker that is one of the greatest importance, and if a newly created symbol enables you to visualize and energize in an effective fashion, then it is a perfectly satisfactory symbol. It is not necessarily the outward form of the language which carries the message but its inward essence, for it is this which is transmitted either to oneself or to others by way of the talisman.

"All truths lie waiting in all things," said Walt Whitman, and in talismanic magic it is possible to feel that all energy is held within the one talisman and given direction and specific powers by either the passionately felt belief and interest of the maker or the finder.

Epilogue

And even in England and America at the present time large numbers of people are influenced by beliefs which were common in Babylon four or five thousand years ago. No amount of development, culture or education will make men abandon wholly the use of amulets and systems of divination. For amulets give their wearers a sense of comfort, and protection and well-being, and they harm no one.

Sir E.A. Wallis Budge

Rather than intrude my personal experiences upon this survey, I have chosen to write about them in an epilogue. This is partly because my own approach to the practice of talismanic magic differs in many ways from the patterns suggested by other authorities I have adduced, and partly because it would have been extremely irritating had I interjected my own views earlier.

I have made use of talismanic magic very frequently over the last twenty years and feel I must bear witness to the effectiveness of this branch of magic, or otherwise it may be dismissed as hokum. Perhaps I should begin by stating that, as a witch, I am bound by the Witches Law: "Do what you will, but harm no-one". I do not create talismans to harm others. I must however point out that while almost all the talismans I have described are positive in effect, either protecting or bringing blessings, talismanic magic may also be used to harm people.

Energy has no ethics; electricity, after all, may be used to cook a meal or destroy a human creature. The kind of talisman that does harm is often not intended to do so, however. In my *Memoirs of a Literary Blockhead*[1] I told the story of a woman suffering from a talismanic curse. She was sent to me for help by her hairdresser. My account reads:

> She had been married several times, and her last husband had died from the consequences of alcoholism. She sat on the edge of the sofa and accepted a small glass of wine as if she thought it would bite her. She told me she hated living alone and therefore took rooms in people's houses where she would share the kitchen and feel, at least a little, part of the household. Everything always went well for the first ten days and then the family "turned against" her, and she became unhappy and had to move on. This kept happening. She was now so nervous she could not even contemplate getting a job and working with people. She knew they would "turn against" her too. It sounded like paranoia, but I probed a little further and discovered that her husband shortly before his death had given her a ring with the jovial words "I'm putting my brand on you, my girl". She always wore the ring. I said, "Let me have it," and as I held it I could feel the energy field of the thing. It was like holding a hot coal. I said, "May I keep this for a week?" and she said I could. I cleansed the ring of its energy field and she came back a week later to get it back. This time she sat on the sofa in a relaxed manner, accepted two full glasses of wine, chatted easily, and spoke of getting an apartment for herself and maybe taking a few courses and visiting her family in Alberta. I told her that I would vet any apartment she found, as she was clearly sensitive to psychic influences, but she never came back to me, though I did make inquiries and her hairdresser told me she was doing fine. I am sure that her husband had not really intended to curse her; he had done so unwittingly.

He had bound her to him, made her his own, to such a degree that she could not establish even a friendly relationship with anyone else.

---

1. Macmillan, 1988; now distributed by Reference West.

That was one of the first instances of cursing that was brought to me as a consultant witch. A later one had some of the same characteristics.

A woman in her fifties came to see me. She was from Austria and had been in Canada for a number of years. She said that she had suffered an extraordinary run of ill-luck over a long period. Nothing went right for her, either in her business or in her relationships and her health was failing. My initial response was, of course, to wonder whether or not this was caused by quite usual and commonplace factors, and so, over an hour or so, I explored her life and she told me her story. I was looking for a point in time when this misery had clearly begun, and I wanted to discover if a particular person was involved in that beginning. I got the time straight at last. It had all started around eleven years previously, just after she had left Austria. Had she upset anyone? Had she made an enemy? Had there been a disastrous love affair? Love affairs often cause this kind of disturbance if they end with ill feeling or involve a jealous possessiveness. The answer to all these questions was No. And then she told me that just before she left Europe a man she called a "magician" had given her a pendant, which she wore. It had her own horoscope on one side of the flat metal disc and a magical sign on the other. I took it from her and immediately knew that it had, even after eleven years, a great deal of energy. I told her that it had been the cause of at least some of her troubles and that I would cleanse it, which I did, by burying it in salt for a couple of days. She said she did not wish the pendant to be returned to her and I still have it. Her depression eased and her self confidence returned.

The clue here was the engraving of the zodiac signs on the metal, for the "magician" had, by writing her "signature" upon the pendant made her part of his life. It was a possessiveness that would prevent her ever being completely her own self. It bound her to him. Now, I do not know what happened to the magician. I cannot say whether or not he had himself had a bad time of it and transferred his depression to her by way of this link, or whether, even, he had died and she had found herself affected by the loss of part of herself. I only know that this pendant had prevented her from being successful. It could be from jealousy. It could be from a number of reasons.

Possessiveness is often a cause of this kind of suffering. Often the possessiveness is not really culpable. The intensity of a person's concern for another may well limit their freedom of thought or feeling. The originator of the curse wishes good things to happen, but in so doing also has views about what those good things are. Thus a young man came to me feeling that he could get nowhere with his life and was being held back by some psychic force. He himself was something of a sensitive, and knew that the psychic waves were emanating from his family in another province. They were concerned about him and his way of life and they were emotionally very strong people. He gave me a photograph of them and pointed to the most powerful personality in the group. This was a trickier proposition and I therefore dealt with the problem in two ways. Firstly, I gave him a protective mirror talisman. It was a mandorla-shaped piece of polished steel, curved so that one side was a convex and the other a concave mirror. This is quite a common fishing lure that can be found in most stores that sell fishing equipment. Before I gave it him I empowered it, by placing it on a mirror on my spell table, summoning up the energy and putting the message "Protect, return all harmful thought and feeling" into it, saying these and other words until I felt sure that the message had been firmly implanted. I tested the talisman for energy both before and after my implanting it by using an amber pendulum, suspending it above the thing with my elbow on the table so that no shaking of my hand could affect the movement. The first test showed little movement of the pendulum; the second sent the pendulum moving very quickly indeed. I told him to wear this talisman beneath his clothing so that no one but his wife would see it.

In addition to this I took the photograph and performed a bond-breaking spell. I took a reel of black thread in my right hand and then pulled a length of it out with my left hand and broke the thread in a candle flame. Thinking of him and of the people in the photograph, I said "Brow to brow the bond is broken (snap), Eye to eye the bond is broken (snap) and so on down the whole length of the body.

A week or so later the young man reported that his career had vastly improved and he no longer felt shackled. Whatever had been preventing him getting ahead and giving him fits of melancholy had disappeared.

The simple solutions are often the best because they enable one to concentrate more easily. The more theatrical a ritual, the more lines there are to say or movements to make, the more difficult it is to keep the power at full strength.

The mirror or fishing lure talisman is remarkably effective. I gave it once to a young man who was being unmercifully harassed by his superior at work. Within ten days the superior left for another business.

It is hard to say how much of the effect of the mirror talisman is due to suggestion and how much to magic. Does the conviction that one can reflect back the psychic attack lead to the ability to do so, or does the talisman itself do the job? In several of these instances it is clear that a kind of possessiveness is involved. The husband who gave the ring; the family that wished to control the behaviour of its members, the magician who inscribed the pendant; these are all instances of an intrusive possessiveness. The same might be said of the tormenting superior, though one could call this kind of possessiveness power-lust. It is important to recognize this, for behind many of the fears of people of the past, many of the concerns about the Evil Eye, was less a fear of a specific disaster than a fear of being taken over of being "possessed". We are none of us so secure in our personalities that we cannot feel sensitive on this point: we have all suffered the bully, the tyrant, the petty dictator, and some of us have suffered torture, brain washing and other evils.

I make this point because talismanic magic, like all positive magic, is in defence of the individual human spirit, even while it is aware of the power that spirit, that field of energy, possesses. We are aware of the talismanic power in the gifts we are given. At times of falling out gifts are often returned. This may be why it is usual for couples who have broken up return each others rings or sometimes throw them away or sell them. Rings are powerful talismanically. Other objects, however, can also be formidable. When I come across a person who feels that he or she has been cursed I always look for a talismanic source first of all. This applies to more than the kind of talisman we have been discussing. A haunted house that Jean Kozakari and I exorcised was haunted largely because a list belonging to the previous, now dead, owner had been left on the fridge. I remember it as a list of duties for a home-help to perform for the person who had died; it was a shopping list and the owner thought it fascinating and kept it there. We took it away and, after a little more work, the ghost went on to her next phase of existence.

This may seem irrelevant to a book about talismans, but in my experience I have found that almost anything can carry an energy field and therefore, intentionally or unintentionally, carry talismanic energies and commands. Knowing this makes it a great deal easier to function as a talisman maker. Still, there are limits to the kind of thing that will work effectively over time, and limits, also, to any object's ability to retain energy. My favourite example of this concerns a particular sleepstone.

While a number of talismanic stones and talismans of country lore have been credited with curing insomnia and giving sound dreamless (or dream-filled, come to that) sleep, I never myself found any reference to a sleepstone. The certainty that a sleepstone could work, and that a sleepstone should be of a certain kind, came to me entirely intuitively. Firstly the sleepstone is a polished stone just big enough to be held comfortably in the closed hand--not so big that it needs to be gripped, not so small that one can hardly feel it. The colour of the stone should be white, or creamy, or transparent. White agates or milk stones are fine and so are quartz pebbles. Although rose quartz is not white or cream, it will do, because the colour is gentle. The same would apply to any very faintly and gently coloured stone. The stone must, of course, be smooth, not jagged, but it need not, perhaps indeed should not, be one that has been deliberately shaped by machinery. Once I have my stone--actually I keep a box of them and empower them in batches--put it, or them, on a mirror that is placed in front of a lit candle, or three lit candles, on my spell table. The spell table also contains salt, water and an image of the Goddess, for this helps the atmosphere. The spell table, incidentally, is painted white and the mirror is silver backed.

I talk to the sleepstones saying "Peace...comfort, easy sleep, calm, calm," and such other words as I feel get the message across. As I do so I rock back and forth on my heels so that the reflection of the candle flame licks the reflection of the stone or stones. When I feel convinced that the message has been completely embedded in the stone I test the energy field with an amber pendulum in the manner I've already described. If it is energy-filled then I put the sleepstone or stones in a wooden box together with other sleepstones and soft feathers. I may wrap them in silk, or I may not. The important thing is to have them neighboured by similar energy fields.

When I am consulted by someone who has trouble sleeping I take a sleepstone from the box and put it in a small bag, which does not have to be silk. This, I think, is a sophistication which is pleasant but not necessary. I give the bag with the stone in it to the sleepless one and tell him or her to place the bag under the pillow on the bed. When sleeplessness occurs the sleepless one should take the stone out of the bag and hold it in his or her hand; calm untroubled sleep will soon follow.

I had been giving people sleepstones for some time and they had usually proved successful, when I was asked by a friend in Toronto to provide one for her husband who was suffering from hypertension and sleeplessness. I duly sent her one by post and it had absolutely no effect. This puzzled me, and then I wondered if the post office sorting machinery might not have affected the stone's energy field. I was due to visit Toronto in a little while, so I wrapped another sleepstone in the lead foil from a bottle of wine and took it with me.

My friend and her husband threw a small party for me on my arrival and it was a very jolly affair. When it was all over I gave the husband his sleepstone. That night having drunk a little more than usual he was extremely loquacious and also wide awake. After some time his wife said, rather testily, "Why don't you use Robin's sleepstone." He reached under his pillow where he had placed it in its small pouch, according to instructions, took it in his hand and said "It's fighting me...it's fighting me..."and fell fast asleep. I would have ascribed this partly to the drink were it not that it worked just as well the following night when he was absolutely cold sober.

The implication was obvious. The talisman does contain an energy field and that energy field can be disrupted by electro-magnetic fields emanating from postal or other machinery. This is perhaps hardly hot news any more for several studies have shown that there may be a connection between the incidence of bodily disorders and the proximity of power lines and electrical substations. Still, it led me to emphasize to those to whom I gave talismans that, if possible, they should not be subjected to strong electrical fields or magnetic influences.

Another instance of the sleepstone's efficiency involved a further consideration. A student of mine asked if she could bring me a man who had suffered from severe insomnia for fifteen years and nothing seemed to be able to cure it. Sleeping pills, of course, worked but not invariably and, in any case, they left him feeling out of sorts. Drugged sleep is not, as we well know, healthy sleep. He was unfortunately leaving Victoria the day after our appointment. There was no time to be elaborate.

When he and his wife came to see me I explained how the sleepstone worked and gave him one. By fortunate chance my daughter, Alison, was present at this occasion and I asked her if she would work out a Bach Flower Remedy for the man. In order to create a Flower Remedy for anyone there must be quite a thorough examination of the sufferer's life, character, and, obviously, symptoms. Alison had little time but she made her diagnosis and in a couple of weeks the remedy was posted away. Not long afterwards my student told me that the insomnia had been cured. I cannot in this instance be sure whether Alison or I had the greater part in the cure, but, again, the implication is clear. One should not rely upon one method only. Wherever possible one should attack the problem in several ways.

How great a part suggestion plays in talismanic work is hard to determine. Certainly one talisman I have found effective may owe a great deal to its obvious connotations. This talisman is a key, an ordinary small key of the size usually needed for old fashioned attache cases or small pieces of hand luggage. Yale keys are not satisfactory, for they do not remind one of the images of the key that are found everywhere in drawings and paintings. The notion of age, of tradition, is important.

This talisman occurred to me when I was asked to help find a house for a single mother with two children. I gave her not one but three small keys, for it seemed to me that all three persons involved required the home, required a door to be unlocked. Within three weeks she found a suitable place on a quiet street on which there were several families with small children of the same age as her own.

The key is an image of opportunity, of doors opening. I have also used it for people seeking employment, and it rarely fails. When it does fail there is usually an obvious reason. One young woman who asked for help to find work did not really wish to find work at all; she was simply saying something that she thought would convince me of her seriousness as a person and her sense of commitment to her own life. Another young woman quite simply did not wear it except very casually. This talisman only works if it is supported by the will of the wearer.

This aspect of talismans requires a comment. The effect of the key talisman is to enhance the wearer's own "radar" for finding opportunities for work. This "radar" may be regarded as an aspect of the will that operates by intuition. Many people have experienced it. Collectors of first editions, old china, matchboxes, or indeed anything, have always found themselves "knowing" that a certain store or fleamarket has something for them. They are drawn to it and they are almost never wrong. I myself have told my wife to stop the car when we were about to pass a bookshop, not knowing why I had to go inside, but knowing that something was waiting for me there, and my instinct has rarely been wrong. Other collectors have told me the same thing. This kind of "radar" is reinforced by the key talisman, but the talisman cannot do the work alone.

Some talismans are less obvious in their connotations. A young man who had reason to believe that his blood cells were not behaving properly and that he had a debilitating virus was given a ring with a red stone it. The association of red with blood is obvious. He wore it for a long time but eventually he found it interfered with his manual work, and then it was broken. I replaced it with another ring, but it became troublesome for him to wear, and so he put it aside. His body had, however, got the right habits by that time and he has been in good health for several years.

It would be foolish to maintain that the talisman was wholly responsible for his improvement, but it would be equally foolish to suggest that it had no effect at all. Whether the effect was due to suggestion or to talismanic power who can tell? In all probability it was a combination of the two. The same may well apply to the use of green jade as a talisman. Traditionally, in Chinese thinking, green jade is said to calm nerves, to bring relaxation. I was asked to help a child who was suffering from hypertension and insomnia and I found a small green jade pendant. Her father gave it to her one bedtime and she fell asleep almost immediately. Was this due to the talisman, or to the father's conviction that it would work being transferred to his child? Again, one cannot be certain.

Crystals make admirable talismans because they suggest energy; they reflect and refract light and they have been associated with mysterious powers for centuries. Crystals are capable of carrying almost any kind of message. They are certainly effective in healing, or causing the wearer to heal himself or herself. In one instance a young woman was suffering badly from bowel and stomach difficulties. I gave her a small crystal bead or button and advised her to tape it into her navel, so that its influence would be felt most immediately in the right area. Taping talismans to the body had its difficulties, however. The crystal, being somewhat sharp edged, proved uncomfortable and had to be discarded after a while. Nevertheless, the condition improved.

The uncomfortable talisman has some advantages; it cannot be forgotten by the conscious mind of the wearer and therefore its message is continually in mind. This is the reason why some people prescribe talismans bound around the forehead or talismans whose size makes the wearer uncomfortable. The jewish phylactery, bound round the forehead and carrying a religious text, is one example of this type. The inscriptive talisman most usually consists of a text taken from a sacred book, but this means that the wearer must believe in that book. Texts from other sources may be used, as long as the wearer believes in the power of the words. One might, for example, give someone an inscriptive talisman bearing the words "Peace of mind, peace of heart, peace of understanding" or some such.

One of the problems one faces is where exactly a particular talisman should be placed. My personal tendency is to make use of rings, pendants, and, occasionally, throat and navel ornaments, but there is no reason to avoid other places and it seems clear that the traditional use of the left arm makes sense as this is on the heart side of the body and juxtaposition in talismanic work is important. One can, of course, get very complicated when dealing with rings in deciding exactly which finger should carry the talisman. I myself do not worry very much about this; one finger is as good as another, I feel, unless the talisman wearer has a strong belief that the finger of Venus, say, would be appropriate.

There is one kind of magic which must be mentioned because, while it does not involve actual physical talismans, it involves talismanic thinking quite definitely. If I had to give this kind of magic a name I would call it The Doctrine of the Invisible Talisman. It is one type of what in my book, *The Practice of Witchcraft*,[2] I called Projective Magic. The point here is that the talismanic image is "projected" or imagined onto the site of the sufferer's pain or disorder. One example I gave was:

To Ease Soreness of the Throat

To ease a sore throat, project a wreath of small ivy leaves around the throat; it draws the inflammation into itself, just as ivy feeds upon a tree.

There is absolutely no justification for thinking of ivy in this

---

2. *The Practice of Witchcraft*. Porcépic Books, Victoria, B.C. 1990.

connection. It has no herbal virtues to suggest that it could cure laryngitis, and in mythology it is associated with Bacchus-Dionysus and drunken revels. And yet I have found it, in combination with hand-magic, to be effective. Here it may be that my own intuition followed by my own explanation was strong enough to make it work. Maybe my belief did the task. And yet I find myself wondering exactly why I had the intuition in the first place, and why I found myself accepting that explanation in terms of talismanic thinking so easily.

Why, again, did I use red thread to cure my younger daughter's nose bleeds, and why did it work? I did not, at that time know, had never read, that tying red thread around a person's wrist--the left one--would cause frequent nosebleed to disappear. I simply "knew" it, did it and it worked. Statements of this kind are irritating because they are unhelpful and simply ask the reader or hearer to accept a phenomenon without question. Nevertheless this intuitive procedure is absolutely essential to efficient talismanic magic. It seems, occasionally, that if one opens up one's mind, not thinking consciously, just letting images float around one central concern, a solution to a problem will arrive, just as it can in sleep as many notable scientific discoverers have told us.

I myself perform this manoeuvre both in my head and while wandering around my room idly opening boxes that contain polished stones, pebbles, rings, pendants and so forth. Quite often a particular object will leap out at me, saying "I'm that one." It is rather like working on a jig saw puzzle, trying to find a piece that will fit. This is almost a commonplace activity of mine when faced with the necessity of giving someone talismanic help. In order to perform this task effectively, though, one does need quite a large supply of material. Most of this need cost little. Although we have talked of precious and semi-precious stones we need not use them. Pebbles of the right colour, of the right clarity, will do just as well. Costume jewellery can be picked up quite cheaply in junk shops and flea markets, as can polished pebbles. Pendants can be made easily from a polished pebble a glued-on split ring and a cheap metal chain, or even a piece of string, or a leather thong. If one wishes to make more elaborate talismans, then one can make use of anything that is practical. It is the energy and the intent that does the work, though I should obviously add that a metal or stone that carries and contains a lot of electrical energy will always be more effective than cardboard. The energy and the intent, however, must be supported by a visual (or sometimes tactile) image, and, while there are no rules about this in that each person reacts differently to different stimuli, there are some general principles, particularly as regards colours.

Colour has, of course, been found to be of use in healing and there are a great number of books on colour symbolism and on working with colour.[3] We are told, by some, that the colour of what we wear affects us; we are told by others that coloured light can also affect us. This is certainly true, but here we are concerned with colour in talismans, for if we make our talismans from other than expensive materials of tradition and legend colour is going to be the most obvious attribute of whatever we construct. Let us begin with Black which is the colour of Saturn and associated with night and morning. It is also, however, a colour that suggests knowledge, wisdom and the strength that wisdom brings. Black stones such as black onyxes are powerful and, most importantly, suggest power. I would pick a ring or pendant with a black stone to help someone who was already set upon a particular path, but who needed more strength. I'd be careful about this, though. Black carries so much energy that it can overload the sensibility of the wearer.

The colour Brown is not much use for talismans as, being a mixed colour, it sends only indefinite vibrations. White, on the other hand is quite definite. Associated with the moon, and Virgo, as is silver, it not only brings purity of mind and emotion, but clarifies and heals in general. A white ring is an excellent healer for people under stress; it brings out the intuitive in the wearer, eases pain, and, especially if round, gives a sense of completeness.

Yellow, especially "hot" yellow, is the colour of the sun--or is regarded as being so, and therefore it is associated with Leo and Ra the sun god. It is an agitating stone and does not work too well in talismans, whereas orange has a warmer presence and gives the wearer increased vitality. It is also a disturbing colour. Such colours should only be used when increased energy is required and, in the case of orange, increased energy in passion and in sexuality. Increased energy is also gained from a red talisman. Red is a colour of Mars or Jupiter, but it is also the colour of blood and, in making a talisman, blood red is the colour we need. Red strengthens the blood, the heart, the immune system, as well as gives confidence. It should, ideally, be on a ring rather than a pendant, for it responds positively to people's stares, not negatively as

3. See, notably, Linda Clark: *The Ancient Art of Colour Therapy*, Devin Adair, 1975

do some paler colours. It has been used for magical purposes it seems for ever. Phalluses have been painted red in both Greece and India in order to increase the corn crop. Red bands, cloths, cords, cloaks are found everywhere in many cultures,and all are intended to promote strength, virility in men and cure illness of all kinds. Red flannel was long a traditional cure for childhood chest ailments in England and many people were wrapped in red blankets to cure them of smallpox in earlier centuries. Red is, therefore, a most valuable colour, for the wearer of a red talisman is already convinced it will work because of the numerous associations red has for him or her; it is, after all, pure authority. It is the red wax that seals documents and laws and it is the colour of the royal robe. Red should not, of course, be used when subtle help is needed and the actual shade of the red should be controlled carefully. The opposite of red, in the optical sense is Green which has sometimes been regarded as unlucky because of its association with faerie. In fact green is, both physically and psychological, a peace-bringing colour, as well as a colour of vitality. Again, the shade matters quite a lot. A yellowish green may exacerbate a disorder whereas an emerald green will cure it. A deeper green presents calm amounting to sloth and helps in dealing with insomnia.

Blue, as we have already noted several times, is the colour of Venus and of the Mother Goddess in all her various guises. It is a colour of harmony and helps to give people easy and comfortable sleep and blue should be worn by nursing mothers. It cools fevers and soreness, and reduces tension. Purple or Magenta is good for heart disorders and stabilizes blood pressure, and the colour Turquoise is also an aid to tranquillity and balance. Other colours and colour combinations obviously occur. Should one, for example, give someone suffering from anxiety and physical weakness a red talisman, or perhaps a red talisman with clear quartz in it, not only to promote vitality but also clarify of perception? It sounds sensible.

Other questions must be asked, especially about the nature of the talisman. Would a red belt be suitable for a woman who needed to improve a sluggish digestion? Would a blue night-dress help a woman to go to sleep? The answer in both cases is Yes, but it must be realized that unless the belt is metal it will lose its energy fairly quickly and the blue night-dress, while retaining the power of the colour as such, will not have much talismanic power after if has been washed.

It is more difficult to get people to accept talismanic clothing and accessories than it is to persuade them that rings and pendants can be of use. If you suggest a different fashion in dress you are, after all, meddling with the wearer's identity and sense of himself or herself. People do, nowadays, discuss the "power tie" or the "power dress", but this is only in terms of the theatrical effect of such clothing, not in terms of the actual energy fields; they are however admitting the effectiveness of Identity Talismans.

No matter what we as talisman makers attempt, we come up against the question of authority. However strongly the message has been implanted in the talisman it will not work at full intensity if the conscious mind of the wearer rejects it or is overly sceptical. The consultant witch (or, come to that, the priest, doctor, teacher or shaman) must induce faith in his or her "patient". Sometimes this trust may derive from the known track record, the reputation, of the consultant. Sometimes it is created by rather theatrical means; the patient is presented with an incense-laden room, a darkened place, an altar with candles, and so forth. This may or may not be legitimate; in some circumstances a degree of ritual is needed to bring the psychic energy into play. In other instances it may be mere charlatanry to impress the highly suggestible or even gullible. I myself avoid theatrics and prefer to see people in my own ordinary cluttered living room, give them a glass of wine or tea or coffee, and chat for a while until we are comfortable together, before even getting down to questioning. Everyone will have his or her own best method of working, and the method may well be different for each visitor. If one can set aside a particular room for working magic with people it is good to do so, but if one cannot then one should be able to work in ordinary surroundings.

There may be many legends and myths surrounding talismans and many esoteric practices are connected with them. Exploring them has taken us to Ancient Egypt, to Greece, to Rome, and we have found ourselves glancing at astrology, kabbalism and magical alphabets. For all that, however, talismanic magic is based upon something entirely simple and human. It is based upon the energy fields of the world that surrounds us and upon our relationship with them. Its history may be complex and even, sometimes, lurid, but the talisman is a part of our ordinary thinking and our day-to-day behaviours. It is also a practical way of helping, healing and bringing happiness to other people.